D0900353

SEXUAL
DEVIANCE

Readers in Social Problems

DONALD R. CRESSEY, CONSULTING EDITOR

UNIVERSITY OF CALIFORNIA, SANTA BARBARA

SEXUAL DEVIANCE

EDITED BY

JOHN H. GAGNON

&

WILLIAM SIMON

WITH THE ASSISTANCE OF
DONALD E. CARNS

LIBRARY
OF
MOUNT ST. MARY'S
COLLEGE
EMMITSBURG, MARYLAND

INSTITUTE FOR SEX RESEARCH, INC.
AND
DEPARTMENT OF SOCIOLOGY
INDIANA UNIVERSITY, BLOOMINGTON, INDIANA

HARPER & ROW

Publishers

NEW YORK, EVANSTON, AND LONDON

TO OUR WIVES

FOR BEING MANY MORE THINGS

THAN ALTERNATIVES TO DEVIANCE

SEXUAL DEVIANCE / Copyright © 1967 by the Institute
for Sex Research, Inc. Printed in the United States of
America. All rights reserved. No part of this book may
be used or reproduced in any manner whatsoever without written permission except in the case of brief quotations embodied in critical articles and reviews. For information address Harper & Row, Publishers, Incor-
porated, 49 East 33rd Street, New York, N. Y. 10016.

Library of Congress Catalog Card Number: 67–15788

CONTENTS

PART IV / FEMALE HOMOSEXUALITY

PREFACE

THE VIOLATORS of major social norms are always strangers—strangers either in the literal sense or strangers in the sense that they are the products of highly exceptional processes. It is a common tendency to create a sense of social and psychological distance between ourselves and deviants: they aren't our kind of people. While we can understand this kind of reaction, understand how it makes possible support for the sanctioning of deviant actors in a way that serves, in turn, to reinforce conformity to social norms, we must also understand that this reaction can be costly. These costs take the form of generating elements of nonrationality in the conduct of societal affairs and of an inability to utilize the study of deviance to enrich our understanding of the more general human experience.

All works in the social sciences are subject, in one degree or other, to the biases of authors or editors; where possible, such biases should be articulated in the most explicit manner. Our major biases are relatively simple. We feel that the most extreme deviant still shares more in common with the rest of humanity than he holds as unique attributes. We think that the propensity to develop a deviant career depends not upon some exceptional attribute, but upon attributes that we tend to share with others. The deviant is really not a stranger. Rather, given the right circumstances, we are all potential deviants. It is our conviction that remarkably few deviants invent their own patterns of deviance, and that the learning of deviant patterns can only be understood with the application of the same conceptual language with which we approach the learning of conformity. To the degree that it represents a bias, we are deeply concerned about the heavy costs to our society that follow from the typical ways of thinking about deviance and the deviant; we are concerned about the nonrationality that permeates the question, about the fears, anxieties, and cruelty that it can promote.

Among the debts accumulated in the process of producing this book we must acknowledge one to the late Professor Robert E. Park who, with his colleagues and students, created what became known as the "Chicago school" of sociology. A major characteristic that marked this group was a fascination with the urban community and the forms of social life it contained or gave rise to. On reading the works that came out of this tradition, one cannot help but be impressed with the sense of richness and the varied texture of social life in the urban community that they convey. It was an exposure to this tradition that made of us walkers and watchers in the city; it was a source for learning to recognize the appearance of deviance and for learning to see it in context.

Further, we are indebted to the pioneering work of Alfred C. Kinsey and his associates. All who currently work in the area of sexual behavior owe a substantial debt to their work: they provided both legitimacy and a starting point. More directly, we have drawn a great deal from the resources and accumulated wisdom of the institute that Professor Kinsey created. This could not have been possible without the generous and tolerant support of Paul Gebhard, Director of the Institute for Sex Research, and Cornelia V. Christenson, our fellow trustee of the Institute.

Donald E. Carns provided invaluable service in the preparation of these materials. Karin Ford assisted in a number of phases of preparing the book, working with a quiet competence that significantly lightened our burden. Lenora Key, Bettie Silverstein, and Sue Williams worked dependably and diligently in producing the manuscript of this book.

WILLIAM SIMON
JOHN H. GAGNON

SEXUAL
DEVIANCE

Introduction:
Deviant Behavior
and Sexual Deviance

For the student of sociology a concern for social behavior must soon begin to focus upon a concern for the sources and modes of regulating behavior. For the sociologist the existence of norms covering many aspects of behavior takes on significance not because the norms exhaustively describe what people actually do, but because they represent a constraint to do or not to do things. This constraint molds not only the behavior of those who act in conformance with the norms but also the behavior of those who violate them. From classical sociological theorists (such as Durkheim and Weber) to contemporary theorists (such as Parsons and Merton), the structure of social behavior has been viewed not as a fixed relation between behavior and norms, but as a dynamic process. The consideration of the normative structure of collectivities, or behavior in conformity to norms, would thus be incomplete without considering, at the same time, nonconformity or deviance. The reverse of this proposition is also true: despite the understandable tendency to conceive of many forms of deviant behavior as exotic and strange, it is important to view deviant behavior, including sexual deviance, in terms of its essential relationship to the conventional structures and processes of collective life.

The major criteria of what is deviant are not to be found in the behavior as such, but rather in its definition as norm-

All footnotes appear in the Notes section, grouped by article, at the end of this book.

violating behavior. There is no form of behavior, sexual or nonsexual, that is intrinsically deviant or deviant because of the behavior that it involves. In the area of sexual deviance (as well as in other forms of deviance) there is wide variation between cultures in which specific behaviors are defined as deviant. With the possible exception of incest (and different societies define differently the extent of family relationships that are covered by the prohibition), there are no age preferences or gender choices or styles of sexual behavior that are universally prohibited. Thus, social structures of considerable variety have existed in the past (or do exist now) which were (or are) capable of integrating widely disparate forms of sexual behavior. To repeat: a form of behavior becomes deviant when it is defined as violating the norms of some collectivity. Usually, the collectivities that are relevant are those formally empowered to sanction deviant behavior in general, though for certain forms of sexual behavior only informal and covert sanctions are applied by selected collectivities.

Deviance, then, may be considered one of the facts of social life. While the "why," the "what," and the "how" of its definition and the response of those so defined may vary from society to society, or from community to community in more complex societies, or even from one period in the history of a single community to another period, the probability of the occurrence of deviance is great, for to speak of norms is to anticipate their violation.

Almost all persons, one may be sure, can recall some act of deviance from their own experience; it is virtually impossible to grow up in the context of American society, or indeed any relatively complex society, without having committed, knowingly or unknowingly, such an act. For most persons, however, the deviant act was an isolated event that did not lead to a social career as a deviant.[1] Thus deviation, as a social act, must be conceived in terms of social structure, social situation, and the character of specific actors rather than in terms of a fixed and seemingly immutable set (or sets) of moral postures.

This approach to deviant behavior makes systematic study extremely difficult, since it requires going beyond merely describing and categorizing behavior to the task of tracing out the complex processes of societal definition, the emergence of the deviant self-conception by a so-labeled actor, and the contingency-laden career that follows the labeling experience. Thus the task becomes a multiple one of determining the role and character of the deviant-defining processes, detailing the interaction between the person so identified and the way he deals with the definition, and then following the career processes of a specific kind of deviant life style. In many cases this last element is more complicated and problematic than any of the others and contributes more to the ultimate character of the persons involved. Thus, the kind of life led after entering a career of deviance may be more influential in shaping the person's behavior than any of the etiological characteristics that brought him to the point of committing the act or acts in the first place.

When one turns to the question of sexual deviance, the issue becomes increasingly obscured. It is important to bear in mind that sexuality is, perhaps more than any other aspect of human behavior, intertwined with moral imperatives, conscious fantasy, and unconscious desires, all of which combine to compromise even the most scientific of observers. Moreover, sexuality has the dubious distinction of being the only biological drive that has been proscribed in nearly all of its physical manifestations.

Given the tendency to proscribe most forms of direct sexual expression, there should be, and there are, a relatively large number of forms of sexual deviance, particularly if we choose to move beyond those that are legally proscribed and include forms of sexual behavior that do not involve legal liability (or at least are not actively pursued by the police and other norm-enforcing agencies) but are commonly defined as wicked, immoral, or perverted. (The reader should bear in mind that from a sociological perspective acts are not deviant simply because they are illegal, but because they meet with social disapproval. Moreover, we would expect that the deviant actor—even if never observed in his deviance by others —can be expected to anticipate the imposition of sanctions of one sort or another.)

DEVIANCE: LAWS, MORES, AND BEHAVIOR

The actual fact of defining something as deviant is an outcome which usually reflects a complex interaction between institutionalized norms (laws, both in terms of statute and precedent), shared and internalized norms of a populace (mores), and the actual pattern of behavior exhibited by that population. In normatively integrated communities (that is, where norms do not conflict with each other to any significant degree and where these same norms are effective in fulfilling the needs of people, singly and collectively) these three elements should stand in relatively high correlation most of the time. In addition, it is possible that in communities and societies which do not reflect a uniformly high level of normative integration there should be some kinds of behavior about which there is such an ordered consensus. Thus, just as the law strongly sanctions incestuous behavior, almost all persons strenuously disapprove of incestuous behavior, and relatively few of them commit acts that could be defined as incestual. This consensus, indeed, may be observed about many forms of sexual deviance, e.g., rape or sexual contacts with children.

There are, however, a number of forms of sexual activity not characterized by a high correlation between laws, mores, and behavior. While there is no specific law proscribing masturbation, it is formally condemned by many religious groups and defined negatively by most individuals. Nonetheless, masturbation is, at one time or another, engaged in by all but a few males and about two thirds of all females. Indeed, for some segments of the male population masturbation is the most important element of their sexual experience prior to marriage. The negative character of prevailing mores with respect to masturbation obviously does not constrain the behavior, but does manage to produce feelings of guilt or marked ambivalence on the part of those who masturbate. A similar example is premarital intercourse, which, unlike masturbation, can be construed as a legal offense in most states and is also disapproved in most circumstances by most

Americans. However, the research by Kinsey and his associates, as well as others, indicates that two thirds of males with college educations and some 80 percent of men with grade-school educations report such premarital coitus, as do about half of all females at all social levels. A further example is provided by heterosexual mouth-genital contact which is proscribed under sodomy or other statutes, yet is reported to occur usually in marriage among approximately half of college-educated adults.

These three forms of sexual deviance—masturbation, premarital coitus, and mouth-genital contact—might almost be termed "normal deviance." This term applies not merely because large numbers of persons are involved, though this is a consideration, but rather because the behaviors themselves either articulate with a fully legitimate expression of sexuality (marriage), or because they are basic to, or reinforcement for, the continued maintenance of other prohibitions about sexual behavior. In addition, they typically become public only by accident and consequently do not publicly challenge formally stated laws and conventional morality. Situations like this frequently give rise to such widely expressed judgments as: "It is wrong only if you get caught." Moreover, the integration of these behaviors with approved aspects of sexuality, as well as widespread involvement in them, tends to soften the intensity of the sanctions and render relatively inactive most proscriptive statutes. Thus, even in those cases where the behavior represents a legal offense, the law is rarely invoked.

There are also forms of sexual deviance for which the correlation between laws, mores, and behavior is somewhat greater and for which, unlike the behavior discussed above, the intensity of sanctions invoked both on the level of the mores and on the formal legal level remains high. Such forms of deviance usually involve smaller though still sizable numbers of persons (such as homosexuality) or involve larger numbers of persons, but only episodically (such as clients of prostitutes). It is clear, however, that these forms of deviance, which are more strongly sanctioned at both the formal and informal level, fail to articulate with legitimate expressions of sexuality and are more likely to be defined as a challenge to conventional morality. Nonetheless, the sheer persistence of relatively large numbers of persons engaging in such deviant behavior is sufficient to constrain norm-enforcing agencies to attempt to regulate either the deviant behavior or the deviants themselves rather than attempting to suppress it or them entirely. In effect, the function of the police in these situations is to keep the behavior under control either by harrassing the deviants and preventing them from congregating, or by confining the behavior to places where it is not easily visible to the general public, but still readily accessible to those who are involved. In this manner the function of norm-enforcement agencies is not to suppress the behavior completely, as it would be if there were a fairly complete consensus between the three factors (law, mores, and behavior) and if the population of deviants were not so large.

Clearly the degree of correlation between laws, mores, and behavior is itself a complex outcome, dependent on many factors. For example, size and degree of urbanization are variables that are generally associated with differences in these correlations. The large urban community offers more anonymity to the individual than the small community, and this fact may encourage the acting out of deviant tendencies. Indeed, such an urban community may provide a social structure which will facilitate some forms of deviant conduct. As Robert Park pointed out over a quarter of a century ago, a person who might be a socially isolated and sexually inactive homosexual in a small community can, in the large urban metropolis, be a member of a community of homosexuals. (It might be added that this is true of poets, drunkards, atheists, druggists, and business executives as well.)

Moreover, the urban community encourages more professionalized and formalized enforcement of the law which, in turn, tends to reflect the lesser effectiveness of the informal controls (mores). To the degree that deviant behavior is private and its control is dependent on the reinforcement of informal sanctions, as is a great deal of sexual conduct, the behavior in question becomes less amenable to the sanctioning power of the community. This reduced effectiveness of informal controls (in the form of public opinion) may, in turn, reflect the problem of expressing the responses of a mass of persons, the relative lack of extended interpersonal involvement in the large city, and a greater probability of value heterogeneity that can insulate the deviant and make the translation of private opinion into public opinion more difficult for the nondeviant. In the urban situation the outraged citizen communicates not with other citizens but with trained officials for whom the specific form of sexual deviance is not an unusual, highly emotionally charged event, but a routine everyday fact of life. Indeed, in these situations law enforcement agencies tend to respond to those offenses that involve specific complainants or victims (such as burglary and car theft) rather than to those that involve persons acting in complicity (such as prostitution or homosexuality). With the latter the outraged citizen is reporting what the police already know to be occurring, and they therefore do not normally respond by making an arrest.

All of this does not suggest that smaller communities are not, or do not become, environments in which deviant behavior occurs, nor that the urbanized community itself is the cause of sexual deviance. Rather, it is important to understand that the forms that sexual deviance takes, the nature of its impact on the community, and the community's response to it will vary from one social setting to another as that setting shapes the relation between the mores, the law, and behavior.

TYPES OF SEXUAL DEVIANCE

As should already be clear, the activities that fall under the rubric "sexual deviance" far from comprise a homogeneous category. To the contrary, all that such behaviors appear to have in common, at least at first glance, is that they involve sexuality and are disapproved by either the formal code of the society or by the normative judgments of a population, or both. In the previous section there was a consideration of ways in which the forms of deviance could be differentiated. There is another and related manner of subdividing this category of behavior, but it is one that focuses more immediately on the social dimensions of the activity itself.

Three rough categories of sexual deviance can be distinguished. The first of these involves acts that are generally disapproved, but that either serve a socially useful purpose and/or occur so often among a population and with such a low social visibility that only a small number are ever actually sanctioned for engaging in the behavior. This type would correspond to the second pattern of relations between law, mores, and behavior, or what has been called "normal deviance." The kinds of behavior that fall into this category include masturbation, premarital coitus, and heterosexual mouth-genital contact. All of these acts are performed by large numbers of people in our society, and they can all be construed as—to use the language of our earlier discussion—articulating in some way with more fully legitimate expressions of sexuality. Masturbation, to take the first, is manifestly a substitute outlet that is most frequently utilized by males during periods when access to legitimate heterosexual behavior is limited. This is most prevalent during adolescence (especially for middle-class males), or when the spouse is absent during marriage, or when men are deprived of females while in prisons or armies. Premarital intercourse and petting, in many cases, relate to a process of progressive intimacy and emotional involvement that appear to be part of generating the conditions for marriage. The exchange of increasing levels of sexual intimacy on the part of the female for increasing levels of emotional commitment on the part of the male is a recognized part of the courting ritual in this society. It is noteworthy that approximately half of the females who engage in premarital coitus do so with only one male—the one whom they later marry. A large proportion of the remaining half have nearly all of their premarital experience within the context of serious courtship. The third example, mouth-genital contact, may also be viewed as articulating with marriage in a fairly direct way; for a number of observers this activity is viewed as an important part of the de-inhibition process that aids in making the sexual exchange a binding force in marriage.

A basic characteristic of this type of normal deviance is that it does not give rise to a specific form of social structure organized around the deviant act or its consequences. While some forms of "normal" deviance occur in social relationships, no special groups—that is, any more special than the category of men or women—are organized around this activity in order to teach it or to maintain people in it.[2]

The second type of sexual deviance corresponds to the general case where there is a high correlation between law, mores, and behavior. This type of deviance might be termed "pathological deviance." Examples include incest, sexual contact with children of either sex, exhibitionism, voyeurism, and aggressive or assaultive offenses. These types of deviance, unlike "normal deviance," involve very few persons, but are like it in that pathological deviance does exist without supportive group structures that serve to recruit to the behavior, train participants in it, gather partners together for its performance, or provide social support for the actor. Except for the gang rape among lower-class men, these kinds of offenses rarely involve more than one offender who is acting alone out of particular psychological needs. While the behaviors involved represent learned responses, understanding the sources of deviant learning and the reinforcement of continued behavior generally necessitates a psychological or social-psychological perspective rather than a sociological one. In these cases the causal nexus of the behavior appears to exist in the family and personality structure of the individual and is linked to the contingencies of his biography rather than to those of social structure.

The third type of sexual deviance involves precisely those kinds of behavior that generate specific forms of social structure. Clearly, among those to be included in this type of deviance are female prostitution and both male and female homosexuality. While it is possible for some instances of homosexual behavior to occur in a manner more typical of "pathological deviance," as in the instance of a person who develops a homosexual commitment and engages in homosexual behavior without necessarily having had contact with other homosexuals, the largest portion of homosexuals engage

in and, in many ways, depend upon contact with other homosexuals. The emergence of what has been called "the homosexual community" with its particular institutions such as bars
and steam baths, formal homophile organizations, homosexually oriented publications, and a community wisdom and
language, would indicate just this. And what is important is
not only that such a community represents a clustering of
homosexuals, but that significant parts of the social and
sexual life of the homosexual—particularly his ability to me-
diate his relationship with the larger society—may be shaped
not by his homosexuality per se, but by the degree of development or elaboration of the community in which he plays a
role. To some extent the ultimate social and psychological
adjustment of the homosexual will be conditioned by the
structure of role opportunities provided by the homosexual
community.

Similar to the private homosexual it is possible to conceive
of the private prostitute, where prostitution has been initiated
on an individual level and then is carried on in isolation from
other prostitutes (prostitution defined here as the exchange
of sexual access on a relatively indiscriminate level for monetary reward that is specifically for the act itself). Undoubtedly
some amount of prostitution does take place in this way in
our society. However, occurring over longer periods of time
and representing by far the largest proportion of sexual encounters that may be described as prostitution are those acts
committed by females who are part of a social world which
includes as its elements specialized knowledge, language, and
relationships with other persons. Being "in the life" involves
existing inside a prostitute's occupational culture. In socially
structured prostitution the reference is not to "organized vice"
or to "syndicate vice" (though these are not entirely unrelated), but more specifically to the fact that most prostitutes
exist in social networks consisting of other prostitutes and
allied occupational and social roles (e.g., pimps, steerers, the
police, customers). As with the homosexual community, this
is a network of social relationships that both facilitates and,
in some measure, determines the sexual and the social activity
of the prostitute.

In one sense these two worlds are quite different. The social world of prostitution does articulate with the broader sexual world in that it provides direct sexual services for segments of the conventional community, and it tends to recruit its members from particular social levels in the community. The lower-class girl who becomes a prostitute frequently does so from an earlier career of active heterosexual contact and simply slides into the life. The transition is often not traumatic, and there are persons available in the community who willingly recruit such females into prostitution. The factors that produce homosexuality seem to operate across class boundaries, and the organized homosexual world accepts persons who have already acquired some knowledge of their sexual commitment to persons of their own sex. In this sense the world of prostitution may be seen as a system of recruitment in, and maintenance of, deviance, while in the homosexual community it is only the maintenance of the deviant career that is provided.

THE ORGANIZATION OF THE BOOK

It is homosexuality and prostitution that will be most extensively treated in this volume. What is important about these two forms of deviance is that a study of the emerging and continuing social structure that surrounds their performance requires essentially a sociological perspective. The book will not treat those forms of deviance that we have described as pathological, since these behaviors are acted out in isolation, and their understanding would require considerable reference to particular kinds of crimes that would be too great for a very short book. Indeed, for adequate coverage of the variety of factors that enter into these types of deviance, there would have to be materials covering each type of offense as well as all of the subvarieties of men that commit these kinds of acts. For example, an adequate treatment of sexual assault would have to take into consideration those men who assault small children, those boys who rape as members of a small peer group, as well as other men whose assaultive behavior seems to represent a fundamentally aggressive pattern in all spheres of behavior. In most cases the roots of such behavior cannot be easily located by a sociological perspective. To the degree that a sociological perspective is useful for dealing with the sex offender, the article by Stanton Wheeler attempts to provide a framework for it.

Treating the problem of normal sexual deviance is significant since it lies within the realm of sociological explanation, but its dimensions are too great for this kind of book. It would require specifying quite clearly the relationships that exist between sexual conduct and the rest of social structure in a way that has not yet been attempted and for which data do not yet exist. In a preliminary way the articles by Gagnon and Reiss attempt to set the background for a general overview of the dilemma of sexuality in American society and the problem of dealing with it among children and adolescents.

The remainder of the volume is divided into three parts, the first composed of articles dealing with female prostitution, the second composed of articles dealing with male homosexuality, and the last a single long article by the editors on female homosexuality. The decision to write an original article to deal with this last area was a difficult one to make and arose from a basic dissatisfaction with the literature as it relates to female homosexuality. Through the entire volume there is an attempt to deal with sexual deviance within the context of sociology and the forms of discussion and explanation that the discipline requires. A point to be reemphasized is that deviance is not something special or bizarre, but subject to the same kinds of explanations as is conforming behavior. Deviance exists in social systems as a necessary complement to conformity, for as we have suggested before, to speak of one is to imply the other.

PART I

An Overview

Sexuality and Sexual Learning
in the Child

JOHN H. GAGNON

The patterns of adult deviant conduct considered in this book are those that are most affected by conditions that exist after childhood; however, there are those patterns that rest upon earlier training for sexuality. This paper attempts to assess some of the factors that control childhood sexuality and sexual learning, and the way that the latter is linked to sexual value systems of adults. The lack of a fully developed societal consensus leaves many opportunities for the experimentation with deviant behavior. The dilemma for the child is that learning about sex is heavily laden with guilt and anxiety without a corresponding specification of the particular behaviors that result in the invocation of sanctions. What is important, then, is not that specific acts are prohibited, but rather that the entirety of sexual life is permeated with a sense of guilt and shame even when specific behaviors themselves are prescribed (such as coitus in marriage). The salience of the child's peer group may be greater in this area of learning than in practically any other, due to the usual lack of sexual information supplied in the home and indeed the prohibitions that frequently exist between parents and chil-

REPRINTED with the permission of the author and the editors from *Psychiatry* 28:3:212–228 (August, 1965). This is a revised version of a paper originally published in Italian as "Sessualità ed apprendimento sessuale del bambino," *Scuola e Città* 15:249–258 (1964).

This research was supported by the National Institute of Mental Health Grant No. MH-07742.

dren in terms of talking about sex. The conditions of learning about sex and its attendant values are thus highly unstable for any given individual and are located with those persons least likely to give adequate and valid information. For children entering adolescence, a period containing their first confrontations with sexuality, only confusion and avoidance are likely to be the case. The negative functions of this adolescent state, in terms of experimentation with deviant behavior, are apparent. What is less apparent is that the capacity of young people to experiment with "normal deviance," as described in the introduction, may also depend on this same ambiguity in the norms that have been learned.

One of the most impressive aspects of this century is its exceptional concern with children. This is not to say that our children are loved more intensely or that their loss is mourned more deeply than in previous times, but that there is a special awareness of them as *children.* Only occasionally in preninteenth-century literature is a child depicted in present-day terms; rather children are represented as smaller and weaker versions of the adults surrounding them. A reading of Chaucer and Shakespeare fails to reveal a special world of the child, and it is not until the nineteenth century that such writers as Wordsworth in poetry and Dickens in the novel attest a new and prepossessing concern for the life of the child,[1] and childhood becomes a unique stage during which perceptions and learning are related to age as well as to station. In contrast, the execution of the Princes in Shakespeare's *Richard the Third,* and even the labor of children in the mines and factories in the nineteenth century, were consequences of children sharing with adults the assets and dangers of their common social positions of nobility or proletariat. There was no universal dispensation for age independent of social status even in the nineteenth century, though a change of consciousness was beginning to appear in the genius of the era.

This newfound concern, not only in England, with the child as an entity unlike an adult presaged the fundamental assessment of the impact of a child's experience on his character as an adult, which was the basic contribution of Freud. While much of the discussion of childhood in the late nineteenth century was idyllic and asexual, this tendency would seem to be partially a result of the honorable desire to protect the child from the vicissitudes of adulthood. At the same time, however, the quality of protection given to any individual child often depended upon his presumed innocence. Concurrent with this increasingly prevalent image of children, which is often conceived to have been universal and wrongheaded by modern scholars reacting to "Victorian prudery," there was writing about the sexual capacity of children in British medical literature, focusing upon its dangers, but certainly not denying its existence.[2] Thus the shock for adults of Freud's discoveries was not that children might be involved in sexual activity, but that this activity was not confined to a few evil children and was, in fact, an essential precursor and component of the development of the character structure of the adult. What superficially appeared to be an aspersion on the innocence of childhood was an assault upon the antisexuality and asexuality of adults. Freud pointed out the many permutations of the sexual impulse, the most important of which was that it never failed to be manifest.

In this process of realization that there was a special character to childhood, and indeed that it might require a special psychology, a new consciousness of children developed. While this change has not been universal, it is a characteristic of the United States and other countries of the Western European tradition, and more than likely it will be the dominant orientation of the future.

One of the consequences of this recognition is that adults now have a greater conscious concern with the processes by which children learn about sexuality. During the nineteenth century the popular method of dealing with childhood sexuality when it intruded upon adults was either to suppress the behavior or to deny its existence, and to avoid thinking about it at all as long as it was not a public issue. These methods are to this day the most popular ways of dealing not only with the sexuality of children, but also with that of adults.

However, as sexuality has become more and more of a public concern in the United States, a growing desire has been expressed to instruct children appropriately in sexual matters. Appropriate instruction is usually considered to be that which teaches without provoking either discussion or overt behavior. In this way, it is hoped, the alleged traumas that result either from incomplete information or mislearning may be avoided, and the essential nonsexual character of the child is preserved. In addition, the development of textbooks of sexual knowledge relieves parents of the anxieties and embarrassments of talking about sexuality to their children.[3] Part of this reluctance to talk about sexuality to one's offspring arises from the fact that such discussion may suggest to the child the sexual character of the adult. If the parent describes coitus to the child, then there is the risk that the child will make the correct supposition about parental participation. As will be discussed later in this paper, only a minority of sexual information is in fact learned by children in a legitimate, formal manner either through the school or the parents. However, when discussions are held about the methods of such instruction, it is usually these formal informational channels that are emphasized. Thus such questions as, "What, how much, by what means, and when should I tell my child about sex?," are always cognitively framed as if a rational pedagogy were the solution to the proper ordering of the sexual life, not only of the child, but of the adult. Out of these questions a small but growing literature on how to tell children about sex is appearing, oriented not only to parents but to formal youth groups; in addition, there is some interest in programs of sex education, to be carried on usually in the high schools for children of 15 to 18 years of age. It is in this mode that the majority of effort is directed, even though there is some evidence that it is misdirected and that, even if directed properly, it occurs at considerably later ages than it should.

The rest of this paper is concerned with what seem to be some of the central elements in the development of sexuality and sexual knowledge in children and the role that the formal processes of information-giving may have in this development.

THE SEXUAL VALUE SYSTEM OF ADULTS

A prerequisite in any discussion of the sexuality of children is some description of the sexual value system of the adult members of the community. The discussion here, as elsewhere in the paper, is restricted to the United States, less specifically to Western Europe, and probably not at all to non-Western cultures.

The most apparent element in the sexual culture of adults is the degree to which there is no real community of values.[4] There is a cluster of negative values that represents the total body of public sexual norms, but as Lionel Trilling says in evaluating the larger cultural significance of the book, *Sexual Behavior in the Human Male*,[5] "Nothing shows more clearly the extent to which modern society has atomized itself than the isolation in sexual ignorance which exists among us.... Many cultures, the most primitive and the most complex, have entertained sexual fears of an irrational sort, but probably our culture is unique in strictly isolating the individual in the fears that society has devised."[6]

What consensus there is usually is worked out by indirection or through the behavior of sexual pairs. The public system of values in reference to sexuality is clearly supportive of only marital coitus as a legitimate expression of either virtuous or mature sexuality. However, there is a substantial body of evidence that marital coitus has not been the only source of sexuality for the majority of adults, especially males. This capacity of the system of values and the system of behavior to exist side by side not only within groups, but within the same person, is indeed remarkable, so that it is possible for the same individual to report the majority values as well as behavior contradictory to them.

An examination of the specific sexual adjustment of pairs of persons reveals that it is quite possible for extensive and long-term sexual relationships—even, and possibly especially, in marriage—to work out to the apparent satisfaction of the two persons involved without a word being spoken about sexual behavior and its consequent pleasure or pain. This seems to be primarily a function of the character of the male and female roles brought to the marriage. The exchange of information between males in American culture is not sexually informative except in an indirect sense. The information comes as part of tales of sexual prowess or of humor in which emphasis is placed on heterosexual expertise or exploits. What evolves from this male-to-male interaction is an image of the sexual self rather than knowledge about sexuality. Among females, on the other hand, while a certain amount of sexual information is exchanged, by far the majority of discussion is related to affection and love. Thus the male is cast in the role of the technical expert, and this expertise is related to his masculine role. Even if he is not expert, there is a substantial constraint on the female not to point this out and not to help in the sexual adjustment, because there is always the problem of revealing to the male how she acquired her knowledge and arousing his anxiety about her ability to make invidious comparisons. Consequently the sexual relation is learned by and large through the exchange of cues and gestures rather than through discussion or direct experimentation.

The development of adult sexual consensus about acceptable overt behavior through the interaction of pairs of individuals rather than among larger social groups in the community has serious consequences for the nature of public discussion of sexuality, especially in times of controversy. The privatization of sexual consensus means that no one can be sure of the behavior of others, and this insecurity is accompanied by a belief that statements that differ from the conventional norms will be taken as evidence of sexual deviation. The only system of values that can be invoked in a time of sexual controversy is the most conservative, and this often results in the most puritan of the community defining the content of public sex education for children.[7] This lack of consensus makes it very difficult for a body of disinterested opinion about sexuality to exist. Any statement by an individual about sexuality is commonly presumed to be related to the sexual preferences and desires of that individual. In this sense all sexual statements are assumed to be ideological in character. Another consequence of this lack of knowledge and consensus is the degree to which fantasy may be projected into and then shape the sexual situation. In most areas of social activity, a reality check upon individual fantasies is provided either by interaction with other persons or by contact with the mass media; but the sexual area lacks such checks, and the proportion of fantasy probably outweighs the proportion of reality. With these conditions prevalent in the adult sexual community, it is not difficult to see some of the difficulties inherent in parent-child interaction, out of which come the primary experiences that shape character structure and sexual behavior.

PARENT-CHILD INTERACTION

It was Freud who developed the first fully articulated theory of psychosexuality,[8] and the stages of psychosexual development, which he called the oral, anal, and genital, have now passed into what might be called the "conventional wisdom." Freud conceived of the sexual character of the child and the processual changes by which the undifferentiated drive becomes the infrastructure of adult sexual life. To a striking extent, Freud's hypotheses were put to use as part of therapeutic programs without conventional empirical testing— except as they were tested in relation to individual patients. The result of this historical accident was that instead of the ideas being adequately judged, two warring camps developed, one believing in Freud as revealed wisdom, and the other rejecting his insights as absolutely unscientific. It is only in recent years that these ideas have received serious treatment from a scientific point of view—that is, one that treats the ideas as subject to confirmation or disproof. This is, in fact, the most important honor that could be done to Freud's work.

There are two primary difficulties in the Freudian scheme that are relevant to the problem of childhood sexuality. The first is the location of the instinctual energy within the child;

the child is invested with initiatory capacities that would seem to be better allocated to the parent. The second is the rather overgeneral presumption that all contacts with or stimulation of the end organs of the infant have either a protosexual or completely sexual meaning.[9]

The first of these difficulties has been the emphasis on the instinctual character of the sexual energy source in the child. The child is seen as possessing certain sexual character- istics which express themselves regardless of parental action systems. These actions of the child are viewed, in an older sense of the concept of instinct, as rooted in the constitutional nature of the organism. It is possible to reconceptualize this notion to include that of a transactional information system which exists between the child and the mother, and while maintaining many of the clinical insights of Freud to abandon the psychic instinctual model.[10] To suggest this does not require that such central insights as the unconscious and the irrational bases of action be abandoned, but rather that they be reorganized into another noninstinctual theoretical system. It is interesting that Freud should have allocated certain initiatory elements in the interaction between parent and the child to the child's own "nature." This theory projects upon the child—who is less differentiated sexually and there- fore less initiatory—the sexual desires of the parents, who are the primal agents in developing, promoting, or repressing the sexual behavior and attitudes of the child. In some sense this may have made it easier for the parent to accept a sexual element in the child by placing it in the realm of constitutional forces. However, it seems more likely that parents may un- knowingly be sexually initiatory to their children, and may interpret nonspecific behavior as sexual and respond to it, giving it such a definition to the child.

The second difficulty is the primitive Freudian view that all actions of parents that impinge upon the child or that all of the child's actions of a specific class—for example, thumb- sucking—have direct control over or stand in place of certain sexual actions or functions. It is clear that this is too general a formulation, but it does lead to fruitful considerations of the relationships between "nonsexual" parent-child interaction and the resultant sexual behavior of the child. The specific mechanisms by which the parents' behavior in reference to, say, bowel control is related to the sexual functioning of the child, and the hierarchy of significance of the various activities involved in the teaching of this earliest form of control, are currently unknown. However, there is substantial evidence that the experiences of the child early in life have certain lasting and defining influences on the way in which he conducts his sexual life.

The convergence of the early work of Spitz[11] on mother-deprived infants and that of Harlow and others[12] on the Rhesus monkey are two of the most important examples of research pointing out the significance of early learning for sexual development.[13] Spitz found that infants observed in normal homes with excellent mother-child relations had a significantly greater incidence of genital play in the first year of life than did children reared either in an institution with mother-child relations of varying emotional quality, or in a foundlings' home without mother-child relations. Spitz concluded that genital play was part of the normal pattern of development of the healthy child in contact with an accepting mother. This remains rather global terminology since the acts and attitudes of the mother are not so much specified as hidden in the description; however, it still points to the importance of the early experience. The work of Harlow in rearing Rhesus monkeys in a variety of experimental situations is of equal significance, and, since the adult activities of the monkeys were observed, of even more convincing character. Some of the monkeys were reared with surrogate mothers made alternatively of wire or cloth; others were reared in various combinations of play groups and present or absent mothers. A series of powerful findings was generated by these researches. One was that adult monkeys who had been reared in isolation from both mothers and peers were completely incapable of adult heterosexual contacts, and exhibited symptoms which looked very much like human mental disease. In addition, an important element in the development of the sexual capacity of these animals was the presence of peers; when the infant monkeys were reared with peers but without mothers the sexual capacity did not seem to be disturbed. Deprivation of peers from the age of three to six months, Harlow contends, "irreversibly blights the animal's capacity for social adjustment."[14] He further suggests, "It is apparent also that sexual activity is stimulated by the mother's grooming of the infant."[15] In this research there is specific evidence that particular patterns of activity of a mother with an infant animal have lasting and permanent impact on the sexual life of that infant when he is an adult.

Thus there exists the beginning of a body of empirical evidence that is supportive of the general Freudian presumptions about early childhood experience. Further, there is some value in viewing the original Freudian conceptions which specified basic developmental sequences as a prototype of the critical-period hypothesis. This hypothesis, which originated in ethnological research, has, as pointed out by Caldwell, two possible meanings. One is that beyond a certain point in time the organism becomes immune or resistant to certain types of stimulation, and the second is that during a particular period of time the organism is especially susceptible or sensitive to certain types of modifiers.[16] This is, of course, what is involved in the Harlow findings about deprivation of peer interaction during the period of from three to six months of age in the Rhesus monkey.

It would appear reasonable to suggest that the developmental sequences suggested by Freud might well be of the critical-period type.[17] However, at this point, while there is evidence that the early period of life is extremely significant, the systems of transactions which are causal are not as yet clearly delineated.

Much of the behavior described above may have sexual consequences for the child; however, except for a few adults who are conscious of Freud, there is little recognition of the significance of differences in parental behavior that have different outcomes for the child. Indeed, even among those who have some recognition of the current fads in child-rearing, there is little evidence to suggest that conscious planning of child-parent interaction has done any more than confuse the child about what to expect next. The parent often seems to be working out fundamentally unconscious needs in a pattern of habitual response rather than planning his interaction with the child.[18]

One of the obvious areas in which the behavior of parents toward children has clear-cut sexual consequences is the separate behavioral syndromes that are related to the rearing of male and female children. The work of Money and the Hampsons[19] indicates clearly the early development of gender role, which they describe as "... all those things that a person says or does to disclose himself or herself as having the status of boy or man, girl or woman, respectively. ... A gender role is not established at birth, but is built up cumulatively through experiences encountered and transacted—through casual and unplanned learning, through explicit instruction and inculcation, and through spontaneously putting two and two together to make sometimes four and sometimes, erroneously, five."[20] These scientists demonstrated that in their cases gender role was usually set by a little after two years of age, and attempts after this time to change the orientation in children who had been placed in the incorrect sex category because of external genital ambiguity had various negative psychic consequences for the child. Other criteria—gonadal or chromosomal—for sex assignment were of minor importance even though they have been assumed to have biological priority.

It is possible to argue, as indeed Money and the Hampsons do, that their research is antithetical and in basic contradiction to theories of innate bisexuality such as those of Freud. However, a more modest middle ground which will admit directionality based on prenatal potentiation of the organism through hormonal effects on the nervous system seems to be the one to take at present.[21] It is possible, as has been pointed out by Diamond, that the abnormal cases studied by Money and the Hampsons may have been less directed toward maleness or femaleness because of lowered hormonal levels and therefore more labile to misprinting in the sense that the latter authors use the term.[22] The biological substrate produced by prenatal hormonal effects may differentially ready the organism to receive the definitions and inputs of masculinity and femininity from the parents. The gender role and

LIBRARY OF MOUNT ST. MARY'S COLLEGE

its components will then be built on the bisexual biological character, and the gender role will be a resultant of these two kinds of forces rather than the unique product of either. Further, data have been gathered that suggest that persons with anomalous genitalia who have been reared in a gender role opposite that of their biological internal structure have made successful shifts in gender role late in life, and these shifts were often made because the patients felt "something was wrong."[23] This finding suggests that the management of the sexually misidentified child should also take into account his own self-conception and desires rather than simply adhering to one or another rigid therapeutic orientation derived from a specific theory.

Since many of these inputs of information to the child occur without thought upon the part of the parent, it is clear that the actions that are involved even in the development of gender role are quite obscure; however, the fact that the parents are clear in their belief that the infant is either male or female has permanent consequences for the child.[24] Thus the vigor of play, the frequency of father-child as opposed to mother-child interaction, and the tolerance for aggression in the male as opposed to the female infant and child all contribute to the development of the self defined as masculine or feminine. Indeed, one of the purely physical elements that may be connected with the greater intensity of the Oedipus conflict when compared with the Electra conflict is the sheer frequency with which the mother handles the genitalia of the male child in contrast to the frequency with which the father handles the female, and the period in development when the contacts take place. In addition, the mother may have a more sexual definition of the phallus than she does of the vagina. The period of contact, the frequency of contact, and the psychological set of the parents can be expected to have differential consequences for gender role development.

This is an example of sets of actions which spill over indirectly into the sexual area. The phenomenon of indirect learning is probably more important in sexuality than in any other zone of development. These early experiences are primarily important in setting the capacity of the organism to respond to information that comes later on. Therefore the child in the first years of life does not develop a fully articulated sexual structure, but rather there are limits and parameters set, within and around which the growing child will operate. Thus the experiences of the child with nurturance and the character of his toilet training define to a greater or lesser degree his capacities to deal in the future with situations which are homologous or analogous to the early experience.

NEGATIVE LABELING, NONLABELING, AND RIGIDITY

Upon examining the interaction of parents and children, one is struck by the frequency of both negative injunctions and what appear to be—at least to adults—unambiguous instructions given to children in their early years. A simple household item like the stove is an example; the toddler is taught that the stove is hot, and whether it is hot or cold at any given moment he is told not to touch it, for a single failure in learning might well be disastrous. As the child grows older, more flexible information and attitudes about fire, temperature, and the stove are learned. The stove may be touched when there is no fire, cooking may be experimented with, and finally a series of rather fine discriminations are learned in order to deal with a common household object. This new information comes in both positive and negative forms and overlays the original information about the hot stove. This form of training is necessary for the child who is operating in a complex environment where the dangers of injury are high. However, as the child grows older, explanations of negative injunctions tend to be based more and more frequently upon rational calculations. Thus the infant who has been warned only about "hot" when he approaches the stove, is informed as he grows older about the dangers of burning himself, and is given a complicated set of responses to use in dealing with the stove.

This early instruction of the child comes from adults in

whom the child invests considerable affect. However, in most areas of behavior the influence of the parents, while setting limits upon the capacity of the child to respond, is made less pervasive by the impact of other and later experiences. It is in the area of sexual behavior that this body of apparently unambiguous and negative instructions is least modified by later experience. If the child exhibits behavior which the adult perceives as sexual—and, as I have noted before, the majority of adults often do not understand the relevance of most of these behaviors to sexuality since in the adult state sexuality and genitality are usually assumed to be congruent —the adult's response is one of two types. The first is to tell the child that it is wrong to behave in that way—that is, to label the behavior as unequivocally wrong. This type of information often will not come as a shock to the child, since parents who respond in this way have already communicated some elements of this attitude to the child in nonverbal learning situations. The second type of response is to nonlabel or mislabel the behavior.[25] When the behavior is observed, the parent attempts to distract the child from what he is doing by interposing tasks which are suggested to be more enjoyable, or by pointing out negative consequences which are not related to the sexual aspect of the behavior—for example, giving hygienic reasons against kissing. As part of the process of mislabeling, the infantile words for the genitals and for the acts of excretion are only replaced fragmentarily by another vocabulary. The negative control of sexual information extends to single words, and the child is left to nonparental agencies for learning the specific informational content of sexuality.

The nonlabeling phenomenon has two major consequences. The first is that the primary negative and dichotomous informational inputs to the child are never revised. The primitive form of conditioning, which constructs only black and white consequences for behavior, maintains itself independently, since the parental figures, who create the sexual capacity of the child through both direct action and indirection, are not reassessed or newly judged. This may be partially related to Freud's discovery of the requirement of transference for successful treatment of neurosis. One of the commonplaces of our time is the ease with which people adjust to a changing technological environment; however, an even greater commonplace is the difficulty in the treatment of mental disease. Freud says in reference to this:

> In the absence of such a transference (bearing a 'plus' sign) . . . the patient would never even give a hearing to the doctor and his arguments. In this his belief is repeating the story of its own development; it is a derivative of love and, to start with, needed no arguments. Only later did he allow them enough room to submit them to examination, provided they were brought forward by someone he loved.[26]

Thus it is possible for the child to reevaluate his parents' attitudes toward politics, vocations, and religion, for in these areas the parents have interacted with the child not only in the primitive negative manner, but also in a more complex and rational way. The child, as he matures, construes the parent as a religious, political, vocational being, and therefore the original inputs to the child are modified by consequent experience. This is not to say that even such reevaluations, especially if negative, are not accompanied by pain and grief and that in many cases they never take place; however, there is little doubt that most children and most adults are unable to consciously conceive of their parents as sexual creatures. Even those persons who remember having observed the primal scene—as well as the larger numbers who have repressed all such memories—should be included in this class. This observation of parental coitus, even if it occurs more than once—which is more likely to happen to those living in poor and crowded circumstances—is not sufficient to create an articulated sexual image of the mother or the father, whatever else it might do.[27] It is very difficult for children to believe that their parents even existed prior to their birth, and this primacy of mother as only mother and father as only father continues long into adolescence. Even after the experience of coitus, it is extremely difficult for a young man or woman to conceive of his parents in the same roles. It is of great significance that the original organization of sexual learning and attitude is never challenged in any major way, and it is not easily possible for the growing child to revise these early conceptions. Of course, in addition to the parents, other agencies of socialization serve to modify early nonsexual learning, but once again the absence of such processes in the area of sexuality should be noted.

The second consequence of nonlabeling is that of spillover from one training experience to another. As pointed out above, there is an influence on sexual behavior arising from early contact between parents and children which is not recognized as sexual by the parents, and the character of which is not clearly understood at the present time. However, there is one element which seems of greater significance than many others —the problem of the control of aggression and the manner in which training for aggression spills over into sexuality. If the sexual domain is left relatively empty and undefined by processes of nonlabeling, there seems to be a flow of aggression into this area. This has very basic consequences for both males and females, for if the sexual area is left empty, or if only the primitive forms of learning are in the child's repertoire, the differential training and control of aggression in the boy or the girl can come to characterize their sexuality as well. The fact that male children are usually more aggressive than females, and that this aggression is aided and abetted by parents, suggests that it is through the aggressive component of the personality that the male child frees himself from the repression of the sexual drive. In the case of females the sexual component is both nonlabeled and repressed, and the aggressive component is repressed as well; and so the typical adult female has a more responsive and less initiatory personality structure.[28]

This phenomenon of nonlabeling or ignoring sexuality may not always have deleterious results for children. Since many parents have intense anxiety about their own sexuality, the manner and content of their direct instruction about sexual matters might be more damaging to the child than the non-familial and informal structures that actually supply the information. In addition to protecting the child from parental anxieties about giving sexual information, it is possible that lack of recognition by adults of the sexual consequences of certain kinds of contacts with children—such as cleaning the genitals or body contact—may free the adults to perform such tasks with lowered anxiety. If they did recognize the fundamentally sexual character of certain of these experiences which are necessary for the development of the child, they might be inhibited from performing them or at least be unable to do so without displaying considerable guilt and upset.

Even after infancy parents create, unawares, situations of sexual learning. Mother-daughter look-alike costumes are an example of this. The mother wears the costume because it makes her attractive, which is an ultimately sexual consideration, while the child ostensibly dresses the same way because it is "cute." The child is modeling elements of adult female sexual attributes without the conscious awareness of the parent. In this example the linkage is relatively direct. In other situations, such as those involving cleanliness and aggression after the child is verbal, and types of handling and contact with the preverbal child and infant, the adult is even less likely to see these relationships—possibly properly so.

Adult provocation of childhood sexual experiences as actual occurrences, rather than as part of a universal childhood fantasy as posited by Freud after the first crisis in psychoanalytic thought, has been of concern not only to present-day analysts, but to the contemporaries of Freud.[29] The position of Johnson and Szurek, as well as others, is that certain sexual acting-out may be a function of unconscious provocation by the parents, serving to gratify their repressed desires which they project onto their children.[30] Since the acting-out of the children is often restricted to a single area of behavior— often nonsexual—Johnson and Szurek have labeled this phenomenon as superego lacunae.[31] Since it is the function of parents to provide and indeed call forth certain sexual functions in the child, the acting-out of the child who needs therapy must be distinguished from the patterns of development of "normal" children who at least do not make the kinds of signs of distress that provoke the interest of treatment agencies. What is distinctive of the parents of the acting-out child is the openly sexual content of interactions between parent and child; and even though the parents may not be conscious of the consequences of the interaction, they remember (without analytic uncovering of repressed material) specifically sexual discussions and characterizations of the child's behavior.[32] It would seem that the distinction between these parents and those who do not have acting-out children is the fact that the latter are less likely to freely and aggressively define the children sexually. Indeed, it may be really impossible for any adult to consciously intervene in the sexual life of the child without a burden of guilt that will perhaps overwhelm both him and the child. Ferenczi suggests that in this situation the child will come to identify with the adult and will introject the adult's guilt and anxiety so that the child feels both innocent and culpable at the same time.[33] In the case of certain pathological adults, the calling forth of sexuality on the part of the child by the adult—a customary characteristic of the learning of sexual patterns—becomes a disorganizing and disruptive sexual experience.

THE CHILDREN'S WORLD

The capacity for specifically sexual pleasure (as defined by orgasm) has been observed in both male and female children as early as four months.[34] This is clearly not present in all children; however, the capacity seems to develop steadily over time, with more and more children at each age level being able to respond to specifically sexual stimuli. Shortly after puberty most males in the United States (90 percent by age 16) have had orgasmic experience, and this same figure is attained by age 29 among females.[35]

However, the development of the physical capacity to respond in a specifically sexual manner probably only complicates the already difficult situation in which children learn to deal with sexual information. As noted above, the phenomenon of nonlabeling or mislabeling leaves the young child without a vocabulary with which to describe his physical or psychic experiences.[36] This specific absence of terminology has two major consequences. The first is the tendency for fantasy to overrun the sexual life of the child. The mysterious penis that must exist behind the female pubic hair, the feeling that females have been castrated, and other childhood fantasies are common because there has been no system of naming which will adequately control the child's nascent interest in his own or others' bodies.[37] The second consequence of the lack of a controlling set of symbols is probably related to the tendency for children to identify their sexual organs with excretory functions, and many psychoanalysts have noted that the emphasis on the dirtiness of the excretory function utilized to enforce sphincter control surely has consequences for the child's perception of the cleanliness of his own genitalia and of their sexual function. This may also be related to some of the sexual differences between girls and boys; since boys may get dirty—therefore dirt is not so bad—and girls may not, the association may be more firmly entrenched among the latter.

In addition to the fantasy-proneness of childhood, there is the tendency for the unsatisfied curiosity of children to lead them directly into sexual play. This is probably true of many aspects of childhood behavior where the child does not possess a meaningful vocabulary with which to communicate or to elicit information. From the data on adults in the United States gathered in the samples of the Institute for Sex Research, about 57 percent of the males and 48 percent of the females who were interviewed as adults remembered sociosexual play prior to puberty, with most of it occurring between ages 8 and 13.[38] Of a small sample of males interviewed before puberty, about 70 percent reported such sex play, suggesting that it is an even more widespread phenomenon, and that the memory of it is apparently often repressed by adult respondents.[39] Most of the play was sporadic and primarily motivated by curiosity about the body of either the same or the opposite sex.[40] Similar to children's other patterns of behavior, the learning situation was usually initiated by a child slightly older either in age or experience, and most commonly the behavior did not continue. The lack of labeling may make experimental play more likely in that it creates a zone of the body about which there is some fundamental mystery and concern.[41]

Given this framework of repression and avoidance by parents, it is not surprising that the child gets the bulk of his sexual information, though not his attitudes, through peer relationships. Though the parents are not providing cognitive information about sexuality for the child, they are creating attitudes and orientations through which information from other children will be filtered. In the peer relationships, since no children—or, at most, few—have accurate information about even reproductive functions, they will systematically misinform each other just as they are systematically misinformed by their parents about being brought by the stork, being brought in the doctor's bag, or having been found in a cabbage patch. Unfortunately these belief systems and their origins among children have not been systematically studied, and the most likely reason for this is that the research itself must be a form of sex education.[42] In the exchanges between child and interlocutor the child will not remain unchanged, and even if he is asked only the meaning of certain terms, he will be in that moment informed or made curious. In this case there can be nothing but action research.

In all of the American studies it is clear that the primary source of sex information is peers. This has been a stable characteristic of most populations studied beginning with the Exner study of 1915 (85 percent of 948 college men),[43] and continuing through Hughes in 1926 (78 percent of 1,029 schoolboys),[44] Ramsey in 1943 (90 percent of 291 high school students, either from peers or by self-discovery),[45] Gebhard and co-workers in 1965 (91 percent of 477 lower-class men, 89 percent of 888 incarcerated criminals, and 89 percent of 1,356 convicted sex offenders).[46]

In approximately one half of the cases in all of the studies, neither parent contributed any information. In the Ramsey study of 1943, 60 percent of the mothers and 82 percent of the fathers had given no sexual information.[47] In the study by Gebhard and co-workers, approximately three quarters of the parents of both sexes had failed to give any direct sexual information.[48]

The information that mothers give is usually related to menstruation and pregnancy; however, less than one boy in four in the Ramsey study received even this information from his mother. Learning about contraceptives, prostitution, and coitus was practically restricted to peers (over 90 percent in each instance). The role of the father is most ambiguous in this whole area; the myth of the good heart-to-heart talk between father and son seems to be exactly that. The father even less than the mother serves as a source of sexual information, and this seems to be a surprising finding. Apparently the father either assumes the boy will learn in his own good time, or that he has no real role to play in this area.[49] Unfortunately the questions asked have not ascertained whether the father ever made an attempt to teach his children anything about sex and then found out he was too late.

The Ramsey study also focused upon the age at which learning took place, and it is clear that pregnancy was learned of first (69 percent by age 10), intercourse usually next (57 percent by age 10), and masturbation next (43 percent by age 10). By age 14, the point at which it is suggested that most sex education programs should start, nearly all (92 to 100 percent) of the boys had learned about the previous three categories, and as many had learned of female prostitution. They remained most ignorant of menstruation (38 percent) and venereal disease (57 percent).[50] However, there is nothing in this learning process which suggests that the children have any integrated body of sexual knowledge. The young boy with experience in sex play may not associate his firsthand knowledge of the anatomical differences between boys and girls with the fact that babies grow inside of his mother, and the biological facts of fertilization may never dawn on him at all. Even though the large body of data on females in the files of the Institute for Sex Research has not been analyzed for these variables, it would seem safe to speculate that except for menstruation females are unlikely to have learned the facts in any more logical or coherent order. In the case of females it is clear that the mother may often play a more decisive role because it is more appropriate that she inform her daughter of the dangers of sexuality and the possibility of menstruation. This is certainly not always the case, since a fair number of females in our sample report that they first

learned of menstruation when it occurred for them the first
time.

What is learned is important; however, it is the context
in which it is learned that is more important. The exchange
of sexual information among children is clandestine and
subversive, and the manner in which parents attempt to teach
their children reinforces this learning structure. The admonitions of parents, since they are general and diffuse, do not
result so much in cessation of either interest or behavior, but
in their concealment and the provoking of guilt. It is clear
that few males have been deterred by the horror stories attached to masturbation. Madness, degeneration, and physical
stigmata have all at various times been attributed to this
behavior in the face of the evidence that the majority of males,
especially in adolescence, have masturbated and that they
have suffered none of these consequences. Those they have
suffered have been related to the anxiety produced by worry-
ing about the nonexistent consequences.

Thus children interact and exchange information on a
sporadic and unconnected basis, usually but not always with
some guilt.[51] The novelist Richard Wright recalled in his autobiography that in his early childhood he repeated an obscenity
to his grandmother and received a ferocious beating for it,
but did not know why he had been beaten.[52] This seems to
happen fairly often—that the child behaves in a manner an
adult perceives as sexual, and the child is punished without
being able to make a connection between stimulus and response. The punitive action of the parent may have little
inhibitory power since it is nonspecific to the child's behavior,
but it may provoke intense anxiety.

The development of guilty knowledge occurs extremely
quickly, and the children's world resembles a secret society
keeping information from parents.[53] This secret society is
under enormous strain from two sources, both of them pointed
out by Simmel. One is the tendency of children to express
spontaneously what they know or feel, and the second is the
difficulty of keeping a secret in a "small and narrow circle."[54]
There is a positive value set on the ability of adults to talk
to children about their problems, and the quality of child-

rearing is often judged by whether the child will go to the parents with his difficulties. Even with all of these tensions organized to force the communication of sexual attitudes and information between the parents and the child, the barriers of mutual distrust and anxiety are too high. Thus the sexual learning process contributes another element to the child's character structure—the capacity and need to keep sexuality secret, especially from those one loves.

After adolescence a different set of sexual problems appears, many of which are more or less restricted to the United States and relate less to the areas of Western Europe. Free dating and open intersexual social contact result from very special American conditions. Even with these special conditions many of the preparatory attitudes and belief systems that originated in childhood and infancy continue to play a powerful role.

Despite a rapidly changing society, especially in the technological realm, the power of these early experiences may be attested to by the stability (for the last fifty years at least) in patterns of overt sexual behavior. For the male the only basic overt behavioral change in his sexual repertoire has been a substantial decline in the frequency of coitus with prostitutes, although the proportion of men who have had at least one such experience seems not to have changed.[55] The use of prostitutes as a stable and substantial source of coitus seems to be a phenomenon of the past. Two attitudinal changes have occurred that are of some importance. First, the intensity and duration of anxiety about masturbation have declined (although the incidence and frequency of the behavior have remained remarkably constant) and, second, the proportion of males who seriously adhere to the "double standard" has declined, with a shift to a position described by Reiss as "permissiveness with affection."[56] The most radical change in sexual patterns has been the substantial increase in the incidence of premarital coitus among females born after 1900, who grew up during the 1920's, when contrasted with females born before 1900, who grew up before the first World War.[57] There has been no recent change similar to this, as surveys of college students have shown.[58] The bulk of this coitus is restricted to one male and to the year before

marriage, indicating that premarital coitus in the female
seems linked more directly to age at marriage and falling in
love than it is to the attributes that are most important in
determining male sexual behavior.[59] Attitudinal shifts have
taken place among females, but often they are situation-
specific, changing from a more permissive stance when the
girl is in the process of courtship and is about to get married
to a less permissive one when she has teen-age daughters.[60]
The connection between these changes in attitudes and how
they are translated into overt behavior is still obscure.

The long predicted change in American sexual patterns has
not, in fact, occurred, despite the advent of the automobile
and other artifacts of a changing technology. Since most of
the sexual orientations of the adult personality are results of
events that are not reversible through conventional means,
there are no grounds for predicting that the sexual life can be
easily changed. Given our difficulties in changing the behavior of schizophrenics, drug addicts, or juvenile delinquents,
or even of changing the political party affiliation of others,
there seems to be a curious contradiction in the belief that
sexual behavior is immediately amenable to change from the
slightest external impulse. This anxious belief may arise from
the facts that practically all sexual behavior is taboo, that violations of the norms are widespread, and that the transgressions are systematically ignored. These violations, which are
as constant as the norms, are assumed, when discovered, to
be the product of changes in behavior rather than to represent the persistence of previous patterns.

PLANNING AND THE UNPLANNABLE

The forces that mold childhood and thereby provide the
structure around which the personality of the adult is formed
are still only vaguely understood. Even such an insightful
work as Erikson's *Childhood and Society* primarily provides
a set of labels, albeit useful, and only intimations of possible
explanations of process and change.[61] Even if these processes
were understood at some high level of scientific sophistica-

tion, it does not follow that many parents would be able to utilize the available knowledge. A large portion of the actions of parents toward children is based upon irrational grounds, often repetitive of the experiences that the parents had as children. I am not suggesting a simplistic cyclical theory, but attempting to point out a differential amenability to change in various areas of both the personality and social life.

It is experiences in infancy and childhood that ready the child for integration of sexual knowledge and sexual behavior. This readiness is the consequence of systems of parental behavior that have no direct sexual bearing but spill over into the sexual area. The actions of the parents are not planned or rational, and, when there is an attempt to make them so, the child often becomes confused—he must respond at one level to the habitual character of the parents and then at another to the parents' rational plans. In the midst of these plans the irrational components of the parents' character tend to erupt, and the child is unclear as to the actual nature of the parents' expectations.

These confusions on the part of parents and the consequent disorderliness of the child's life are now commonly placed at the door of permissive child-rearing. It is now suggested by psychiatrists as well as Dr. Spock that discipline—when not carried too far—is a good thing and that good discipline is needed for the child's own sense of security.[62] The sentiment of psychiatrists that parents should return to punishment— administered "wisely" is the usual codicil—is based on two disparate but mutually supporting experiences. The first is related to the stresses of the therapeutic life for the therapist, for whom treatment failure and changes in the presenting syndromes of new patients have endlessly complicated the problems of traditional psychoanalysis. (In contrast to Freud, it is possible to argue that the success or failure of psychoanalytic therapy is unconnected to the explanatory value of the theory in reference to human behavior; however, since psychoanalysis has been primarily used as part of a treatment program, this distinction is usually not made.) As Freudian analytic techniques are rejected, so are the pronouncements about the processes of normal childhood development and the role of permissiveness. This reaction is especially notable among those therapists who deal with criminal or other deviant populations or mass groups such as school children.[63] The intractability of the case or the dimensions of the problem (often simply in terms of size) are enough to make people suggest a return to techniques which are applicable in the mass and by the number.

The second experience is the difficulty which parents have in applying the suggested methodology and the responsibility that it implies. The popular literature is replete with anxious parents unhinged by the dangerousness and difficulty of the child-rearing task, and much talk to parents is bent upon reducing parental anxiety. The opening line of Dr. Spock is the summation of all such reassurance: "You know more than you think you do."[64] The current mode is to tell parents to rely upon their common sense, whatever that might be. The import of these admonitions is to remove the onus from the parent of the terrifying (and rightly so) responsibility of rearing children, for this is often too much for the consciousness of the parent; he cannot reconcile the seriousness of his task, the lack of accurate guide rules (as opposed to clichés) for his behavior, and his emotional involvement in the child who is demanding his attention. The new literature even deflects from parental responsibility by pointing out elements such as inherent differences between children, as if this provided an exclusionary clause. It is not that the techniques of permissive child-rearing are necessarily indicted by the failures of parents in using them, but rather that parental incapacities have made adherence to the principles so sporadic and of such uneven intensity that they resulted only in confusion for the child.

In addition to the parents' incapacity to deal with the indirect elements which affect sexuality, they are also unable to deal with the problem of the supply of specifically sexual information. Since the parents persist in patterns of information control that are mostly composed of negative sanctions and nonlabeling and mislabeling of behavior, the child must search for information in the meager resources of his equally misinformed friends. As has been suggested earlier, given the troubled quality of adults when they deal with sexuality, it may be better for the children to learn through the informal channels of other children, since material from parents that might be overloaded with anxiety is reduced in significance and impact.

The overwhelmingly unplanned and unplannable elements in the development of the sexual life of children make it extremely difficult to discuss the role that planning in sex education might play. It is, however, possible to suggest that information imparted to children in schools or in other educational contexts should be communicated in each grade as part of the general curriculum. While it may be too rapid for some children and too slow for others, in general, if there is a source of accurate information that the children may tap anonymously and which is presented in a nonpejorative manner, at least the methods of communicating the information to the children will not in themselves be particularly destructive.[65] The specific age at which a child receives this information, as well as the specific items of information to be imparted, are of less significance than the preparation of the child for receiving this knowledge. The child who is traumatized by the sight of a nude body, or by learning that intercourse occurs, or by learning that babies grow inside of the mother, has previously developed a background of experience such that sooner or later, in one context or another, he would have been unable to cope with similar sexual stimuli. The specific triggering event is less important than the accumulation of readying experiences that prepared the child for such responses.

Planning of sex education should then be viewed as a rather secondary force in the development of the sexual life of the child, and while humanitarian values suggest that such planning should be done, the bulk of the evidence suggests that it will play a minor role in setting patterns of sexual life. There may be some long-run value in the teaching of sex education in schools, since it reduces the role of the parent who may only reproduce his own anxieties in the child. Whatever patterns of sexual life are considered desirable to maintain in a society, or whatever changes men may seek to

make in these patterns, it is certain that it will be more difficult to resist or accomplish these goals because of the roots
of sexuality in childhood. Even the accumulation of scientific
knowledge about human sexual behavior may not accelerate
much the pace or direction of change, for in this area of
behavior—as is probably true in others—the statement that
"Ye shall know the truth, and the truth shall make you free,"
may not apply. In a society that is addicted to the ideology
of limitless possibilities in human engineering it is perhaps
important to focus on some of the refractory elements in
human development. While it is possible to be more hopeful
about the human capacity for change than was Freud in his
later years, his statement about the limited potentials of sex
education should be kept in mind. It occurs during his discussion of the limited consequences for mental health that
either the purely intellectual discussion of instinctual conflicts
or the reading of psychoanalytic writings has. Freud says of
these activities:

We have increased his knowledge, but altered nothing else in
him. . . . We can have analogous experiences, I think, when we
give children sexual enlightenment. I am far from maintaining that
this is a harmful or unnecessary thing to do, but it is clear that
the prophylactic effect of this liberal measure has been greatly
over-estimated. After such enlightenment, children know something
they did not know before, but they make no use of the new knowledge that has been presented to them. We come to see that they
are not even in so great a hurry to sacrifice for this new knowledge
the sexual theories which might be described as a natural growth
and which they have constructed in harmony with, and dependence on, their imperfect libidinal organization—theories about the
part played by the stork, about the nature of sexual intercourse
and about the way in which babies are made. For a long time
after they have been given sexual enlightenment they behave like
primitive races who have had Christianity thrust upon them and
who continue to worship their old idols in secret.[66]

Sex Offenses: The Marginal Status
of the Adolescent

ALBERT J. REISS, JR.

The dilemma of the adolescent encountering his newly found biological capacities for sexual behavior in the context of moral and legal sanctions against his expression of that behavior is clearly expressed in the following article by Professor Reiss. While the adolescent is biologically an adult, he is not socially considered adult nor considered capable of the social and sexual activities of the adult. He finds himself still in the context of childhood, but without the kind of forgiveness that is normally available for the transgressions of the child. At the same time, the adolescent's biological imperatives are much more intense for the performance of sexual behavior. In this stage of life, as in childhood, the sexual environment is ambiguous and laden with traps for the unwary. There is no set of sexual behaviors that is considered appropriate for this stage of the life cycle except, of course, a lack of sexual behavior. While risk is involved, however, the application of specific sanctions for specific behaviors still does not occur unless the behavior itself somehow becomes visible or disturbing.

As Professor Reiss points out, there are substantial differences in the kinds of sexual behavior that are acted out, depending both on whether the adolescent is male or female and on the social class environment of the actor. Thus, the expectations of normal behavior are very different and far more permissive for males than for females. The social-class

REPRINTED with the permission of the author and the editors from a symposium, *Sex Offenses*, appearing in *Law and Contemporary Problems* 25:2 (1960), published by the Duke University School of Law, Durham, North Carolina. Copyright, 1960, by Duke University.

The writer gratefully acknowledges his obligation to Clark E. Vincent for helpful comment and criticism.

factors affect not only the overtly sexual behaviors that are performed, but also the psychological and social meanings that are applied to these behaviors. The lower-class boy begins heterosexual coitus in the context of the peer group, whereas, in contrast, the middle-class boy defers sociosexual gratification while continuing to masturbate. To the degree that the coital experiences of the lower-class boy are confined to the ranks of girls who are defined as morally bad, his coital activity, like the masturbation of the middle-class boy, is construed as "normal deviance."

One of the problems indicated in this article is the variable character of the sexual standards of persons who are members of deviance-locating and deviance-defining groups (such as policemen and judges), which influences the ways in which the law is enforced and the severity of punishments applied to the deviant. This further contributes to the unevenness of law enforcement and to the differential selection of persons to be labeled and treated as deviant.

INTRODUCTION

Adolescence is not a highly institutionalized position in American society.[1] It is a transitional status between childhood and adulthood, but it is less institutionalized than either of the two age-based status positions that it borders and connects. The adolescent is a marginal person who is no longer accorded the privileged status of the child, nor as yet many of the rights and responsibilties of the adult.

The relatively low degree of institutionalization of adolescence as a status position and the marginal position of the adolescent in terms of role expectations in American society are reflected in the fact that most of the norms governing adolescent behavior do not have adolescent behavior patterns as their reference point. Rather, the norms and expectations governing adolescent behavior have either child or adult behavior patterns as their reference point. The exhortations of parents and other adults admonish the adolescent either to "behave like a grown-up" or to "quit behaving like a child." They rarely encourage him to "behave like an adolescent." There are, then, no highly institutionalized expectations of how one is to behave like an adolescent, in the sense that achievement of these status expectations is a positive transitional link with the adult status.

This article is an attempt to show that the failure to accord adolescence a distinct status position that is closely integrated with the larger structure of American society and the resulting minimum institutionalization of norms for governing adolescent behavior has several very important implications for defining and sanctioning the sexual conduct of adolescents in our society:

1. The perception of adolescent sex offenders as neither children nor adults tends to (a) encourage considerable variation in definition of their sexual offenses; (b) lead to preferential treatment and differential adjudication of their cases of sexual behavior on the basis of age, sex, socioeconomic status, and jurisdictional considerations; and (c) obscure the degree to which they are denied the due process of law.

2. The age-based status reference point for evaluating adolescent sexual offenses is a factor in the sanctions applied to their deviation. When adolescent sex offenders are viewed as "not adult," they are generally overprotected and absolved from moral responsibility for their behavior, thereby weakening the moral integration of the total society. When they are viewed as "not children," there often is a tendency to deal more punitively with them than with adults who commit similar sex offenses.

3. The sexual behavior of adolescents is primarily peer-organized and peer-controlled. As such, it reflects the attempt by adolescents to achieve a compromise between being encouraged to behave like adults and being denied the rights and privileges of that status. An examination of the peer-organized basis for adolescent sexual conduct provides a normative basis for evaluating their behavior in relation to the larger social structure in which they are held accountable for their behavior.

I. THE EFFECT OF ADOLESCENT STATUS ON DEALING WITH SEXUAL CONDUCT

What acts committed by adolescents will be defined as violations of sexual conduct norms? And how will his status as "not child" and "not adult" encourage variability in the definition of an adolescent's sexual conduct as a sex offense?

Despite some variation in the legal codes from state to state in our society, the statutes define the acts for which violators are classified as adult sex offenders. But the problem is not as simple for defining the juvenile as a sex offender. Most juvenile court statutes not only define the violation of all criminal statutory codes as sufficient ground for a finding of delinquency, but also hold that if the child is growing up in a situation inimical to his welfare, he or she may be adjudicated a delinquent. For all practical purposes, then, the definition of a juvenile sex offender rests with the standards followed in each juvenile jurisdiction.[2] The statutes, in fact, prescribe that the finding be that the child is a delinquent person, and not a specific type of offender.

Going beyond the immediate jurisdiction of the court to the legal institutions for the care and treatment of juvenile offenders, one finds that still other standards may be applied in defining what is a sex offense. Reaching out into the social environment of juveniles, one quickly finds further variation in what is a sex offense, depending upon the status environment of the juvenile's family, his adolescent peers, and the institutional organizations within the community. There is no question but that in any of these contexts—the family, peer group and community, including the organizations administering justice—all forms of sex activity, including nocturnal emissions, may be prima facie evidence of the violation of sexual norms, so that negative sanctions may be invoked against the person engaging in the behavior.

The governing statutes are phrased in such general and inclusive terms that *any* sexual act or conduct can be defined as a delinquent offense. The omnibus provision for "immoral conduct or behavior" can be construed to cover all deviations from sexual conduct norms. The body of legal opinion and decision for delinquent acts similarly reflects considerable ambiguity as to what sexual conduct is to be defined as a violation and what is permitted sexual behavior for adolescents. Juveniles who are held to be guilty of a sex offense often are not charged with a specific sex conduct violation. The categories of "ungovernability," "loitering," "immoral or indecent conduct," "runaway," and similar designations frequently are the preferred charges, particularly if the court has a policy to avoid stigmatizing an individual with a sex offense. The terms "sex offense" and "sex offender" are not clearly defined, then, for adolescents in legal codes or in the adjudication of cases involving the violation of sexual conduct norms.

Most forms of behavioral deviation from norms or legal codes are linked with other forms of behavioral deviation, at least for a substantial proportion of all known deviators. For this reason, a person classified as a violator of legal or other conduct norms governing sexual behavior also may usually be classified as violator of other legal conduct norms. An adolescent boy or girl who is arrested for stealing almost always has also violated sexual conduct norms, and the reverse is usually the case as well. In behavioral terms, then, it is not particularly meaningful to define a person as a sex offender. This, of course, is true of most other delinquency classificatory terms as well. One technically violates the sexual conduct norm through behavior and thereby commits a *delinquent* offense. The term sex offender should perhaps signify no more nor less than this. Certainly, it should not imply that this is the only major kind of delinquent activity the person has committed. To classify a person as a sex offender may only serve to develop self and public definitions of the person as a sex offender.

The term sex offender, of course, is very ambiguous since it does not specify the specific kind of behavior that is used as the basis for charging a violation. But even if one employs specific behavioral definitions—as, for example, by designating the person as an exhibitionist or an unwed mother—the charge usually would not exhaust the sexual conduct violations for which the person could be charged. As Kinsey and others have shown, total sexual outlet is derived from a variety of types of sexual behavior,[3] almost any one of which could in the case of many adolescents be used to charge conduct violation. Although there is difficulty in classifying a person as a type of offender when an act of sexual behavior violates a conduct norm, the simple cumulation of such acts as a basis for classifying a person as a specific type of offender (*e.g.*, persistence) involves one in even greater difficulty. Not only is it difficult to secure accurate and reliable statistics on violation of sexual conduct norms for adolescents charged with a sex offense, but, as Kinsey observes, the frequency distribution is continuous for any kind of sexual behavior; any cutting point chosen on that curve, therefore, is arbitrary.[4]

The status of adolescent is an apparent factor in the application of adult sex norms to their conduct. The prescribed form of sexual behavior in American society is that of heterosexual coition in private surroundings between partners in a monogamous marriage. The legal norms, however, specifically prohibit adolescents to marry without the consent of parents. Unless this condition is met, therefore, heterosexual coition is proscribed for an adolescent. This example is instructive in that the norms do not specifically prohibit young persons from engaging in heterosexual coition; the limitation rather arises for adolescents because of difficulty in satisfying the conditions for marriage. Adolescents lack both the privilege and opportunities for self-determination of their marital status and thereby for their heterosexual behavior that culminates in sexual intercourse. It is not surprising, therefore, that for adolescents, petting to orgasm becomes a functional equivalent to coition.

Adolescents themselves set standards for what is a violation of their sexual codes. The standards in these adolescent codes vary considerably according to the social status position of the adolescent and his family in the larger society. A comparison of the prescribed heterosexual coition patterns of middle- and lower-status boys and girls may illustrate this variability. Among the lower-status white adolescent boys in our society, premarital heterosexual intercourse is prescribed to secure status within the group, while it is not necessary to secure status within most middle-peer status groups, even though it does confer some status.

Heterosexual behavior with prostitutes is not very common among adolescents up to the age of fifteen, although it is more common after that age. For adolescent boys, however, intercourse with female prostitutes comprises only a relatively small proportion of their total sexual outlet. Premarital sexual intercourse apart from organized prostitution is far more common among boys than is intercourse with prostitutes.

Among young lower-status adolescent boys, perhaps the most common mode of heterosexual intercourse is the "gang-shag" or "gang-bang." A gang of boys usually knows one or more girls who are easy "pick-ups" for the group who will consent to serial intercourse with the members of the gang. To understand this behavior, several peer normative factors need to be taken into account. First of all, the girl in the "gang-bang" almost always is one who gives her consent. She is not being sexually exploited in any sense of forcible rape. In fact, when she consents to being picked up, she understands that she is to be a partner in heterosexual coition. Lower-status boys clearly distinguish between "putting it to a girl" (she consents) and "making a girl" (she does not consent). Few lower-status boys, particularly delinquent boys, will "make a girl," although almost all frequently engage in heterosexual intercourse and most have at least participated in a gang-bang. Most lower-status adolescent boys express the view: "Why should I *make* a girl when I can get all I want without it." The opportunities for heterosexual coition with consent are ever present to lower-status boys, so that they negatively sanction forcible rape. This is not to say that some adolescent girls are not forcibly raped by an adolescent boy or even a gang, but the proportion who are is, without doubt, very small.

The girl who consents to sexual intercourse with the gang loses her reputation as a "nice girl," and they no longer regard her as a possible partner in a marriage relationship.[5] Her status becomes that of a prostitute. Similarly, a girl who consents to sexual intercourse with a number of boys, even if the acts are separate and private, risks her reputation as a partner in marriage. The status of an "easy mark" in sexual intercourse sharply reduces her life chances for marriage, at least among the lower-status boys who are acquainted with her. As a consequence, sexual behavior becomes her only competitive claim to masculine attention. This very loss of status as "marriageable," with the substitute status as "easy-to-get," gradually forces the girl either to withdraw altogether from the competitive struggle for the attentions of boys or to bargain increasingly the only thing she has—*i.e.*, sexual favors.[6]

The adolescent girl faced with the status dilemma described above is likely to adopt one of two solutions to the problem. One of these is the "steady date," which includes the "understanding" that he has sexual access to her and she is guaranteed a steady date—she does not have to compete with other girls for a date. Under these circumstances, the girl can defend her behavior in terms of romantic love ideals. Many middle- and upper-status girls undertake heterosexual coitus under these circumstances, since it protects their status within the group. They are "in love," "going steady," and "intend to be married"; *ergo,* if coition is a private act between two who are as married, it can be permitted. The other major alternative is some form of prostitution, either in organized prostitution or through the acquisition of a status or reputation as a "pick-up" or "easy-to-get" girl. The major risk a girl encounters in either solution is that of pregnancy, while in the case of prostitution, she also runs a fairly high risk of venereal infection.

It is not so much the sexual act of coition that brings the girl to the attention of legal authorities as it is either of these consequences of the act—premarital pregnancy or venereal infection. The couple is seldom caught in the act of coition. Since girls are more likely than boys to be defined as the carriers of venereal infection, a girl who is picked up by police or juvenile authorities is almost always given a physical examination to determine whether she has had sexual intercourse, now has a venereal infection, or is pregnant. This is particularly true for runaway girls. Boys seldom are given as complete a physical examination for venereal infection as are girls. Even less often are they questioned as to their sex experiences. There is a great variation among jurisdictions in this respect, however. Personnel in some are more likely than in others to learn about the sexual deviation of girls. The life chances of a girl before police and juvenile authorities, therefore, are more favorable to definition as a sex delinquent than are the life chances of the boy.

A number of other factors are important in the greater relative frequency with which girls, as compared with boys, are defined as sex offenders. Many policemen come from lower-status social origins. In their youth, many of them, therefore, shared the sex patterns of the lower-status boys and accepted the norm that deviation in heterosexual intercourse is permissible. So long as the boys do not forcibly rape a girl, or so long as the girl's parents or others do not file a complaint, the police are generally accepting of this form of sexual deviation. They may make a concerted effort to limit the opportunities for deviation, since that is expected of them in their work role, but they seldom arrest on discovery. Discovery in the act of intercourse is difficult, so that evidence is almost always obtained by confession or circumstances.

Adolescent boys come to the attention of the court as heterosexual sex offenders usually only when the morality of the girl's family is offended. The most common form of complaint is for the family to define coition as "rape" of their daughter. Research evidence shows that in most cases, the boy is not a rapist in any technical sense that force or coercion was used. The act occurred through common consent. The complaint arises because the girl, under family pressure, charges that she did not consent. Although many complaints arise in this way, it does not follow, of course, that some delinquent boys gangs do not forcibly rape a young girl nor that boys individually do not engage in such acts; it is rather to emphasize that available evidence strongly indicates that most heterosexual coition between adolescents occurs through mutual consent. The girl has a reputation. She is sought out or picked up. She knows what is expected of her, consents, and services one or more boys. No money is exchanged.

Middle-status boys do not prescribe premarital intercourse, and certainly not at as early an age as do lower-status boys. Experience in heterosexual coition confers status, however. The middle-status white adolescent boy assumes no obligation for premarital pregnancy, and marriage under these circumstances is to be avoided. The preservation of a middle-status boy's reputation is more important than the preservation of the reputation of the girl, particularly if she is of lower social status. Community organizations will strive to preserve his reputation, even at the expense of the reputation of the girl.

It has been suggested that a major difference between lower- and middle-status adolescents in respect to premarital intercourse is that lower-status girls commonly enter into the relationship by perceiving it as fun morality—"if it's fun, it's good"—while middle-status girls see it as one involving love morality—"it's good because we're in love."[7]

Status within a peer group is a very important factor determining whether an adolescent girl will engage in coition with boys. Courtship patterns in American society require that girls use a variety of means to attract males as dates or potential marriage partners when in competition with other girls for these boys. One of the competitive advantages a girl has available to her is her sexual attractiveness to males. Yet, the male norms prescribing the ideal marriage mate require that the girl one marries cannot have a reputation among other males as being sexually immoral. A girl's competitive advantage, therefore, is easily lost if she gains the reputation that she will enter into a sexual liaison with a boy if she is dated. Recent research shows that the adolescent girl who fails to acquire status within a conforming adolescent peer group of girls is at a competitive disadvantage in securing dates with boys, since dating is largely controlled by peer groups of boys and of girls who enter into "diplomatic relations" with one another. The failure to acquire status within a peer group of girls forces a girl to date by herself rather than "double date," to use more overt means of sexual attractiveness to get a date, or to withdraw from dating competition altogether. The use of any means to get dates other than those controlled by the peer group of girls results in her further exclusion from the peer society and leads to a definition of her as "sexually loose." Girls often communicate such definitions to groups of boys before the boys have formed a similar evaluation of the girl. An adolescent girl's status as being sexually immoral, therefore, often arises among girls rather than among boys.[8] Having acquired such an unfavorable definition then further deprives a girl of using conventional dating attributes as a means for getting the attention of boys in competition with other girls. Gradually, her only means for getting a date, therefore, is her reputation of ease of sexual access. She progressively is forced to resort to the use of this means if she hopes to attract boys as dates, and her behavior must conform to the boy's expectations once she gets the date.

The single most important reason, perhaps, why most adolescents who engage in premarital coition are not defined as delinquents is the difficulty in detecting couples in the act of violation and obtaining evidence of coition. For the most part, adolescent violators have a strong social status investment in not being discovered. This renders detection even more difficult. Violators, therefore, seldom come to the attention of the police or juvenile officials unless a girl involved in heterosexual coition, or her family, enters a formal complaint. Interrogation then is the principal means for determining whether the accused boy or boys are guilty of the offense. In some jurisdictions, even a lie-detector then is used on the boy, without any regard for his consent, in an effort to determine whether or not the behavior was as charged. Middle-status families generally will not risk the reputation of their daughter by bringing heterosexual violations to the attention of the police and courts, while lower-status families are less likely to see such a risk for their daughter. The lower-status family, in fact, sometimes sees formal complaint as necessary to protect the status reputation of their daughter. The effect of these status differences in the discovery and reporting of sexual violations is that the lower-status boy or girl is more likely to come to the attention of the police and courts as a sex violator than is the middle-status adolescent.

One is impressed with the fact that the judge and personnel attached to juvenile courts produce considerable variation in defining what is to be regarded as a sexual offense and who is to be classified as a sex offender. Some years ago, the writer observed delinquency petition hearings before a metropolitan juvenile court and examined the records for some 1500 cases of the court adjudicated by a single judge. During this time, the judge refused to treat any form of sexual behavior on the part of boys, even the most bizarre forms, as warranting more than probationary status. The judge, however, regarded girls as the "cause" of sexual deviation of boys in all cases of coition involving an adolescent couple and refused to hear the complaints of the girl and her family; the girl was regarded as a prostitute. Observation within a southern county jurisdiction some years later, where a religious fundamentalist judge presided, showed almost the opposite pattern in decisions. The girl was invariably seen as victimized by the boy.

Much of the variability in juvenile court jurisdictional standards as to what is a sex offense and who is a sex offender is attributed to differences among court personnel, including the presiding judge. The question can be raised, however, as to why such variability is possible. What is it within the juvenile court structure that permits such variability in standards and practices? The answer can largely be found within the structure of the juvenile court itself and the definition of delinquency in the statutes.

Juvenile courts were founded largely on two principles: The individual rights of the delinquent child were to be safeguarded by the court acting in the role of *parens patriae,* and the minor was to be protected from the association with adult criminals and from the application of rules of law for adult criminals that were deemed inapplicable to minors in many instances. The putative advantage of the court was that it would prevent juveniles from moving into a life of adult crime.

This is not the place to examine in detail whether the juvenile court has operated within these principles. It seems clear, however, that most juvenile court jurisdictions do not operate to safeguard the rights of minors in terms of the due process of law, that facts in juvenile court proceedings are subject to considerable interpretation and opinion, and that the probability of appeal from decisions of juvenile court decisions is, for many reasons, quite low. The result is that individual prejudice and opinion on the part of arresting officials and of court personnel are particularly likely to play an important role in adjudication of juvenile court cases. The word of police officers and of court investigators and the opinion of judges largely go unchallenged, particularly if the juvenile is from a low-status family. The juvenile may even be forced to take a lie-detector test without his consent, and almost any kind of evidence is admissible in reaching a decision that he is to be adjudicated as a delinquent.

These violations of civil rights and the disregard for due process arise from the ambiguous status position of the adolescent in American society. The adolescent is held accountable for violations of adult sexual norms, but is not entitled to the rights and privileges of adults before the courts. Put in another way, juveniles are assigned a special legal status where they are "not adult" and "not child," but where punishment or justice is administered for not conforming to adult norms. In general, it might be said that the principles and procedures of juvenile courts need to be carefully examined from the standpoint of assigning definite rights and privileges to the juvenile. These rights should be consistent with an adolescent status position that is integrated into the total structure of society. The assignment of such rights and privileges and the recognition of their importance in adjudicating an individual delinquent seems imperative in a society that is increasingly becoming conscious of problems of civil rights.

The ambiguities of adolescent status and the variation in procedures for adjudging an individual delinquent granted to juvenile court jurisdictions make it possible for prejudice and opinion to enter into decisions about juveniles more than it does in the case of adults. Since interpretations of sexual deviation are particularly fraught with prejudice and opinion in American society, the court is particularly prone to adjudicate cases of sex violation where these factors are operative.

Mention has already been made of the fact that juvenile

court statutes permit a wide range of behavior to be defined as delinquent. This is, of course, owing in part to the fact that in a technical sense, juvenile court judges do not enter a finding of guilt for a specific crime. The minor is simply adjudged a delinquent.[9] This legal technicality, however, obscures the fact that the decision to enter a finding of delinquency is based on a prior finding that behavioral acts violate either criminal codes or provisions of the juvenile court act. Proof of delinquency is a necessary part of adjudication.[10] The difficulty in adjudicating cases involving sex offenses lies in the fact that there is at least a double standard for adolescent and adult.

Only two states, Indiana and Wyoming,[11] have ever held it a crime to encourage a person to masturbate, and none makes it a criminal offense for an individual to masturbate. Juvenile court statutes, however, permit masturbation to be defined as immoral conduct, particularly if it occurs in a group setting, as it sometimes does among adolescent boys. But it is only rarely that the court will adjudicate such cases.

Many Americans, particularly at the lower-social-status levels, still condemn masturbation. Nowhere is this condemnation more apparent than in the codes governing sex behavior in institutions for adolescents. Masturbation is usually severely condemned within these institutions, and punishment is administered for its practice. At one such institution, a state training school for boys, the writer recently discovered that boys were physically punished if caught in the act of masturbation. Repeated violation resulted in confinement to the disciplinary dormitory of the institution. Such administrative policies within institutions to which delinquents are committed by the court or in which delinquents are held in detention by the court appear only to heighten the ingenuity of adolescents to seek more clandestine modes of sexual outlet. Among other consequences, the policy may only serve to exacerbate the problem of controlling homosexual practices in these single-sex institutions.

Homosexual behavior takes many forms and over a period of time involves such a large proportion of persons that it is difficult to treat these behaviors as having very much in common from a sociological or a psychological viewpoint. The laws regarding homosexual behavior appear as statutes against sodomy, crimes against nature, unnatural acts, buggery, indecent behavior, and lewd or lascivious conduct. To avoid the stereotyping of a boy as a "homosexual," some juvenile court jurisdictions, in fact, charge either "indecent behavior," "lewd and lascivious conduct," or "loitering." The penalties prescribed in criminal statutes for homosexual behavior are generally so severe that acts of sexual deviation are not punished as severely in any nation as in the United States. There is a tendency for juvenile court jurisdictions to ignore homosexual behavior among adolescent boys of the same age, so long as common consent is involved. At the same time, there is a countertendency to treat boys involved in homosexual acts as mentally ill. The problem of homosexual behavior among adolescent girls seems almost altogether ignored. There is one instance, however, in which the court may define the problem as a serious one, and that is where the boy or girl is involved in a homosexual relationship with an adult. This type of relationship is particularly common among lower-status boys and adult males. Lower-status, career-oriented delinquent boys often are involved in some form of sexual relationship with an adult male.

The sexual mores for single adolescents in American society are ambiguous. If the conditions for the prescribed form of sexual behavior are not met, then abstinence is prescribed. Basically, this norm assigns all other forms of sex behavior to a lower normative order. Not all other forms are tabooed, however, since who does what to whom, how, and under what circumstances will determine public reaction and sanctions to the sexual behavior. There are several basic elements that will determine the reaction to the kinds of sexual behavior between persons in different combinations of social positions under varying social circumstances.

The first of these elements is the *social visibility of the offense*. The more public the circumstances in which any sexual behavior takes place, the stronger the taboo and the sanctions against violators. By way of illustration, masturbation is generally permitted in private, but it is strongly tabooed in public as a form of exhibitionism.

A second element is the *social visibility of the offender*. The offender may be socially visible apart from the offense. Thus, an unmarried woman whose pregnancy is noticed is known to have transgressed the mores.[12] The transvestite, by reversing sex roles, is perceived as guilty of a sexual offense, although sexual acts are seldom actually observed for them. In adopting the clothing of the opposite sex, the transvestite invites strong public reaction, since the reversal of social roles becomes socially visible.

An extremely important element determining public reaction to acts of sexual deviation is the *degree to which the status and role of the participants in the sexual act depart from the status and role expectations for these persons apart from the sexual act itself*. In American culture, the male is expected to assume active roles and the female, passive roles. The degree to which the male departs from the masculine, active sex role or the female departs from the feminine, passive sex role, therefore, is a factor in public reactions to the deviating sexual act. The "pansy" and the "castrating female" both seem more likely to be sanctioned for homosexual deviation than are the participants who fulfill conventional active-passive sex-role expectations. The socialization of children requires that parent-child authority relations be maintained. Incest is universally tabooed primarily because the status and role expectations for family members cannot be fulfilled when heterosexual behavior is permitted between members of the same nuclear family.[13] Upper- and particularly middle-status persons in American society are regarded as the guardians of morality; women are so regarded more than men. Lower-status persons are regarded as persons to be condemned or saved from their immoral behavior. These norms apply as well to sexual behavior. The lower the social status of both participants, the more acceptable the behavior. Proscribed sexual relations between parties who have low social status, such as Negroes, criminals, or "low class," are more readily accepted than proscribed sexual acts between whites, conformers, or middle-class persons. The middle-class white woman, who is regarded as the custodian of American morals, is most strongly sanctioned for her behavior if it is defined as voluntary, but her involvement is most likely to be seen as that in which she is the victim of sexual aggression; it is intolerable to think of her as sexually aggressive.

The norms of American society permit a woman to use sex, particularly sex enticements, as a means to other ends—most specifically in her attempts to find a marriage partner. The male, however, is not permitted to use sex as a means; rather, he must seek it as an end in itself. The social status of adolescent boys in our society, especially within lower-status peer groups, rests in part on their sexual conquests. Among adolescent boys, in fact, it appears that gratification is less important in the sexual relationship with a woman than is the act of conquest itself, since conquest confers status within the peer group. *Acts of sexual deviation that depart from the expectation that females must seek sexual activity as a means and males as an end in itself* are more likely to arouse public indignation. It is more acceptable, therefore, for a low-status girl to advance her social position by coition with a higher-status male than it is for a low-status boy to initiate a sexual act toward a higher-status girl. For this reason, too, it is more acceptable for males socially to degrade themselves in the sexual act than it is for women to do so. Men are viewed as seeking sex as an end in itself, but women are allowed to seek it only as a means to other ends. For this reason, too, boys are allowed greater versatility in their choice of sexual partners (including animals) than are girls.

The degree to which the behavioral act departs from the model of heterosexual coition also is a factor in public reaction to deviating sexual behavior. Although mouth-genital fellation is a felony in most states, it is much less likely to be treated as a felony in heterosexual than in homosexual contact. Likewise, since infrahuman contacts depart most from the expectation, they have the lowest relative incidence of all major types of sexual activity and are most condemned.

Within American society, there are important subgroup differences in codes governing sexual conduct. The lower-status
groups in American society, for example, generally sanction
premarital sexual intercourse with the expectation that culmination in pregnancy prescribes marriage if the girl is "nice"
—i.e., not sexually promiscuous. Similarly, this lower-status
subgroup prefers (but does not prescribe) virginity in the female chosen as the marriage partner, but prescribes that the
single male have regular outlets for heterosexual intercourse.[14]
There are subcultures, too, such as that of the beatniks, that
prescribe any form of sexual act so long as it maximizes sexual
gratification,[15] or some delinquent ones that legitimize the
role of prostitute with adult male fellators.[16] Still other sub-
groups positively sanction celibacy and/or sexual continence,
as, for example, men and women in religious orders.

There also are differences in structural opportunities for
sexual deviation from community to community and in the
life situations of adolescents.[17] A boy or girl residing in a
lower-status, urban slum area has more opportunities to come
into contact with certain forms of organized prostitution. The
single-sex social structures and arrangements as found in
school and college dormitories and training schools for boys
and girls, with their increased sex segregation limiting heterosexual contact, lead to the availability of other forms of sex
behavior. The typical state training school, for example, increases the exploitative homosexual contact between boys or
girls of the same age and creates the role of the "punk" or
"queer" among others. The differences in availability of contact with subgroups that hold norms positively sanctioning
sexual behavior at variance with the legal norms of the larger
society and the actual availability of opportunities to engage
in deviating forms of sexual conduct are important factors,
of course, in accounting for the patterned differences in sex
behavior among adolescent subgroups in our society. In general, the lower-status adolescent boy living in a large metropolitan subcommunity that is homogeneously lower-class is
most likely to have experienced and positively to sanction all
forms of sexual conduct.[18]

II. THE RELATION OF ADOLESCENT STATUS
TO SOCIAL SANCTIONS FOR
SEXUAL DEVIATION

There is informal recognition among adults responsible for enforcing the sexual codes in our society that much sex deviation among single adolescents must be tolerated—that it is "normal" behavior and, therefore, it is a permissible, although not a preferred, form of behavior. This is particularly true of premarital heterosexual intercourse among adolescents. So long as an unwanted pregnancy does not occur and the partners are reasonably close to one another in age, the behavior seldom invites strong legal sanctions. Our culture, in fact, goes so far as to allow one to teach adolescents contraceptive behavior and the importance of recognizing and receiving treatment for venereal disease at the same time that it exhorts adolescents to shun premarital intercourse and legally prohibits it. The pragmatic in the culture requires at least that adolescents "be prepared" when they deviate (as we expect they will).

While heterosexual intercourse is permitted if it is a private act between an adolescent boy and girl, society clearly does not tolerate the behavior if it becomes public and thereby flouts the mores. Nowhere is this more apparent than in public reaction to the illegitimate child of the single adolescent girl. The boy is not treated as problematic in this case, but rather it is the girl who is the offender. It has been suggested that the reason for this is that pregnancy by its social visibility challenges the mores. The challenge must, perforce, be met with negative sanctions.[19]

While data on the incidence of premarital pregnancy are difficult to obtain, it seems clear that the lower-status girl, particularly of low-status ethnic minorities, who also is of borderline intelligence and social skill is most likely to be made a legal offender for premarital pregnancy. From a social-problems perspective, of course, this type of girl poses the greatest risk for recidivism, so that it is not too surprising that she is selected for definition as a sex offender. But it must be remembered that she also is least able to defend herself before the courts or to seek extralegal assistance, given her life chances. Thus, a girl is more likely to be negatively sanctioned for premarital pregnancy if she is in the weakest power position to affect the legal sanctioning system and has least opportunity (and perhaps wish) to hide the social visibility of her deviation.

The failure to accord adolescents a distinct status position in American society, so that there are clear-cut expectations regarding their behavior, has implications for the degree to which punitive sanctions are employed in dealing with sexual deviation and the degree to which the adolescent is seen as morally responsible for the deviating act.

When the adolescent is defined as "not a child," the adolescent often is treated more punitively than an adult for the same act of sexual deviation. This is especially the case when the adolescent is viewed as a morally responsible agent who deliberately or voluntarily enters into an act of sexual deviation. An unmarried adolescent girl who is to bear a child often is sent to a delinquency institution for her act of sexual deviation, while an older woman who similarly bears an illegitimate child is not usually so sanctioned by the courts. (In both cases, of course, the babies are socially valued for their adoption status.) To choose another example, in New York State, adults are permitted to practice homosexual acts as private behavior, but juveniles are punished for private homosexual acts if it is known they have engaged in this form of sexual deviation.[20]

When the adolescent is defined as "not adult," society and its legal arm tend partially to absolve the adolescent from moral responsibility for the deviation and to protect the child from the full force of the sanctions, or altogether fail to sanction the behavior. This is usually the case when the adolescent is socially defined as the "victim" or "exploited party" in the sexual deviation. An adult who is viewed as exploiting an adolescent for sexual ends will be more severely punished for this than for the same act with an adult. The relationship between an adult male and an adolescent boy requires special discussion in this connection, since the social and legal definition of the relationship is one in which the adult male is defined as a homosexual who is exploiting the juvenile.

Recently, research has shown that the social definition of the sexual relationship between an adult male and an adolescent boy is in many cases erroneous. The homosexual act in a large proportion of cases occurs within a prostitute-client set of expectations, where the adolescent boy is the prostitute and the adult male is the client. From the standpoint of the lower-status delinquent boy who usually gets involved in this sexual relationship, the act is an instrumental one in which the boy seeks adult males, particularly fellators, to minimize the risk in making money. A brief description of the way this behavior is organized in a number of metropolitan areas may serve as an illustration of what is involved in the relationship.[21]

Adolescent boys in delinquent gangs quite commonly seek out older males—"queers"—to perform mouth-genital fellatio in exchange for money. These boys, however, have no conception of themselves as homosexual, although they view the fellator as a "gay" or "queer boy." The relationship, however, is quite clearly defined and prescribed as a part of the culture of career-oriented delinquents. There are a number of elements in this definition. Peer-hustling of "queers" is defined as an acceptable substitute for "legitimate" delinquent earnings (theft, for example) when one cannot afford to risk being caught. The *"peer-queer"* sexual transaction of mouth-genital fellation provides "easy money" for the delinquent boy at very low risk of being caught.

The delinquent boy often is inducted into this form of hustling by his older peers. He learns how contacts are to be made and where they are easily effected. Above all, he learns the norms and sanctions attached to the relationship. There are several such norms. He learns first of all that the sexual transaction with a "queer" must occur solely as a means of making money, that the relationship should be restricted to mouth-genital fellatio, that it must be affectively neutral, and that violence must not be used against the "queer" if he conforms to these expectations. For many career-oriented delinquent boys, then, hustling of "queers" is permitted. For other delinquent gangs, the practice becomes one of "queer-baiting," to roll the "queer" for his money, since he fears legal recourse to charge he has been robbed. In either case, the adolescent boy exploits adult males in the homosexual transaction, if exploitation is a meaningful term in this context.

The point to be made about legal sanctions in this context is that in many instances, the sexual transactions between adult males and adolescent boys arise precisely because both parties are outside the law. The laws of our society and the mores of the public define both delinquents and adults who engage in homosexual practices as deviators and restrict their opportunities to pursue their respective goals. Under these circumstances, it is not surprising to learn that the adult male who engages in homosexual acts and the delinquent pursue a mutually instrumental relationship.

In a fairly large number of cases involving an adult male and an adolescent boy in a sexual transaction, it is questionable whether the adult male seduces the adolescent boy. There are, of course, cases in which such seduction occurs. These cases of seduction, however, do not appear to involve large numbers of adolescent boys—certainly not to the point where the boys in the long run become involved in homosexual practices. Most of the delinquent boys who become involved in the "peer-queer" relationship described above do not continue the practices after adolescence. A small proportion of them undertake hustling careers,[22] but most assume the typical lower-status adult male role of husband and father. The relationship never was defined by the boy as one in which he was in the social roles of either homosexual or prostitute.

The socioeconomic status of the adolescent is of some importance in the sanctions attached to sex violations. The higher the socioeconomic status of the adolescent's family in the community, the more likely the family is to afford legal counsel and, therefore, to require that the evidence clearly support the charges. In cases involving a sexual offense, it is particularly difficult to provide the necessary evidence to substantiate the charge. The court, therefore, is less likely to enter a finding of delinquency in cases where legal counsel are involved. It is unlikely that the boy or girl from a high-socioeconomic-status family who gets involved in a sex violation will be sent to a state-operated juvenile institution, since other and private means will be found to treat him or her— means of which the court will approve. For example, the lower-status pregnant girl who is single often is committed to a girl's institution as a sex delinquent. If a middle-status girl who is premaritally pregnant comes to the attention of the court at all (and she seldom does), the court will usually agree to her voluntary entry into a maternity home. Similarly, the middle-status family will seek the services of a psychiatrist or a clinician to treat its adolescent child involved in deviating sexual offenses such as exhibitionism or handling small children, and the court will adjudicate the case unofficially. The lower-status child with a similar offense often is committed to a public institution, where clinical treatment is given.

III. SOME PROBLEMS IN THE APPLICATION OF LEGAL CODES TO ACTS OF SEXUAL DEVIATION INVOLVING ADOLESCENTS

Perhaps the most difficult problem in legally dealing with sex violators is that the incidence of sex offenses among adolescents far exceeds their adjudication. Although it is impossible to obtain precise estimates of the incidence or prevalence of deviation from the sex mores or legal codes defining sex violations, the rate for adolescents undoubtedly is very high. Kinsey estimates:[23]

On a specific calculation of our data, it may be stated that at least 85 per cent of the younger male population could be convicted as sex offenders if law enforcement officials were as efficient as most people expect them to be.

A comparable estimate is not available for the younger females, although it is guessed below this figure. The simple fact is that it is quite difficult to detect persons in the act of committing a sex offense, given the essentially private circumstances under which they may occur and the circumstance that no other law is being violated. In addition, our social organization provides considerable support for evading detection for a sex offense, so that it is difficult to obtain sufficient evidence to enter a finding of sex delinquency. Most persons, including police officers, hesitate to risk the publicity associated with sex cases, including juvenile sex cases. While it would seem that the juvenile court procedures offer sufficient protection against publicity to persons offering testimony in such cases, the general public is unaware of this fact.

The result of this discrepancy between incidence and detection is that only the most socially visible offenses and offenders come to the attention of the court. Chance, therefore, may be the major factor in detection.

The interpretation of legal sex codes in our society is based on the assumption that juveniles are incapable of consenting to some kinds of sexual behavior or to a sex act that does not involve other adolescents. The adolescent in these cases is seen as exploited or seduced by others, usually older persons. Preceding discussion has emphasized that such an assumption is untenable, given the sex behavior of most adolescents in American society. Disregarding masturbation that may occur within a group setting, available evidence supports the view that (1) the majority of acts of sex deviation involving an adolescent occur only with other adolescents or at least persons relatively close to them in age; and (2) probably only a minority of sex contacts that adolescents have with older persons may be viewed as an act of exploitation or seduction on the part of the older person. A brief summary of some of the evidence in support of this proposition may serve to introduce the discussion that follows.

A majority of all boys and girls in the preadolescent years experience either homosexual and/or heterosexual sex play contrary to the mores.[24] By the way of contrast, less than half as many boys and girls ever report they were approached by adults with sexual intent, and the large majority who report being approached report it was either verbal or exhibitionistic. When it is remembered that most such approaches to the preadolescent appear to come from adolescents rather than from older adult persons, it seems clear that the preadolescent sexual experience is largely confined to persons at their age level or that of an adolescent.

Heterosexual intercourse is primarily limited to partners within several years of one's own age. Intercourse with persons in organized prostitution does not involve a large proportion of boys or girls with a high frequency of contact. Among lower-status boys and girls, the group culture sanctions practices of heterosexual coition in a group setting. The older the adolescent boy or girl, the more likely, however, that the partner is an older teen-ager or person in the twenty-year age group. There is considerable evidence, however, that the major basis of induction into heterosexual intercourse is the peer society itself, and not through seduction by adults.

Homosexual practices often begin in the preadolescent period with other preadolescents. For lower-status boys in particular, the contact with adult males in sexual behavior is an instrumental one of "queer-baiting," described where the boy seeks out the "queer" to roll or assault him for his money or to steal his car, or enters into a prostitute-client sexual relationship with him because the sexual practice provides income with a minimum of risk. Induction into these homosexual practices, as noted, is defined and supported by the delinquent peer society, and its members often initiate younger members into the practices.

Thus, while some adolescents are seduced by older persons into acts of sexual deviation, the majority are not. Adolescents either mutually consent to the practices or they establish relationships with older persons in some form of organized prostitution in which the delinquent is the entrepreneur and purveyor of service.

It should be clear that these adolescent group determinants of deviant sex behavior may be more true for boys than for girls, and for low- than for middle- or high-status adolescents. It also seems to be the case that the low-I.Q. person is more likely to be victimized by older persons, although the evidence on this is not altogether clear, since low-I.Q. persons may be more socially visible in their acts of sexual deviation.

If this thesis is correct—and to some extent it must be

regarded as a tentative formulation—then the question arises: Why is it commonly thought that most adolescents are victims of sexual aggression? There are a number of ways to answer this question. Not all of them are given in this discussion.

There is, first of all, the obvious explanation that the public and the courts come into contact only with those adolescents who are frightened or traumatized by the sexual activity. Only those adolescents who perceive of themselves as victims will bring their cases to the attention of the public or to the juvenile authorities. Adolescents who voluntarily enter into sexual relations with adults—and who, therefore, do not see themselves as exploited—seldom come to the attention of the public or legal authorities. A public and legal image, therefore, is created that the victimized person is the most common. Research evidence leads to the conclusion that this is not the case.

A second explanation lies in the social definitions we are taught regarding when we are to perceive of ourselves as victims in sexual behavior. We are taught to see ourselves as victims when the person is a stranger and we do not voluntarily enter into the act. Involvement with an older person who is a stranger, therefore, is most likely to lead an adolescent to define the situation as one in which he was a victim. Research shows, however, that in sexual relationships involving an older person and an adolescent or child, more often than not the older person who victimizes the child is a close friend or a relative rather than a stranger. Cases involving a close friend or relative are more likely to be dealt with through informal rather than legal means, however, since it is less easy to express indignation against these persons than it is to express it against a stranger. Courts, therefore, tend to get only those cases where the public definitions lead one to define oneself as a victim and where the adult, therefore, was a stranger.

A third kind of explanation is that the ambiguity in the sexual mores vis-à-vis sexual practices, coupled with the ambivalence most persons have toward sexual aggression, leads to a shared definition that an adolescent involved in any sexual behavior with other persons is a victim of the other person. Regard, for example, the fact that many middle-status parents do not wish to define their children as sexually mature, since this may force them as parents to cope with the sexual maturity of the child on a reality level. So long as the child is regarded as sexually immature, any discovery that their adolescent child is involved in acts of sexual deviation, then, is more likely to be explained on grounds that the child was a victim, since the adolescent is not seen as voluntarily seeking such activity for goal satisfaction. Certainly, parents are relatively unaware that their son, on the average, is more sexually active than he ever will be in his life or that their daughter is about as sexually active as she ever will be, as measured by the average frequency of orgasm in total sexual outlet.[25] Among lower-status parents, there probably is greater acceptance of many of the practices, so that there is less ambivalence toward their child's deviation. The lower-status family actually may support the deviation in more subtle ways, even though it may exact conformity at the verbal level.

Public indignation, as already noted, is more likely to reach its peak when acts of sexual deviation involve older persons and adolescents, particularly if they are publicly defined as homosexual or "unnatural" acts. The agencies of law enforcement, adjudication, and treatment also single out these kinds of acts for special consideration. From the police, who are most likely to arrest such offenders, to the courts and the newspapers or gossips, who are most likely to report them, these acts come to be conceived as the most common forms of sex acts involving preadolescents or adolescents when they are not. Let it be clear that no position is taken that public indignation should not be expressed against such acts. The point expressed here is that out of public indignation emerges a conception of reality that these are the major forms of sexual deviation involving adolescents when this is not the case.

To extend the point further, it appears, on reflection, that there is far more heterosexual intercourse among adolescents than any premarital pregnancy figures would disclose, that our social arrangements are likely to foster homosexual relations among persons of the same age and social origins, and that opportunities for sex deviation are related to one's social position in a community and the availability of organizational structures in it that support sex deviation. These social facts, of course, are the major determinants of the process of induction into deviating behavior, whether it is sexual or some other form of normative deviation. They account, too, for the structural variation in deviating behavior.

The moral concern about adolescents being involved in heterosexual coition cannot be adequately dealt with by arrest and adjudication for a number of reasons. There is, first of all, the fact that it is extremely difficult to detect and apprehend juveniles who engage in premarital coitus. Kinsey and his associates report that their records show fewer than six of each 100,000 copulations are discovered in progress. Furthermore, their records show no instance of legal adjudication arising from any of these discoveries. While some persons are charged with the offenses of premarital coitus, in no instance did the charge arise from actual discovery. Rather, conviction was based on other kinds of evidence and testimony.[26] This very difficulty in detection means that those who are detected must necessarily be the objects of selective discrimination, since they represent only a very small proportion of the total population engaging in the behavior.

The police, who are primarily charged with law enforcement, do not usually think of heterosexual intercourse as an offense. This may be so for a number of reasons, including the fact that the sex histories of policemen usually show similar violations in their youth. The point might be generalized, however. Since a substantial proportion of all males and almost nine of every ten lower-status males experience heterosexual intercourse as adolescents, and most of them are not ever discovered or adjudicated as offenders, it seems reasonable to conclude that most males inevitably are ambivalent toward arresting an unmarried adolescent for heterosexual coition, given the punitive action that may follow arrest.

Since premarital coitus is a moral concern to the families of adolescents and since the status reputation of an adolescent girl depends upon her maintaining her social status as a virgin (she may long since have actually lost her virginity), the adolescent peer society makes it difficult to detect and sanction deviation from the norms. Many violations of the sexual conduct norms, in fact, are maintained as a private concern to protect the individual from both the judgment of the peer society and that of the adult society.

Though tangible evidence is generally lacking, Kinsey and others report there is considerable variation in the way judges handle cases of premarital intercourse, depending upon their social origins. They suggest that the closer the social origin of a judge to lower-status origin, the more likely he is to be lenient in adjudication of cases involving premarital coitus.[27]

There likewise is considerable evidence that the norms of both adolescents and adults do not support either therapeutic or punitive action for acts of premarital coition. It is not the behavioral act of heterosexual intercourse that is to be avoided as much as its consequences. The consequences of contracting a venereal disease, of pregnancy, or of the status of being promiscuous are to be avoided in the view of most adolescents.

Given these fundamental problems in detecting and adjudicating cases of premarital coition among adolescents, together with the problematic aspects of what to do with violators, it seems doubtful that rational legal enforcement of norms is possible. This is not, of course, to deny that heterosexual coition is a problem of moral concern to be dealt with by other institutional forms of organization in the society.

Evidence shows that the homosexual behavior of lower-status adolescent boys—particularly that of career-oriented delinquents—occurs either as an organized form of prostitution or in some exploitative form of "queer-baiting." From the standpoint of the processes of law enforcement and adjudication of offenses, the adult male homosexual who is involved with adolescents should not in most cases be thought of as making the adolescent a victim of his homosexuality. Rather, the adolescent boy in many instances should be viewed as a self-styled delinquent proprietor who purveys an illegal service at a price fixed by fair-trade agreements. The relationship between the adult male homosexual and the lower-status boy is fundamentally rooted in a set of social definitions that the adolescent and the homosexual share as deviators. The relationship is supported by a delinquent subculture and peer society.

There is little doubt, of course, that such behavior affronts public morality and, therefore, is a problem for law enforcement and adjudication. To define it as a criminal violation for the adult homosexual and an exploitation of the juvenile, however, misstates the problem for legal adjudication. Other faulty ideas also interfere with a rational approach to the problem. A punitive approach to the adult male homosexual's offense does not deal with the problem of his homosexuality. To view the delinquent as a homosexual offender would ignore the fact that it occurs within an organized set of understandings commonly referred to as prostitution. It also would ignore the fact that the relationship arises as part of patterned delinquent activity. Making money from "queers" is part of a versatile pattern of career-oriented delinquency. Any legal attempt to deal with the problem under special laws for sex offenders will fail to recognize that fundamentally the act does not represent a sex offense to these boys, but rather an easy way to make money with a minimum of risk. To deal with the problem in moral terms requires a concerted approach to the problem of the prevention of delinquency on the one hand and the problem of adult male homosexuality on the other.

The discussion in this article has in large part proceeded on the assumption that the incidence of sexual deviation in an adolescent population is far greater than statistics on arrest or adjudication show. It has not dealt directly with the question: What would happen if the arrest rate were increased? How would cases be adjudicated? This problem is akin to that which arises for all types of deviation covered by juvenile court statutes. What would happen if we substantially increased the arrest rate for petty thievery, for example? These questions arise, however: Would there be reasons for not increasing the arrest rate? And would there be reasons for handling the sex offender cases differently?

It has already been observed that the problem of deviation from heterosexual premarital intercourse and masturbation norms is probably more realistically a matter for institutional organizations dealing with private morality, unless, of course, the norms governing heterosexual intercourse among adults are violated, such as those for prostitution or public exhibition. Other forms of sexual deviation undoubtedly will continue to be proscribed as institutionalized legal norms, but it is technically difficult to increase the arrest rate for these forms of behavior, given their organized aspects.

The question of what should be done with sex offenders clearly is a difficult one to answer. In attempting to provide an answer to this question, one must bear in mind that the type of sexual deviation influences not only public response, but adjudication and treatment. Should the single girl who is pregnant be placed with the girl who practices homosexuality or the venereally-infected prostitute? Should the unwed mother and the father of the child be dealt with as a unit? Should the career-oriented delinquent who has a sexual liaison with "queers" be treated as a sex offender as well? And so on. From a social and psychological point of view, much more needs to be known about both the causes of types of sexual deviation and the ways to deal with offenders of each kind before the advisability of increasing the arrest rate or of changing the laws governing the incarceration and treatment of sexual offenders can be seriously considered.

The delinquent boy or girl who is adjudged a recidivist often is sent to an institution for delinquents. There are several different kinds of such institutions, the most common of which is a training school. Such institutions house boys who are guilty of almost any kind of offense, including sex offenses. A basic characteristic of these institutions is that the population is highly segregated on age, sex, and even socioeconomic status lines. Thus, they are generally for adolescent girls or boys from lower-status families. Although some institutions may segregate for therapeutic purposes or programs, these criteria of social differentiation remain.

From a sociological point of view, juvenile institutional populations are the most experienced in sex behavior of any subgroup in the population. Furthermore, as already noted, at least among boys, adolescence is the age for the highest total sexual outlet—*i.e.*, at this age, one finds the highest average frequency of sex acts to orgasm. To institutionalize such an adolescent subgroup is to exacerbate the problem of sex deviation. The institution itself becomes a basis for all forms of homosexual and infrahuman sex offenses. Under these circumstances, boys will exploit boys and girls exploit girls.

In delinquent boys' institutions, the most common form of sexual exploitation is that of "punking." A "punk" often is forced to provide a variety of homosexual outlets to the other adolescent boys (although as his status of a "punk" becomes fixed in the status structure of the institution, he may engage in sexual practices in exchange for money or other resources). He may be a fellator, adopt the passive roles in pederasty, bestiality, or "slick-laying," as well as engage in a variety of other homosexual acts. While such acts receive strong negative sanctions from the institutional personnel and some boys refuse to participate in them, a large number of institutionalized boys come to accept them as alternative forms of sexual gratification. In the words of one such boy, "you ain't got much choice, and after you've been here awhile anythin' looks like it'd do."

There seems little doubt that the typical training school for boys or girls fosters highly deviating sex practices within the institution. Yet, except for the "punk," there is little evidence that the homosexual behavior persists when the boy is released from the institution nor that it persists into adulthood, unless the boy or girl also is institutionalized in a closed institution for a criminal population.

There does not seem to be any necessary reason for sex segregation in the institutional treatment of most delinquent boys and girls. The experimental programs begun several decades ago by August Aichhorn and considerably modified by Bruno Bettelheim at the Sonia Shankman Orthogenic School of the University of Chicago[28] and Fritz Redl in the Pioneer House experiments in Detroit[29] provide considerable evidence that delinquent boys and girls—even those who are seriously disturbed emotionally—can be treated in the same open institution in a community without fostering the deviating practices so commonly found in training schools. Parenthetically, it must be emphasized, however, that these institutions are not primarily custodial, but treatment institutions organized on the principle of controlling the milieu of the child within the institution and the community, while gradually reintegrating the child into the community. Still, it must be recognized that social science as yet is unable to demonstrate that such institutions will work for delinquent boys and girls who do not present problems of emotional disturbance, but for whom deviant activity, including sex offenses, is primarily the result of socialization in an environment that positively sanctions the deviation—the behavior is normative within the group; it confers status. Despite this reservation, the single-sex institution of the custodial form is no answer to the problem of the boy or girl who is a sex offender.

EPILOGUE

The problem of adjudicating cases involving sex offenses is a very difficult one. The statutes defining juvenile delinquency are sufficiently broad in scope so that any violation of the sex mores of American society can lead to adjudication of the offender as a delinquent. There is no question then of the kind: Are our juvenile laws sufficiently comprehensive so as to cover all violations of the sex mores as acts of delinquency? The questions which seem more appropriate are: Does there seem to be any way of avoiding the arbitrary application of the statutes to delinquent offenders? And are the criminal statutes regarding the relationship of adults with adolescents in sex offenses sufficiently congruent with the social definition of these acts among the participants? There is a further question: Will the public permit the courts to deal with offenders involved in sex offenses with adolescents or between adolescents themselves in other than punitive terms? Will it accept an approach to the problem that is oriented toward dealing with the causal sequence in the behavior, or will public indignation demand punishment of violators as criminal offenders?

This article has offered some evidence and argument to suggest that private heterosexual behavior involving consent among participants, one or both of whom are adolescents, regardless of their status, cannot be adequately controlled nor can justice be met by legal action. Because it is a moral problem, it is not one for which legal action will be effective. On the other hand, when the heterosexual behavior occurs within such institutional forms as prostitution, or there is clear exploitation or absence of consent on the part of the adolescent, the behavior clearly necessitates legal intervention. How the adolescent is to be dealt with in these situations, however, should be approached in terms of the modern concepts of prevention and treatment.

All other sex behavior, except the private one of masturbation, clearly offends public morality in our society, and the community at large does not appear ready to accept any change in the legal codes regarding these offenses. Despite this limitation, juvenile officials will need to recognize that there is considerable variation in the social organization of these kinds of behavior, so that an approach to the problem where the individual is treated as a sex offender may fail to affect its organized aspects.

Often one hears that the sex mores are changing or that more young people deviate now than hithertofore. Such statements may be correct, but they are essentially without proof. They, therefore, cannot form the basis for any change in our legal institutions. The data now available are for a cross-section of some population within the past few decades. They do not tell us how things have changed. To the degree that there have been changes in the mores, however, the sexual act no longer is regarded as deviating (or at least not as serious), and any attempt to buttress the older mores by legal institutional means will make it a relatively ineffective means of control in American society.

Under some concepts of treatment for delinquent adolescents, the adolescent may even escape moral responsibility for the delinquent conduct. The atomistic view of delinquent behavior and treatment that focuses on treating an individual delinquent and a delinquent as an individual is one such conception of treatment. One consequence of this conception is that adjudication and treatment of offenders often fails to regard the delinquent behavior in the context of the moral integration of American society. The norms of adolescent groups, the status of adolescents in the larger social structure, and their behavior as a consequence of these conditions need to become a focal point of concern if the moral integration of the society is to be preserved. The focus on individual violators to the exclusion of the matrix within which their violation is embedded can only lead to a further destruction of the social and moral integration of the society.

The discussion in this article was offered to show that the failure to accord adolescents a distinct status within the social structure of American society, together with the failure to institutionalize norms governing their behavior as adolescents weakens the moral integration of the total society. It would seem to follow that efforts to define a distinct status position where the expectations are that an adolescent behave as a morally responsible individual within the larger society should alter some of the conditions giving rise to the problems discussed. Attention needs to be focused particularly on what are the culturally-approved goals toward which adolescents are expected to move, what are the means that they may appropriately use to reach them, and what rights and responsibilities are they to have in the total society.

Sex Offenses: A Sociological Critique

STANTON WHEELER

The last of our general papers deals with the problem of sex offenders within the context of a sociological perspective. Initially, Professor Wheeler discusses some of the rationales for the existence of legal sanctions on behavior, focusing on three

REPRINTED with the permission of the author and the editors from a symposium, *Sex Offenses*, appearing in *Law and Contemporary Problems* 25:2 (1960), published by the Duke University School of Law, Durham, North Carolina. Copyright, 1960, by Duke University.

elements: (1) the enforcement of moral codes through setting the boundaries between conventional and deviant conduct; (2) the control of socially dangerous behavior; and (3) the treatment of those who are deviant. It may be seen that (1) would impose sanctions on all aspects of deviance including those that we have called "normal deviance," while the consequences of (2) above would be limited to forms of deviance that appear to be pathological or socially dangerous to others. The role of (3), as Professor Wheeler points out, is more ambiguous, and may cast as wide a net as (1) but with supposedly different consequences.

The second part of the paper deals with the contradictions between reports of overt sexual behavior and the data that exist on adult attitudes toward sexuality. In this regard there is consonance between Wheeler's consideration of the value-behavior discrepancy and the material presented by Gagnon (see pp. 15–42). This problem resides in the fact that expressions of moral sentiments with reference to sex are quite conservative, while the sexual activities of persons who express these sentiments may vary substantially from these sentiments. It is far too easy in order to resolve the discrepancy to suggest that people are being hypocritical when they say one thing and do another; what needs to be understood are the social and psychological conditions that create the hiatus between sexual values and behavior and constrain or allow people to live with such a major conflict between their values and behavior.

Finally Professor Wheeler summarizes a considerable amount of the evidence relevant to sociological factors that surround what we have described as pathological deviance and describes some of the characteristics of persons who fall into these categories.

INTRODUCTION

Issues raised by sex offender legislation cut across a number of problems that are of interest to law, psychiatry, and the social sciences. Three problems are selected for brief review in this paper. The first concerns the basis for deciding what types of sex relationships should be subject to legal restraint. Second, the paper will review objective evidence regarding social attitudes toward various forms of sex conduct between consenting partners. Problems posed by more serious sex offenders will be examined in the closing section, with special attention directed to sex psychopath statutes and to possible sociogenic factors in the development of sex offenders. For reasons of space, the special problems posed by prostitution are not considered. Since other contributions to this symposium deal with experience in other societies and with the special problems of juveniles, the concern in this article is limited primarily to social norms and laws relevant to adult sexual relationships in the United States.

I. PROBLEMS IN THE DEFINITION OF SEX OFFENSES[1]

LIBRARY OF MOUNT ST. MARY'S COLLEGE EMMITSBURG, MARYLAND

A. *Sex Relationships Subject to Legal Restraint*

Most of our sex laws are designed to govern one or more of four aspects of sexual relationships. Strongest legal sanctions are directed to control of the *degree of consent* in the relationship, with many states allowing the death penalty for forcible rape. Other bodies of sex law place limits on the *nature of the object.* Currently, most states restrict legitimate objects to humans, of the opposite sex, of roughly the same age, and of a certain social distance in kinship terms. Thus, sodomy or bestiality statutes prohibit relations with animals, parts of the sodomy statutes prohibit relations with members of the same sex, statutory rape and indecent liberties or child-molestation statutes restrict the legitimate age range of the partner, and incest statutes prohibit relationships with relatives other than the spouse. In addition, many jurisdictions, through fornication and adultery laws, limit legitimate objects to marriage partners. Legal restrictions are also placed on the *nature of the sexual act.* Full legitimacy is restricted largely to acts of heterosexual intercourse. Even if the object is a

legitimate sexual object, the act may be subject to severe
legal sanction. Thus oral-genital contacts, digital manipula-
tion, and common-law sodomy are legally deviant acts, although they may occur by consent between a married pair.
Finally, the law attempts to control the *setting in which the
act occurs.* Relationships that are otherwise subject to no
restraints may become so when they occur publicly or when
carried on in such a manner that the public may easily be
aware of the relationship. States that do not punish single
or even repetitive acts of fornication or adultery may do so
if there is evidence of "notorious" show of public indecency.
Public solicitation statutes as well as indecent exposure laws
are likewise oriented to control of the setting, rather than the
act itself.

B. Aims of the Criminal Law

If there were an explicit and articulate rationale underlying
the criminal law's attempts to control sex conduct, one might
expect that the legal sanctions attached to the various relationships would show an orderly pattern. That nothing could
be further from the case is a frequently-noted and often-con-
demned fact.[2] The wide disparity in definitions of sex offenses
and in severity of sanctions reflects, in part, the differential
judgment of the seriousness of all sex offenses. In addition,
it reflects differing judgments of the *relative* seriousness of
differing types of sex relationships. Some understanding of the
sources of disparity emerges from consideration of the various and conflicting aims of the criminal law as it applies to
sex offenses.

A traditional emphasis views the criminal law as reflecting
the moral condemnation of the community. Emile Durkheim's
discussion of the universal elements in crime stressed the feature of moral condemnation. Crimes "shock sentiments which,
for a given social system, are found in all healthy con-
sciences."[3] Crimes consist "in acts universally disapproved of
by members of each society."[4] The image of a homogeneous
community reacting through the collective conscience was
forcefully presented as the characteristic reaction to crime. A

vigorous statement of a similar position has recently been made from a legalistic perspective. Henry M. Hart has defined crime as "conduct which, if duly shown to have taken place, will incur the formal and solemn pronouncement of the moral condemnation of the community."[5] He has voiced the fear that this element may be lost in sentencing procedure, even if retained in the definition of crime, if corrective and rehabilitative emphases predominate.

The element of moral condemnation in sex laws is vividly portrayed in statutes defining "crimes against nature." The very use of such a vague and ill-defined concept is related to the revolting nature of the behavior. Ploscowe has noted a judge's ruling in such a case.[6]

It was never the practice to describe the particular manner of the details of the commission of the crime, but the offense was treated in the indictment as the abominable crime not fit to be named among Christians. The existence of such an offense is a disgrace to human nature. The legislature has not seen fit to define it further than by the general term, and the records of the courts need not be defiled with the details of the different acts which may go to constitute it. A statement of the offense in the language of the statute is all that is required.

A different basis for the definition and grading of crimes is reflected in the conception that the criminal law should punish only those acts that are socially dangerous, independent of their moral character. The American Law Institute's Model Penal Code[7] and the Wolfenden Report[8] in England have been strongly influenced by this conception in the drafting of recommendations regarding sex offender laws. In recommending the restriction of the crime of fornication to open and notorious acts and those involving adoptive parents and children, the draftsmen of the Model Penal Code justify their position as follows:[9]

The code does not attempt to use the power of the state to enforce purely moral or religious standards. We deem it inappropriate for the government to attempt to control behavior that has no substantial significance except as to the morality of the action.

Throughout the discussion of code provisions, emphasis is

clearly placed on control of behavior that appears to show some immediate social harm, either through the use of violence, through the exploitation of children, or through the nuisance value of public indecency.

The Wolfenden Report reflects a similar concern. It has been noted that "the yardstick applied throughout was utilitarian. If it could be proved that the behavior of an individual was socially injurious, he or she must be restrained."[10] Sex offenses are to be distinguished from sins and controlled in accordance with their objective social danger, rather than the degree of moral arousal they bring about.

A third criterion for the establishment of sex legislation has emerged during the past two decades. It is part of the growing influence of rehabilitative concerns on the administration of criminal law. This criterion reflects neither the moral condemnation nor the social danger of the offense; rather, the stress is on the degree of psychopathology characterizing the offender. The influence of this conception has been extended from sentencing and treatment considerations to the definition of antisocial acts. Some of the sex psychopath statutes have allowed commitment up to life for persons showing such characteristics as "emotional instability, impulsiveness, lack of good judgment, failure to see consequences of act, irresponsibility in sex matters. . . ."[11] Clearly, the emphasis is on personal qualities of the offender, rather than on the seriousness of any particular act.

Finally, there is increasing recognition of the important practical criterion of enforceability. The lack of visibility of most forms of sexual relations between consenting partners means that detection and arrest are nearly impossible for the vast number of cases. Such lack of enforceability may become another basis for judgment of selection of legal sanctions. Practical problems of enforcement are reflected in Model Penal Code recommendations concerning adultery and in discussion of the possible withdrawal of penal sanctions for deviate sexual intercourse between consenting adults.[12]

Current sex statutes reflect these varying aims of the criminal law. They do not fit a single dimension of social evaluation, but instead catch up in differing degrees the aims of expressing a) the community's sense of moral condemnation or revulsion; b) the degree of social harm resultant from the act; c) the degree of psychopathology characterizing the offender; or d) by omission, the practical problem of enforcement. Thus, it is no surprise that our sex laws are inconsistent and contradictory. A consistent criminal code for sex offenders is unlikely to emerge until there is agreement on the fundamental aims of the criminal law in this area.

C.   Trends and Problems

The Model Penal Code and the Wolfenden Report give evidence of a movement toward a consistent framework for the criminal law regarding sex offenses. As noted, this framework places the social-danger criterion at the apex of the aims of the criminal law, assigns a lesser but important role to the aim of enforceability, and restricts the expression of the moral condemnation of the community to such cases as are also viewed as socially dangerous. This shift away from a moral emphasis presents some problems that deserve brief mention.

A chief difficulty in implementing a criterion of moral condemnation lies in the diversity of moral sentiment in modern communities. Durkheim's conception of a universal response to deviance was perhaps overdrawn, even for primitive communities. It seems particularly unrealistic in application to contemporary western societies. The very changes that were indexed by the growth of restitutive law have brought about also a change in the collective response to criminals. Increasing social differentiation makes it difficult to find acts that are universally condemned. To speak of moral condemnation of *the community* is to use the term community in a very loose sense. It may apply to certain acts of violence and to crimes against children. Beyond these areas are many actions where no single community opinion can be said to exist. Responses to gambling laws, to white-collar violations, or to sex offenses between consenting partners depend heavily on the cultural background of the offender or of the person making the judgment. These influences play upon processes of adjudication and help to produce the great disparity in sentencing policies in different jurisdictions. Thus, the conception of a homogeneous community response, as implied by the moral condemnation argument, fails to square with contemporary life.[13]

In the face of these problems, the aim of limiting criminal sanctions to socially dangerous acts has great appeal. It purports to avoid the problem of differing moral judgments by establishing an objective standard of social danger; if acts surpass a certain minimal level, they are to be defined as crimes and graded as to severity according to the degree of danger involved.

The difficulties in working out such a formulation are evident in parliamentary response to the Wolfenden Report recommendations on homosexuality. There appeared to be general acceptance of the argument that conduct not injurious to society falls outside the legitimate concerns of the criminal law. But members of the House of Commons were uncertain that homosexuality between consenting adults was not injurious. There was fear that others might easily be corrupted if the act is not criminal—that persons will be willing to experiment with homosexual relations.[14] There was also the fear that removing the legal sanctions might imply condonation of homosexuality.[15]

Thus, even though there is no clear and present danger of bodily harm or corruption of morals in acts between consenting adults, there is always the possibility of long-term harmful consequences. Arguments to this effect can always be made and are hard to refute on empirical grounds, especially where the effects, if any, are likely to be subtle and only shown over a long time span. Although the history of legal control of sex conduct is largely one of failure,[16] this fact is a commentary on the problem of enforceability of the law; it does not, of itself, establish anything about the degree of social danger of the conduct. It is always possible to argue, as members of Parliament did, that conditions could be worse were the laws not on the books.[17]

This suggests something of the circular relationship likely to be maintained between social danger and moral condemnation as factors influencing public discussions and legislative decisions. The shift to an emphasis on the secular harms of various acts withdraws attention from their moral character. But in the absence of any clear-cut criterion of social danger, moral considerations will enter into and influence the perception of what is or is not socially dangerous. Until the consequences for society of various types of sex relationships are better known, changes in sex legislation will have to be based largely on changes in attitude and ideology, rather than on compelling evidence.

II. SOCIAL NORMS AND SEXUAL CONDUCT

The Kinsey volumes provided the first detailed account of sexual practices in the United States.[18] Public interest in the reports revealed the high degree of curiosity and anxiety aroused by the topic. But precisely because the subject of sex calls forth anxieties and fears, there has been a tendency for behavioral scientists to shy away from the systematic study of sexual attitudes and norms. No study of social norms regarding sexual conduct comes close to matching in quantitative detail the knowledge about sex acts contained in the Kinsey volumes. The result is that we have only meager evidence concerning the social evaluation of sexual conduct, as distinguished from the conduct itself.

Such evidence as is available comes from a variety of sources. The Roper *Fortune* Surveys have included a few items on sex attitudes in their national sample surveys over the past twenty-five years. Attitude questionnaires have been administered to select samples of individuals, primarily college students. Some case studies of particular communities or subcultures yield a modicum of data on normative patterns. Finally, inferences can be drawn from certain gross features of societal concern for sex relationships.

The data bear upon three questions frequently raised in discussions of sex mores: Is there evidence of a trend toward increasing permissiveness? Are there widespread subcultural differences in social norms regarding sexual conduct? Do the norms bear a close relationship to sexual behavior?

A. Trends in Values

Changes in American values during the twentieth century point to a widespread increase in sexual permissiveness, at least as gauged by the increasing freedom and lack of restraint in discussing sexual matters. Instead of the "Society for Sanitary and Moral Prophylaxis," the mid-twentieth century has a "Society for the Scientific Study of Sex." The pervasive influence of Freudian conceptions and the interest generated by the studies of Havelock Ellis are indicators of the same trend. The change has received support in modifications of obscene literature statutes, as brought forth most vividly in the recent case involving Lady Chatterley's Lover.[19] Although commentaries speaking darkly of a "sex revolution" pervading every aspect of social life seem highly overdrawn,[20] there is abundant evidence of increasing public attention and discussion of sexual codes.[21]

There is a vast difference, however, between the change in mores allowing greater freedom of discussion and a change reflecting either greater approval or a higher incidence of particular types of sex relationships. It is more difficult to find solid evidence for the latter type of change. Kinsey's data suggested, for instance, that the major change in rates of premarital intercourse for females occurred with those born between 1900 and 1910. Women born during the period from 1910 to 1930 had roughly the same pattern as those born during the first decade of the twentieth century.[22] And while younger-generation males had slightly higher rates of premarital intercourse with companions, the difference was largely offset by relatively more frequent contacts with prostitutes among the older-generation males.[23] The incidence of homosexuality and adultery also remained relatively constant, although suggesting slight intergenerational changes for different segments of the population.[24]

Caution must be used in interpreting these findings, for there are well-known methodological problems in the Kinsey volumes, the most important being the use of nonprobability sampling, volunteer subjects, problems of recall among the older respondents, and the possible differences between reported and actual behavior.[25] Within these limitations, the findings give no indication of significant changes in the gross features of sexual conduct since the 1920's.

Studies of the social evaluation of sexual conduct reveal a similar pattern. Impressionistic accounts of changes in the mores suggest that intercourse outside of marriage is increasingly viewed as an acceptable form of conduct. Unfortunately, there is no solid empirical evidence that can be used to evaluate this claim over a long time span, for objective methods of attitude and opinion assessment were not in use prior to the 1930's. The best available evidence for a more recent period consists in responses of national samples to an item asked in 1937 and again in 1959 by the Roper polling agency. If major changes in attitudes have occurred during the past twenty years, this fact should be revealed in the Roper data.

The question asked on both polls was: "Do you think it is all right for either or both parties to a marriage to have had previous sexual experience?"[26] Responses are indicated in table one. The results show a surprisingly stable pattern over the past two decades. When it is remembered that the period spanned included publication and widespread discussion of the two Kinsey volumes, it is apparent that the fears voiced in some quarters—that knowledge of the Kinsey results may have widespread effect on sexual standards—have not materialized.

TABLE 1. "Do You Think It Is All Right for Either or Both Parties to a Marriage to Have Had Previous Sexual Intercourse?"

	1937	1959
All right for both	22%	22%
All right for men only	8%	8%
All right for neither	56%	54%
Don't know or refused to answer	14%	16%
	100%	100%

It is, indeed, risky to base a conclusion on such limited evidence. Other interpretations than that of stability could be given. There may have been widespread shifts in opposite directions for different segments of the population, such that they cancel out in the summary findings. There may have been important changes of such a subtle nature that they are not reflected by a single item on an opinion poll. The results may be reliable, but may have caught the population at particular points in a cycle of sexual attitudes, thus giving a false appearance of stability. All of these interpretations are possible and cannot be refuted without further evidence. The simplest interpretation, however, is that there has been little over-all change in attitudes toward this form of sexual conduct over the period spanned by the studies.[27]

B.   Socioeconomic Status and Sex Attitudes

One argument frequently raised in support of a change in legal controls is that communities are no longer homogeneous with respect to sexual standards—that the wide range of standards held in different segments of the population precludes application of universalistic legal standards. Kinsey's data are usually cited in support of this contention.[28] The most important of Kinsey's findings for present purposes are the variations in rates of premarital intercourse and in techniques of sexual arousal. Kinsey found that rates of premarital intercourse for males were highest at low educational levels and were considerably lower among the college-educated segment of his population.[29] At the same time, he found that lower-level couples were likely to restrict their sexual contacts to the most direct form of sexual union, while upper-level couples employed a wide variety of coital techniques, mouth and breast stimulation, and manual and oral forms of genital stimulation. For example, oral stimulation of female genitalia was found in sixty per cent of the college-educated segment, but in only twenty and eleven per cent of the high-school and grade-school histories, respectively.[30] The direction of these relationships suggests that sex statutes limiting premarital intercourse are most frequently violated by lower-class members, while statutes defining various forms of heterosexual perversions are more likely to be violated by middle- and upper-level persons.

There is little systematic evidence to determine whether the normative patterns are consistent with the differential incidence rates for perversions. Kinsey suggests that his lower-level respondents viewed with disgust some of the petting and coital practices of middle- and upper-level persons, although systematic evidence is lacking. The pattern, if verified, is an interesting reversal of the usual view that legal standards of sexual conduct reflect a middle-class morality.

More evidence is available concerning the social evaluation of premarital intercourse at differing socioeconomic levels. Between 1939 and 1943, the Roper agency asked questions about sexual attitudes in three of their sample surveys.[31] Typical results are reported in tables two and three. The question for table two was: "Do you consider it all right, unfortunate or wicked when young men (women) have sexual relations before marriage?" For table three, the question was: "Should men (women) require virginity in a girl (man) for marriage?" Variation in response by socioeconomic status is similar in both tables, although the strength of the relationship varies with the wording of the question.[32] The relationship is also found when occupation is used as the relevant variable. Among males, the proportion who felt such activity was wicked increased from twenty-six per cent among white-collar and professional workers to thirty, thirty-five, and thirty-six per cent among blue-collar, unemployed, and farmers, respectively.

TABLE 2. "Do You Consider It All Right, Unfortunate or Wicked When Young Men (Women) Have Sexual Relations Before Marriage?" (Women Only; N = 5220)

Socioeconomic Status	Wicked for Men	Wicked for Women
Upper	28%	36%
Upper-Middle	34%	43%
Lower-Middle	40%	50%
Lower	53%	62%

What is surprising about the Roper results is not the degree of variation by social class, but its direction. Those in lower social strata are more likely to express disapproval of intercourse outside of marriage than are those in middle and upper positions. This is precisely the reverse of the direction for the behavioral record as found by Kinsey and others. The discrepancy could be due to such factors as a greater tendency among lower-class respondents to give what they perceive as socially desirable responses to middle-class interviewers, or the correlation of social class with religion or other variables. Certainly, the data are not strong enough to accept the finding as confirmed; yet, it does call into question the inference, frequently drawn by Kinsey's interpreters, that the social-class differences in rates are strongly supported by class differences in sex attitudes and values.[33]

TABLE 3. "Should Men (Women) Require Virginity in a Girl (Man) for Marriage?" (Women Only; N = 2570)

Socioeconomic Status	Men Should Require in Women	Women Should Require in Men
Upper	64%	42%
Upper-Middle	66%	47%
Lower-Middle	71%	53%
Lower	72%	52%

There are reasons to believe that the relationship between overt sex acts and cultural values is much more complex than is usually presumed. Thus, a growing body of research has documented the higher degree of intolerance for deviant behavior among those of low education and socioeconomic position.[34] The response to sex may be part of the broader tendency to see the world in a good-evil dichotomy. The tendency is reinforced by the dogmatism of fundamentalist religious groups likely to flourish and have greatest appeal to those in lower social strata.[35] Class differentials in tolerance for sexual expression are also indicated in recent studies of child-rearing patterns. Working-class mothers are found to be far less permissive and to use more punitive measures for preventing sexual exploration.[36] These findings would lead one to expect greater rather than less disapproval at lower socioeconomic levels.

At the same time, the objective life situation of lower socioeconomic groups may predispose them to greater pressure for engaging in the activity. Thus, studies of lower-class urban areas point to the frequency of female-based households in which if the mother is to have any normal sexual outlet, it becomes, by definition, adultery.[37] The greater amount of premarital intercourse among lower-class girls may reflect less a difference in stated values than the use of sex as a means of attracting males of higher status, in the absence of alternative qualities of attraction.[38] A related and important feature concerns differences in the use and effectiveness of social-control techniques. For example, the more punitive methods of child-rearing used in lower socioeconomic strata may be less effective in producing long-term internal controls, even though parental attitudes may be similar to those in other strata.

All of these features may operate to suppress the effect of cultural values on overt conduct. One of the reasons the relationships between socioeconomic status, sex attitudes, and sex behavior are not yet clearly understood is that they are probably quite complex, involving differential pressures for engaging in the behavior and different mechanisms of control. A particular pattern of conduct emerges from many social influences and is rarely a simple reflection of stated cultural values. These influences are frequently neglected in drawing conclusions from the Kinsey research.[39]

C. Other Structural Characteristics and Sex Attitudes

Considerable variation in sex attitudes is revealed when characteristics other than social class are studied. Even a single question on a public opinion poll reveals important differences in attitude by race. Where roughly fifteen per cent of the white females said that premarital intercourse for males was "all right," twenty-nine per cent of the Negro females gave that response. The differences in tolerance for women

who engaged in the same behavior ranged from roughly five
per cent for white respondents to seventeen per cent for
Negroes.[40] Evidence on sex behavior leaves no doubt that
the attitudinal differences are carried out in action. A study
of army recruits located seven virgins among 500 Negro
draftees.[41] Studies of illegitimate birth point to the extremely
high rates for Negro girls in urban areas.

Kinsey's results revealed the influence of religious affiliation
on sexual attitudes and behavior. Increasing rates of premarital intercourse are observed as one moves from Jewish
to Catholic to Protestant groups. For each religious grouping,
the proportion of women voicing regret for having premarital
intercourse was greatest among the most active believers.[42]

Regional and rural-urban differences are revealed in recent
opinion poll results: permissive attitudes are highest in the
urban Northeast (twenty-eight per cent), followed by the Far
West (twenty-six per cent), the South (twenty-three per cent),
and the Mid-west (fifteen per cent).[43] The same data also
indicate that the double standard applies most clearly to
Southern manhood. Thirteen per cent of the Southern respondents, compared to about five per cent in the other areas,
say that premarital sex is "Okay for men only."

The above review of variation in social norms in differing
sectors of society is probably a conservative statement of the
actual variation, for it has been impossible to assess the combined effect of the several characteristics. At the same time,
citation of percentages engaging in this or that conduct or
holding particular attitudes tends to obscure the general lack
of clarity of sex codes. With the exception of certain extremes
found among particular ethnic or religious subcultures, it is
probably fair to say that no single normative pattern is institutionalized in any large segment of the population, let alone
the society as a whole. The wide variation in response to the
Kinsey volumes gives abundant testimony to this fact.[44]

In part, the lack of clarity of sex codes is due to the spec-
ificity of sex attitudes. Whether premarital intercourse is
viewed as acceptable or not depends on many features of
the relationship between the couple. The sociologist William
F. Whyte noted that Italian street-corner boys made a clear

differentiation between "good girls," with whom intercourse was prohibited, and "lays" with whom it was highly desirable.[45] Studies of college students and middle-class sexual patterns suggest that intercourse is more acceptable to girls if part of a love relationship, while males are less likely to view it as acceptable under those conditions (although at any point, of course, premarital intercourse for males is considered more acceptable than for females).[46] Until recently, the social scientists' concern with sexual attitudes and conduct was limited largely to the gross features of such conduct as revealed by frequency counts and general opinion. The meaningful context of the behavior or attitude was seldom studied in detail. The growth of a body of knowledge about the meaning of the activity for participants should provide a more useful set of empirical findings on the social distribution of sex attitudes and behavior.[47]

A more pervasive influence is the lack of visibility of sex attitudes and behavior. To an important degree, no one knows what standards others are employing. Enough life remains in the puritan ethic to prevent persons from expressing their attitudes openly. This quite naturally produces a condition of pluralistic ignorance. Without this element, it would be hard to account for the amazing public interest in the Kinsey reports. And so long as the condition remains, it will be impossible to achieve any genuine normative consensus.

D. Homosexuality

Little can be said about attitudes toward other forms of sexual relations between consenting adults. While much has been written about the homosexual problem, there is almost no objective information on the degree of public tolerance for homosexuals or on conceptions of the desirability of penal sanctions as a means of control. Although mass responses are still shrouded in mystery and fear, the trend is surely toward a more enlightened, dispassionate perspective.[48]

Some inferences as to sources of changing perspectives can be drawn from other studies of tolerance toward deviance. As noted above, an increasing body of research suggests that tolerance toward nonconforming behavior may be a relatively general trait that may cut across many specific forms of deviation.[49] Tolerance is greatest among the younger generation and those with most education. The sociologist Samuel Stouffer's report on political nonconformity found tolerance also greater among community leaders.[50]

Whether these results hold for attitudes toward sexual nonconformity can only be determined by further study. The findings at least suggest the important sectors of the population that may be least resistive to changes of the type recommended by the Wolfenden Report in England. While such proposals are probably still in advance of public opinion, the forces making for greater tolerance are likely to remain and should be a sign of hope for supporters of more liberal legislation regarding homosexuals.[51]

E. Need for More Adequate Information

Review of objective data on social norms and sexual conduct reveals above all else the paucity of useful information. Aside from an occasional item in an opinion poll, a handful of studies of college students, and one or two anthropological accounts, there is nothing that even makes for intelligent speculation as to the sources and types of community reaction to sexual deviations between consenting adults. Such evidence as is available suggests that while there has been no great change in *standards* of sexual conduct at least over the past twenty years, there is a general trend toward greater *tolerance* of various forms of sexual relationships. Some of the more recent proposals for change in legislation invoke distinctions between mental illness, crime, and sin that major segments of the public are probably not yet prepared to understand or accept. Perhaps the single most important factor making for public recognition of these distinctions is the increase in average level of education.

The outstanding fact remains that no major study has been made of attitudes and norms regarding sex conduct. Any conclusions must be tempered by awareness of the flimsy evidence on which they are based. Within this arena of ignorance, the American Law Institute is attempting to design new legislation concerning sexual behavior. Important recommendations are being decided at least partially on the basis of guesses as to how the public or legislative officials will react.[52] Consideration of controversial proposals could benefit from more adequate information on public attitudes.[53]

III. THE SEX OFFENDER

Certain types of sex offenders are either a danger to the community or a nuisance that the community need not tolerate. Their offenses include rape, indecent liberties, exhibitionism, and incest, as well as a variety of related acts. The conception that sex offenders are different from any other types of law violators has led to legislation that results in a placement of sex offenders in a kind of limbo, somewhere between the criminal and the mentally ill. The remainder of this paper directs attention to the problems raised by sex offender legislation and to some possible sociocultural factors in the genesis of sex deviation.

A. History and Critique of Sex Offender Laws

Legislation defining sex psychopaths and establishing administrative procedures for their custody, treatment, and release was passed by some thirteen states between 1937 and 1950, and has been extended to other states since that time. Procedures leading up to the legislation were similar in the different jurisdictions. In a review of the development of sex psychopath laws, the late criminologist Edwin Sutherland noted a sequence characterized by (a) arousal in a community of a state of fear as a result of a few serious sex crimes, (b) agitated community response, leading to (c) the appointment of a committee that gathered information and made recommendations that generally were uncritically accepted by state legislatures.[54] The work of the committees proceeded largely in the absence of facts. Sutherland noted that the laws embodied a set of implicit assumptions that were explicit in much of the popular literature on sex offenses. These included the notion that all sex offenders were potentially dangerous, that they were very likely to repeat their offenses, that they can be accurately diagnosed and efficiently treated by psychiatrists. The laws were passed in the name of science, although there was little scientific evidence as to the validity of the assumptions underlying the statutes.

The act of passing the statutes set in motion the kind of data-gathering process that was needed to establish adequate legislation in the first place. Some of the legislation required study of the effectiveness of the statutes along with studies of sex offenders. These studies drew attention to the weaknesses of the legislation.

Many of the criticisms have been presented in reports prepared for state legislatures and will be mentioned only briefly here.[55] The label "sex psychopath" is so vague as to make administration of statutes unreliable.[56] Sex offenders are less likely to repeat their crimes than are other types of offenders.[57] Very few sex offenders present a grave social danger.[58] Current diagnostic techniques are incapable of distinguishing reliably between the potentially dangerous and those that are not dangerous.[59] There has been no test of the assumption that treatment techniques are effective in rehabilitation of sex offenders.[60]

Given these findings, it is not surprising that members of the legal profession were reluctant to approve of the usual procedures for administration of the statutes. Significantly, the opposition was not along lines usually assumed to separate legal from psychiatric viewpoints: a free-will, punitive orientation *versus* deterministic, permissive orientation. Rather, the criticism has been directed to the possible denial of due process to offenders. Since the statutes typically called for commitment up to life, even for minor offenses, the usual safeguard of a maximum sentence was missing. In addition, the administrative procedure for release, frequently requiring certification that the offender was no longer a danger to the community, made release very difficult. Administrators were understandably reluctant to assert that the patient was cured.[61]

While these problems signify dissatisfaction with many of the procedures built into the earlier statutes, there is still no common agreement on the most appropriate solutions. Some states have dropped the label "sex psychopath" from their statutes, have restricted the scope of the statutes to more serious offenders, and have required that the offender be held no longer than the maximum sentence under traditional criminal provisions. One of the problems posed by these changes is illustrated by the experience in Massachusetts. Massachusetts revised its psychopathic personality statute in 1954. The new law discarded the term "psychopath" and included the requirement that an offender must be released at the expiration of his maximum sentence. The law was deemed inadequate after a double murder was committed by an offender whose release from the state reformatory could not be prevented by provisions of the 1954 act. The law was quickly amended to allow for indefinite commitment up to life for certain types of sex offenders.[62]

The case points to a familiar problem in the visibility of mistakes in the processing of offenders. Errors made in releasing men too early are publicly observable. Under a statute allowing commitment up to life, however, errors made in keeping men who may, in fact, be cured cannot be tested, because by the nature of the procedure, they are not given a chance either to succeed or to fail. While every failure of early release may come to public attention, errors of keeping men too long cannot be detected. Such errors may be quite frequent in the absence of accurate diagnostic procedures. There is always the danger of undue restriction of civil liberties in attempts to provide adequate protection to the community.

B. Developmental Careers of Sex Offenders

Perhaps the single most important outgrowth of recent experience with sex statutes is that we are now aware of how little reliable knowledge is available. Until recently, the major source of ideas about sex offenders stemmed from clinical reports on a wide variety of sex deviants. The case materials have filled most of the books written on sexual deviation.[63] Although the cases may enrich clinical understanding, they do not provide an adequate basis for the development of sound administrative procedures. The clinical interpretations stand logically not as fact, but as hypotheses requiring test.[64] Since the cases are drawn from an unknown population of offenders, there is no adequate basis for generalization. And since adequate control groups are not employed, any claims as to therapeutic effectiveness are claims, and no more. They remain untested.

The impetus to research provided by the sex psychopath statutes has resulted in knowledge that calls into question some of the earlier clinical findings. While the research is still at a descriptive rather than an experimental stage, it has been effective in casting doubt on assertions that all or almost all sex offenders are highly disturbed. Systematic study of 300 offenders committed to the diagnostic facility in New Jersey showed that on the basis of psychiatric diagnoses, fully forty-three per cent of the offenders were classified as normal or only mildly neurotic.[65] This raises the question of what distinguishes the psychiatrically normal from the abnormal sex offender. More broadly, are there systematic differences in the developmental careers of different types of sex offenders? Suggestions of such differences are apparent in recent research.

A distinction can be made between aggressive and passive offenders. The former usually commit offenses involving attempted or completed intercourse with a legitimate sexual object—*i.e.*, a person of the opposite sex beyond the age of puberty. Most rapes and sexual assaults fall in this category. The passive offenses include exhibitionism and noncoital sex play with children. In terms of physical danger, the former category presents the most serious social problem. The sex statutes were passed largely to control the violent acts of rape and sexual assault. Yet, available evidence suggests that as a group, such offenders are less likely to exhibit clear-cut pathological symptoms and may have more in common with nonsexual offenders than with the passive sex deviants.

The report on sex offenders processed through the New Jersey diagnostic center provides information on the characteristics of offenders classified by type of offense. Selected findings from the study are reproduced in table four for the offense categories falling most clearly at the aggressive and passive poles.[66]

The aggressive offenders are more likely to be judged normal by psychiatric diagnosis. They are less inhibited sexually and tend to give fewer indications of severe emotional disturbance. Fewer of them are judged to have been exposed to severe emotional deprivation during childhood. Significantly, their prior arrest histories show few sexual offenses, but many nonsexual offenses. The ratio of nonsexual to sexual offenses is much higher for the aggressive than for the passive offenders. Finally, they are much more likely to show signs of hostility, a characteristic most common among property offenders from delinquent or criminal subcultures.[67]

Evidence from the California studies of sexual deviation supports the pattern noted above. Case descriptions of the most serious and aggressive sex offenses committed by delinquents in San Francisco revealed that over half of the cases were gang-motivated. Furthermore, of the thirty-seven serious offenders studied, half had previous records for nonsexual offenses, only three had previous sex arrests. Reading of the case descriptions further shows that the gang attacks were most frequently directed toward girls in middle or late adolescence, while the offenses against very young sexual objects were more likely to be committed by lone offenders.[68]

Ethnic differences in rates of sex offenses give further support to this pattern. The California research showed that Negroes and Mexicans were overrepresented in the rape category, underrepresented in offenses against children.[69] The New Jersey experience suggested that Negro sex offenders were less emotionally disturbed than their white counterparts.[70] Both of these findings are consistent with studies of racial differences in homicide rates and suggest the influence of cultural differences in restraints on the use of violence to resolve interpersonal affairs.[71]

The evidence thus suggests that the typical aggressive sex offender may be less "sick" than is usually supposed. Their backgrounds have much in common with nonsexual offenders

TABLE 4. Differences Between Aggressive and Passive Sex Offenders on Selected Characteristics[a]

	Diagnosed normal or mildly neurotic	Commitable to mental institution	Over-inhibited	Severe emotional disturbance
Aggressive offenders				
Sex assault	48	24	48	48
Forcible rape	38	25	50	63
Passive offenders				
Noncoital sex play with children	20	45	66	66
Exhibitionists	30	29	72	63

	Previous arrest for sex offenses	Previous nonsex arrests	Underlying hostility	(No. of subjects)
Aggressive offenders				
Sex assault	14	48	72	21
Forcible rape	12	50	75	8
Passive offenders				
Noncoital sex play with children	51	43	35	51
Exhibitionists	34	23	25	89

[a] Each column contains the percentages of each type of offender characterized as indicated by column headings. Thus 30% of the exhibitionists were diagnosed normal or only mildly neurotic. Number of cases on which the percentages are based appear in the lower right column.

who come from crime-inducing cultural settings. Instead of conceiving of their conduct as resulting from a highly specific and grossly deviant sexual motivation, it is perhaps more valid to view their offenses as part of a broader behavior system in which force may be used to attain their goals. It is the use of force, rather than any specifically deviant sexual motivation, that distinguishes these offenders from those who fall within the law.[72] Psychiatric study has revealed the frequency with which sexual motivations underlie such nonsexual crimes as arson and certain types of burglary. The suggestion here is that the reverse may hold for certain types of aggressive sex offenders. In a society stressing active mastery of the environment over passive acquiescence, perhaps it is not surprising that the aggressive sex offender who overresponds is judged less disturbed than the passive exhibitionist.[73]

Brief mention may be made of two additional points where sociological conceptions usually applied to nonsexual offenses may have bearing on deviant modes of sexual response. One of these points concerns the way in which the social structure exerts pressure on persons to use deviant means of achieving culturally acceptable goals. High rates of deviance are presumed to occur among those segments of the population that are least fortunately situated in terms of their abilities to achieve valued goals by legitimate means.[74] The same conception is applicable to the achievement of sexual gratification. Prisons are, of course, an extreme case of a structure that promotes deviant means of sexual outlet. But less extreme instances are in evidence as well. Thus, two studies note high rates of incest in rural populations, where the choice of alternatives to the wife given dissatisfaction with her performance, is severely limited.[75] And prostitution flourishes in lumber and mining areas and in the central sectors of cities, where the sex ratio is abnormally high. These illustrations remind us that the availability of legitimate sexual outlets is itself socially-structured; resort to deviant outlets will reflect these structural features and need not be conceived solely as a result of faulty personality makeup.

Second, the dyadic character of many types of crime means that the victim may play more than a passive role. Wolfgang's recent study of Philadelphia homicides revealed that fully twenty-six per cent were victim-precipitated.[76] Similar findings might result from careful study of those convicted of rape, where the offense frequently follows an evening of drinking and mutual sexual arousal. Consideration of the victim's role means that the offense can be viewed as a product of a social situation; its explanation cannot easily be reduced to a search for the childhood emotional disorders of the party who becomes labeled the offender.[77]

These observations suggest some ways in which sociocultural and situational features may be related to deviant sexual behavior. Assumptions that direct attention solely to psychogenic factors may lead to an inaccurate conception of the causal processes involved, and hence to treatment programs that neglect important sources of the deviation. Specifically, further research may reveal that many aggressive sex offenders are responding to culturally learned patterns of aggression and to situational factors that are unlikely to be relieved by the usual methods of clinical psychotherapy. Patterns of cultural learning as well as psychogenic disorders may be reflected in their offenses. This may partially explain why such offenders are deemed generally less amenable to treatment than the less dangerous but more disturbed passive offenders.[78]

Sociological conceptions of crime are heavily influenced by the sociologist's concern for the impact of culture and social organization. These elements are revealed most clearly in such types of offenses as professional crime, white-collar crime, and gang delinquency. Some of the evidence reviewed above suggests that there may be important sociogenic features in the development of certain types of sex offenders, and that further study could profit from an interdisciplinary approach to the problems posed by such offenders. The growing need for systematic knowledge should lead to research designed to reveal the combined influence of sociogenic and psychogenic sources of sexual deviation. Such research may suggest inadequacies in the conception that most sex offenders are a special breed of criminal requiring unique laws and administrative procedures for their control.

PART II

Female Prostitution

Prostitution

WAYLAND YOUNG

The following is an article by a journalist, not a sociologist; but high-quality journalism often supplies the social reality that the sociologist frequently misses. It concerns prostitution as it exists in London today, with all of the rawness and direct apprehension of sexuality that the term implies. Prostitutes do not speak neatly or in a language that would be easily accepted at the family dinner table. But this is the risk of the profession, that contact with sexuality in the context of money may corrupt not only relationships with the self and others, but with the very language itself. Mr. Young describes the prostitute as extruded from society, in a state of irrelation. The prostitute is indulged in through the exchange of money, and in this exchange the client allows himself all of the sexual freedom that he represses when in contact with women in whom he has invested emotional meaning. The complication of sexuality with the financial nexus allows the buyer to assume that he is dealing with an object, not a person, and therefore any request that he makes he defines as legitimate. As Mr. Young points out, this is not always the case, and the prostitute sets limits on the character and extent of the services that she is willing to extend to her customers.

The world of prostitution is a place where most of the repressions that characterize the sexual life of males are released; this accounts to a great extent for the wide range of

REPRINTED with the permission of the author and the publisher from *Eros Denied*, Grove Press, New York, 1964.

deviant sexual activities that are requested. In this sense the prostitute serves to channel off certain kinds of sexual behavior that are laden with so much guilt that they cannot be performed in the context of other relationships. In this respect the prostitute is the performer in a deviant subculture who is the target for the deviant sexual acts of those who are, for the most part, conventional members of the larger community.

Here too is a vivid description of the life of the prostitute, a life out of time and separated from the entanglements that make up the worlds of politics, religion, and family which contain and bind others to the conventional social order. This lack of connection and life in a half world promotes other forms of deviant involvement with the police and the underworld. The prostitute also runs a high risk of exposure to drugs, alcohol, and venereal disease, all of which are dangers of the occupational setting. The pimp, who is part of this subculture, serves as a basic source of emotional support for those women who have them. He is, for these women, a man who at least speaks in terms of love and affection and with whom the exchange of money is in the opposite direction. Mr. Young highlights the relationship of the prostitute and the larger society by focusing on the sexual-economic functions served by the prostitute and the intertwining of the needs of what he calls the "overworld and the underworld."

> *All women are sitting on a fortune, if only they realized it.*
> *—Prostitute's saying*

There are in our society now two great classes of people excluded from the web of the normal because of their sex lives: whores and homosexuals. Of these the whore will better repay study in the context of this book because she is wholly excluded, all round the clock, whereas the homosexual is only excluded *as* a homosexual; he is accepted in working hours, the whore is not.

There are societies without prostitution; one of them is described in Verrier Elwin's book, *The Muria and their*

Ghotul.[1] But they are very rare. It flourishes almost everywhere, and certainly in all Christian and post-Christian societies. In the Hellenic world it was part of the slavery-pederasty-prostitution triangle, the unruffled toleration of which so sharply distinguishes that world from ours, and so sharply contrasts, in our view, with the philosophic and artistic excellence we find in it. In other cultures, prostitution has been religious in motivation, or at least ritual. In some cultures there have been prostitutes by profession, who are set apart for that work. In others, the occasional act of prostitution has been something permitted to any woman; the function is not localized in this or that person but spread throughout society. Only five hundred years ago, Anglo-Saxon society was one of the latter sort. When Pope Pius II was in Berwick on Tweed as a young man, he was surprised to find that all the Englishmen locked themselves up in a tower at night, for fear of Scottish robbers, but left the women outside, thinking no wrong would befall them, and "counting outrage no wrong." Two young women showed Aeneas Silvius, as the future Pope was then called, "to a chamber strewn with straw, planning to sleep with him, as was the custom of the country, if they were asked." But he ignored them, "thinking less about women than about robbers," and took the fact that no robber came in the night as a reward for his continence.[2]

The custom whereby a man lends his wife or daughter to a guest is a form of prostitution; in return for her kindness the family or the clan expect to receive his good will, or even sometimes the good will of the gods, expressed in fertility of crop and of people. But the wife or daughter does not thereby become a prostitute.

In our society now, prostitution is specialized, mercenary, and reprobated. We confine the function to individual women who become a class apart, and whose characters become formed by their condition and experience. We pay them for exercising their function. We also despise them and penalize them. They are extruded from the body of society, as we like to conceive it, and live a life of their own according to their own values and customs. We know little of what these values and customs are, because we fear the prostitute. We fear her because we fear our own need for her, which conflicts with our formulated ideal of the relation between the sexes. We also project onto her our own guilty desires; because our accepted values declare us low and beastly when we go to her, we feel that she is herself low and beastly. Because we desire her when we go to her, we also feel that she desires us. We punish and blame her with one hand, and pay her handsomely with the other; we see her with one eye as a baited trap, and with the other as a golden haven of rest and warmth. Meanwhile, as Aretino said, she laughs with one eye and weeps with the other.

A whore is a woman who fucks for money. If you pay her enough, she pretends to come.

Let us take, as texts for this definition, first the words of a seventeenth-century pornographer (using the word in the strict sense: a writer about whores), and second those of a London whore today.

Writing in Venice in the 1630's, Ferrante Pallavicino advised the whore to handle her clients as follows:

Let her go along with the humor of these people, and speak as they wish, even though she hold them in scorn. Let her expressions be in general common ones, as my dear, my own heart, my soul, I am dying, let us die together, and such like, which will show a feigned sentiment, if not a true one. Let her add panting, and sighing, and the interrupting of her own words, and other such gallantries, which will give her out to be melting, to be swooning, to be totally consumed, whereas in fact she is not even moved, but more as if she were made of wood or of marble than of flesh. It is certain that the whore cannot take pleasure in all comers, . . . She must nevertheless give pleasure through her words, if not her deeds, and let her put into operation what she can, authenticating her words by closing her eyes, by abandoning herself as if lifeless, and by then rising up again in full strength with a vehement sigh as if she were panting in the oppression of extreme joy, though in fact she be reduced and languid. These lies can be singularly useful, although they are discredited by too common feigning, and often obtain little credence.[3]

And here is a contemporary London prostitute:

There's some of them lies still as stones, they think it's more lady-like or something, but I say they don't know which side their bread's buttered. Listen, if you lie still the bloke may take half the night sweating away. But if you bash it about a bit he'll come all the quicker and get out and away and leave you in peace. Stupid to spin it out longer than you need, isn't it? I learned that from Margaret. Wonderful actress, that girl. I learned from her in exhibitions when I first was on the game. She wasn't the first girl I did an exhibition with, that was a coloured girl who used to pitch near me. I was dead scared of any of that at first, and then one night this coloured pallone comes up to me and says: "Bloke here wants an exhibition; will you help me out? Three pounds each." I was scared, but she said do it just to help her, so I said, "Do we have to go turn and turn about?" but she said she'd lead all the time. Was I grateful! Anyhow, like I say, this Margaret and I used to do exhibitions after that; wonderful actress. Of course you know they're all faked, exhibitions are. We keep our hands down there all the time, which is why I used to shit myself laughing when I saw her pretending to pull hairs out from between her teeth afterwards. It was her I learned to grunt and groan from.

And another thing; when I'm with a client I always put the rubber on him very gently, you know, stroking him and spinning it out as long as I can. "You ought to have been a nurse," they say. That's always what it makes them think of. And then with a bit of luck they come before they even get into me. When they do I look ever so loving and gentle and say: "Traitor!" Well, I'm not paid just to be a bag, am I? I'm paid to make them feel good. It's easy for me, so why not? That's how I see it.

Mark that she learned to "grunt and groan" not from herself, not from a man, but from another whore. And that one word "Traitor!" sums up the whole structure of pretense which is whoring.

The pictures on the wall? I cut them out of a German phorno-graphic book. I don't use photos much. There's some likes them and occasionally it helps to get a bashful client started. I don't know much about who makes them. I did a day's photographic work yesterday, but that wasn't phornographic. I've been asked to, though. Bloke rang up once and offered me fifty pounds for an afternoon's work. Said he'd find the male model. Said he'd take my head out too and put someone else's in, but I didn't believe him. And anyhow, I don't do that.

Here is a poem by a London prostitute.

The Game

Last night
A rather trite
Thought occurred to me. Exactly what pleasure
Is there in being a "Lady of Leisure?"
One has to submit (and grit one's teeth) to a great many men
    who, when the "fun" is at an end
Pretend
They've "never done this before."
And it's really such a bore
To listen enthralled
As they tell you about having called
At the furriers to buy coats for their spouses
(Made from mouses)
And, while wrapped in gorilla-like embraces,
You lie making faces
At your big toe over a beefy shoulder,
And he becomes colder
Because you do not respond as he breathes garlic,
Or worse, alcoholic
Fumes over your pretty neck
And you fervently wish that he'd break his . . .
There are of course so many different types:
Like the one who wipes
His hands all over your bedspread, and though you are very
    sweet to him
And entreat him
Not to do it again, he does—when you turn your back.
And you're just dying to whack
The man who is so "thoughtful" and feels he really ought to give
    you "pleasure" too because you're really far too "good"
For this life. (As if he could!)
And have you ever met the one who is just longing for sex,
But only ever pays with perfectly good cheques?
So when you're fool enough to agree—
(If you wish, he'll meet you at the bank next day, long before
    three)
You find he's hopped it—
And stopped it!
And how about the pound-of-flesher who insists

On being kissed
All over the place, and wants you to remove every bit of your
    clothes, including those nylons you spent your last pound on this
    afternoon,
Which will so soon
Be in shreds.
I'm forgetting the "slave":
On bended knee he'll crave
To be allowed to clean your lavatory,
And when you've stripped him
And whipped him
Mercilessly,
Asks: "Do you get many like me?"

What is the pattern of the whore's own desires and pleas-
ures? Here are several glimpses from different London girls:

I think I have come; I'm not sure. Twice in my life I've thought
to myself, now maybe this is what they talk about. That was before I was on the game. I couldn't bear the sight of the man
afterwards. He couldn't get out quick enough for me.

I get my kicks from dancing, Latin American dancing mostly.
I don't know, there's something about the movements. My first
man was after a dance; I didn't know where I was. And the
father of my child was after a dance too. It's always dancing with
me.

I'm rather abnormally built. You see, my clitoris is very high
—I'm not embarrassing you by talking like this?—it's a long way
round, and so it gets a bit left out in a straight fuck. My womb's
high up too; I guess everything's a bit far apart with me. I can
only come if the man goes down. Well, there's only one man in
ten that I even want to go down, and only one in ten of those
that thinks of it. I can't ask them, can I? They're not there for my
pleasure, I'm there for theirs. That's how the game is. I tell you,
it's not all ninepins.

I don't know why I like girls. It feels safer, somehow. And I'm
not talking about pregnancy. I think everybody agrees now—take
Kinsey—that the clitoris is where women get their pleasure.

The man in the Boat's my mascot. As a matter of fact it's every
woman's mascot, though there's not many men'll recognize it.

You know, the young men's pricks seem to be getting bigger and bigger. It must be the Welfare State. I hate it, though; it splits me.

Sandra would be no good on the game. She likes men and she enjoys fucking.

Perhaps what is most striking about these casual remarks is the feeling they all give of "I'm different; I'm not so well off as some; I can't; I don't; I can't." They suggest a temperament which is already in some way reduced, depleted, disabled, lacking, and that this temperament is a necessary condition of being able to be a whore at all.

It is very difficult to discover how whores become whores. It is difficult to do from a sociological or criminological standpoint, or by observing certain cafés or night clubs, because it is not a thing you *see* anyone doing. They don't enroll through an employment agency, and you don't see thousands of them trooping to work when the whistle blows. It's also difficult to do by asking prostitutes at firsthand. If a whore feels guilty about her trade, feels that the majority society is right to condemn her for it, as many do, then she will naturally have surrounded the memory of how she commenced with a cloud of inhibitions, and may even have suppressed it altogether. On the other hand if she stands up for herself she is likely to have put in some hard thought on what prostitution really is, and to take off into Shavian arguments to the effect that there is no dividing line anyhow, no hard and fast occasion, no key moment. She may throw the question back at you; Is fucking for pity prostitution? For a job? For an apartment? And then of course—for three pounds. Whether she feels guilty or whether she feels defensive or even defiant, she has every interest in slurring over the moment of change. Her present way of life demands it; she could hardly continue to function if she was to admit to herself that at one moment she was one sort of creature, morally speaking, and at the next another.

One of the best of a very small number of good books on prostitution is *Women of the Streets*, by Rosalind Wilkinson.[4] In her account of how girls get on to the game, she lays stress on a preliminary period of vague, floating promiscuity, of what she calls elsewhere "increasing irrelation to society." This is something different from maladjustment, which she sees as a deformed relationship, a warped and impracticable relationship, but one which may be as strong as any other. "Irrelation" is an absence of all relationship. The girl comes to London—most London whores come from provincial industrial cities—and bums around, living with this man or that, and perhaps frequenting one of the drinking clubs the easy establishment of which has recently caused new regulations to be brought in. Or perhaps she finds work as a "hostess" in a night club. There are one or two night clubs which seem to be simply highroads into the game. This intermediate phase is the one when the girl is called a *mystery*: is she going to take to the game or not? Generally speaking, nobody pushes her. This is an important point; the popular conception of well-organized recruiting agencies is a mistaken one. The motive for entertaining the illusion is fairly clear; the more a respectable man idealizes women, and the higher the value he sets on the merits of conventional society, the less will he be willing to believe any girl capable of abandoning it except under pressure or devious corruption. To such a man, all whores will be "poor unfortunate girls," and his imagination will people Soho and Paddington, the main prostitute districts of London, with dope-pushers, razor-slashers, and so forth.

One way on to the game is often open before the girl comes to London. A girl who has been an "easy lay" at school —not usually so much because she likes fucking as because she wants to find out if it isn't possible to like it more—takes work as a waitress or chambermaid at a provincial hotel. She sleeps with the odd traveling salesman, and one day one of them gives her a pair of nylons. The next one gives her a pound to buy her own, and the penny drops. She has been paid for it. Next stop London and the big money.

Here is the commencement of a prostitute, as seen by the man in the story:

I met this girl at a party one night; she'd been sleeping around for some time with all sorts of people. I gave her a lift home after the party and as she was getting out of the car I asked her to have dinner with me a day or two later. She kind of paused, and then she said:—Look that dinner's going to cost you about three pounds. Why don't you just give me the three pounds and come along in and do me now?—So I did.

One does not often hear of the penny dropping so clearly.

But perhaps the commonest way on to the game is by the urging of a friend or elder sister. "Wake up, girl; how much longer are you going to *exist* on eight pounds a week? Why don't you come on out and *live?* You leave things to me, and I'll see you're getting a hundred a week before you know where you are."

Here is a fairly usual "life story." Until the recent law, which cleared most of the prostitutes off the London streets, Dorothy was a streetwalker; she charged three pounds. A pound more for stripping, but she'll do it all the same if the client can't raise the extra. Hates kissing. Undertakes most kinks if she's feeling like it, but no buggery. Buggery is grounds for money back and throw them out. She was illegitimate, and brought up without a father. When she came home after school she would find her mum smooching away in the corner with some man. When she was twelve and thirteen the neighborhood kids used to say to her: "Had your R.C. yet?" She did not know what it meant, but shook her head, and they said: "All right, you can stay with us." R.C. meant "red change," or first period. She had her R.C. one day during an exam at school. She fainted, and was carried by the invigilator to the Headmistress, who said "Are you ill?" "I don't think so." "Well, I mean, er, have you eaten anything?" Yes, she had steadied her nerves by guzzling Rowntrees Clear Gums, and to this day feels sick at the sight of them. So much for sex education.

At sixteen she had her first man, and at nineteen bore a child to an American soldier. While she was carrying the child she took up with a medical student and learned for the first time that she had a thing called a womb. He also taught her hygiene.

And I may say most of the girls don't know a thing about it. They just put some soap on their fingers and tickle themselves.

But he taught me to use a douche, and not more than once a week, otherwise it hurts your insides.

She believes masturbation gives you a bellyache. When her mother asked her who the child's father was, she said she really didn't know. She had passed out at a party and didn't know what had happened to her. Her mother legally adopted the child, a girl, and Dorothy never sees either of them. She blames her mother for her own upbringing, and fears her own child may be brought up the same way, but it's nothing to do with her, it's miles away now.

After the birth of the child she went to London and took work as a barmaid. She went concurrently with a well-off married man every third Sunday, and with the manager of the hotel in the afternoons. One night in a clipjoint she got drunk and started telling the manager of the joint what was wrong with the place; the pattern of the wallpaper was too small, the place was dirty, the girls were badly dressed. This manager took her on the spot as his girl friend and co-manager, and she lived with him for four years. Then it broke up, and she was underfed and began hitting the bottle. (This is the "period of increasing irrelation.") She had a taste for "pretty things and bright lights," as well as for liquor; one night she got drunk at a party and the next morning found she'd been laid and paid for it. (The same story she'd told her mother about the baby.) So there she was, a whore. She began walking the street, though she didn't stand yet.

Before the law virtually put an end to the street trade in London, standing was the end of irrelation; the mystery was accepted. Some older whore invites the walker to share her pitch and makes friends with her. There might be a Lesbian arrangement, and there would probably be something of a team about it. "With your looks and youth you could earn well, that is if you consent to profit by my experience." Perhaps they would do exhibitions together. The older woman might get a rake-off in return for her patronage. The arrangement would be a fleeting one, like everything in the underworld.

Here is another life story, one from the other end of the social scale; prostitution, like everything else in England, is all shot through with class values. Mary was a successful call girl, and occasionally reached the maximum possible earnings, up to fifty pounds for an all night fix. When she was twelve, she was "the only girl without a title" at a snobbish Roman Catholic boarding school run by nuns. Her parents were kindly, but cold. The father was blind, and the mother, having had a total hysterectomy, cut out love not only from her bed but from her whole life. Then, within a year, three things happened. She found papers on her mother's desk which taught her she was the illegitimate daughter of the illegitimate daughter of a housemaid; her true mother had put her in an orphanage when she was three years old, and she had been adopted by the people she thought were her parents on medical advice to compensate for the death of their own, physically irreplaceable, son. She had her first period at school, didn't know what was happening, feared disease, and was told to take an aspirin and think about the Virgin Mary. And thirdly, perhaps not surprisingly, she created a scandal at school by refusing to believe in the Virgin Birth. Her adoptive parents were sent for and she was told to have faith.

At seventeen she wanted to go to a university, but was taken to Cyprus instead by a relative of her adoptive parents. She was not allowed to learn Greek, or to take a job there. She quarreled with the relative, returned to London and took work as a hotel receptionist. Her adoptive parents died, and she set to work to trace her true family. She found her grandmother first, herself the illegitimate daughter of an illegitimate woman; there hadn't been a marriage in the family for generations. The grandmother was not interested. Later she found her mother. This last door slammed in her face with a particularly horrible twist when she learned that her mother had put her away when she was three because she was pregnant again. She had preferred the unborn child to the child of three, and had in fact brought the second child up.

Mary committed suicide at the age of thirty.

A staple of conversation among whores is the "kinkies."

Until recently you could see the ads in Soho shop windows: Miss Du Sade; Miss Du Cane; Miss De Belting (Flagellation). Strict governess: Corrective Training; Corr. and Disc., (the sado-masochistic procedures in general). Miss Kiki This and Kiki That (anything). Lady's black mackintosh for sale. Boots, high-heeled shoes, plastic raincoats for sale (all with the girls inside them). Fifi or Froufrou gives French lessons; recently back from France, French and English conversation (which means *gamming*, from the French *gamahucher*, or *blowing*, or *plating*, or *noshing*, from the Yiddish *nosh*, to nibble, or eat between meals). . . .

The code for kinks is well known to those who need to know it; not many people apply to these girls for French lessons. The code for prostitution itself is more fluid, and it depends what medium is used for the ad. No London newspaper would take an ad for a photographic model, followed by her measurements, but many will take ads for fur coats, and that naturally means that the whore has to contend with a lot of people who really want fur coats. From time to time some paper or other will carry the biggest chestnut of them all: "Demolition agent for temporary erections," until a startled building contractor calls back.

The whole topic of unusual requirements, of perversions, or kinks, is a repulsive one to many people. When the "normal citizen" reads or hears kink stories he may be tempted to consider them as myths, as products of an inflamed imagination which keep on going the rounds out of some sort of unhealthy fascination, but which don't actually happen. Or he may think that all that is old hat; it is all in Krafft-Ebing, and that is where it should stay. But it is a determining condition of the whore's life that she is engaged day by day in enacting the myth, in living through the silly dream, in assuaging the unusual desire. These are not amazing, disgusting or funny stories to her; they are part of her day-to-day work, as real and as normal as dressing wounds is to a nurse; something for which she is paid, and in which she takes a wry pride.

Blowing generally counts as a kink, or a sort of semi-kink,

and costs a bit extra. Some girls confine themselves to blow-ing when they have the curse. Others let the curse make no difference; they plug themselves up and bash right ahead, draining between clients.

Well, as for kinkies, it depends on what I'm feeling like. If I'm feeling cheeky, all right, and good luck to them. But you can't do it every day. When I was working ——'s [a restaurant] the manager said to me one night: "See that fellow over there? He's a member of parliament. Go and see what you can do for him." So I went over and he said: "Listen, have you got manacles and anklets?" I said: "No darling, but I can get them." So I arranged to meet him there a week that day. What he wanted me to do was manacle him and all and then drop candlegrease on his prick. Course I never did it. There he was next week, but I wasn't feeling the same, and I didn't even go over to him.

Beatings are usually a pound a stroke, either way.

Client came to me one night and offered me three quid for three. Fine, said I. So he got into the drag—had it with him in a suitcase, and for me too: black nylons and high wedge shoes and all. He said he was a servant girl called Millie and I was his mistress. They often want that. I had to say: "Where were you last night, Millie?" And he said he'd been out with a boy. And I had to say: "Now it was clearly understood between us when you came to work for me, Millie, that there was to be none of that." He was licking my shoes all the time. "And I think you deserve a beating, don't you, Millie?" "Oh yes, Madam, I do, I do." So then I gave him the three he'd paid for. But I don't know what it was; I was just feel-ing like it, I suppose, but I suddenly lost my temper, oh, not only with him, with everything and everybody. So I gave him four more and took another four quid off him and chucked him out. I really lit into him; he loved it. And yet people ask me why I like cats.

And then another time there was a client took me back to his place. I had to tie him up, you know all the girls have to know how to tie a bloke up to a chair properly. I did him really well, couldn't move an inch. And then I had to strap his prick up against his belly with elastoplast. I was feeling the same way that night, I suppose, because there was some elastoplast over so I put one piece across his mouth and another across his eyes. "There's for you, you bastard," I thought. "You asked to be strapped up, and you get strapped up." He'd told me earlier he had a cleaner come in every second morning. I hope she did, that's all I can say. That was two months ago.

Quite a common one is the client who gets the whore to dress up as a nurse, powder his bottom, put diapers on him and tuck him up with a bottle.

After all, every man has had his first orgasm somewhere or other, hasn't he? But most of them don't get like that. I often wonder about it. And what about women, anyhow?

I was taken back to his place by this bloke. And as soon as I got inside the door he gave me thirty pounds. Ah-ah, I thought; what's coming? But in those days thirty pounds was quite a lot—as a matter of fact it still is. He made me undress and sat me right across the room from him. I had to open my legs, and he took a lot of cream buns from a paper bag and threw them at me. Not a bad shot, he was, either, once he'd got his aim. Then he put marmalade on my breasts and stuffed iced cherries up my cunt and licked the whole lot off. It *was* embarrassing; I didn't know whether I was allowed to wash afterwards.

A variant of this from another girl.

A client used to come to me quite regularly. I had to undress and stand with my arms above my head. He took six kippers—he had them in pairs wrapped in cellophane, you know the things—and threw them at me one by one. If one of them missed he came trotting across the room and picked it up and tried again. Afterwards there was a pine scented foambath waiting for me. He went back to South Africa in the end. I was quite sorry. I used to get fourteen pounds a time.

And again:

A client took me back to his place, and as soon as I got in the door there was a dirty great coffin standing open. He put me in a white nightie with a rosary in one hand and a Bible in the other and a wreath of roses on my head. Then I had to lie down in the coffin. I thought: "Is this a gag to get my money?" But I had my bag in the coffin with me. Then he started nailing the lid down and all the time he was shouting out: "You're dead now, God damn you to hell." He'd told me his wife had died. He'd given me a big spanner to knock the lid up with, but I tell you I was wondering whether I'd ever get out again. I did though, and when I looked round he'd gone.

The Street Offences Act of 1959 cleared the girls off the London streets overnight, as it had been meant to. They went indoors into pubs and clubs, and on to the telephone. Some put up fluorescent red bell-pushes; some hustled by standing at open doors and windows. So much as a nose or a finger in the air space of the street was illegal. Some advertised in the press, and many in shop windows. One put up a neon sign saying: "French Lessons."

Before the Act, the penalty for soliciting in the streets had been two pounds. There was a working agreement with the police that it should not be exacted more than fortnightly, and often a girl could go six months or a year without being booked. There was sometimes a rota system, and the greatest grievance against the police was: "It's not my turn." The routine appearance in the Magistrate's Court and the routine branding as a "common prostitute" played some part in forming the underworld-like pseudo-criminal personality of the prostitute, but the fine itself was fiscal in effect, not punitive or deterrent.

The new Act raised the fine to thirty pounds, with prison on third conviction. Nevertheless, within a year the girls began to come back on the streets. They were forced to by the prosecution of the clubs they used, and of a magazine called *The Lady's Directory*, in which they published their telephone numbers. (The title took up that of a similar publication in the eighteenth century.) The £30 fine works both ways. The girls defend themselves in court, which they had not done against the £2 fine, and this means the policemen who book them have to spend a whole day there instead of half an hour. They, and their superiors, can think of better things for an undermanned police force to do, and so the girls are back on many of the streets. They simply come out later, and close the bargain with less haggling, so as to be less conspicuous.

Among the call girls, one is in a different world. Take the word *whore*. The street and club girls use it quite naturally. It is the simple, obvious word for what they are. The phrase, almost a signature tune, "whoring it along the Dilly" [Piccadilly] has a fine generous ring to it. An occasional highbrow whore who quotes Proust and keeps up with the sexual oddities of the eminent will use the word about herself with a conscious, open-eyed feeling, in the same way that Bernard Shaw used to call himself "an old entertainer." But the call girl uses it to imply all that she is not. She uses it as synonymous with *slack*, which is the call girl's word for a street girl.

I don't look like one, do I? You wouldn't ever know, would you? Not ever? Would you? Would you?

The call girl is tremendously nice. The flat where she lives, and also her gaff where she works, if she has a separate place, are spotless; dusted, shiny, warm, welcoming. The taste will be contemporary, aware of fashion.

The first thing you must realise is that I'm not a whore. I have my friends, but I don't take just anybody. Like for instance if a man rings up and says he's been given my number by so and so, I don't just leave it at that. I put him through it. When did you last see so and so? How was he? Where did you meet? Has he shaved his beard off? He said he was going to. Oh, there are all sorts of ways to find out if they're on the square. All right, then he comes round. Maybe I don't like the look of him. "Ooooh, I'm so sorry. It's really too bad. She's just gone out. Would you believe it; isn't that just too bad." And even afterwards, if I haven't liked him I tell him I'm going off the game, or I'm going away on holiday; he'd better not come again.

You know, half my work's what we call social work. That is, say some friend of mine has someone come to London to visit his firm, and he gives him my number. I have connections with a lot of good firms. All right, he takes me out; dinner, a show, perhaps a party. I go down on his expense account, or something. It may lead to sex, it may not. Often it doesn't. I don't mind. In fact, I'm pleased.

Again:

It's a hell of a life. You know, I imagine the slack is afraid of disease, and afraid of the sex maniac who thinks it'd be fun to strangle her. Well, that's not what we're afraid of. The trouble in this game is when you're afraid you're slipping. Some days you sit and sit by the telephone smoking and smoking, and nobody rings, and you think: "Look out, kid, you're slipping. What have

I done? WHAT HAVE I DONE? Are they telling each other I'm no good?"

The London prostitute comes in all colors and sizes of temperament, but there is enough in common to make it worth saying something about the not so obvious ways in which she differs from other women. She has no sense of time, because her life is without routine. Time is divided into day and night and that's all. She has a sense of obligation, but it is shakier than other people's. It works in an immediate way, because she is used to payment on the spot. If she says she will meet you somewhere in half an hour, she will. To-morrow, or next Tuesday, is another matter. If you take her to a public place, say a restaurant, she is a little awkward or embarrassed, or by contrast flamboyant, coming in and going out; everybody is looking at her, but can they tell? Once settled, she relaxes at once. She is an excellent listener; listening, next to fucking, is the thing she does most of. Her own favorite topics are the wealth and eminence of her clients, the sexual hypocrisy of our culture, king stories, money, clothes, interior decoration, bars, coffee bars, night clubs. She prefers the pageant of life to vicarious involvement through the arts, but she is blind to politics and the organization of society in general. She notices and comments on the women round her more than the men, partly because she is comparing herself to this mysterious competitor the wife, but often also out of straight Lesbian interest. She is probably a fairly heavy drinker. When she is watching her words and thinking what she should say next, she will tell you that she went on the game with a conscious decision, for the loot. She realized she was sitting on a fortune, and made up her mind. She continues on the game because it's interesting, and she's used to it.

When she is relaxed and talking without care or discretion, the picture changes. She is afraid, like all outlaws. She is afraid of disease. Few whores go to a doctor or a V.D. clinic for a regular check-up. On the other hand many seem to believe they are gifted with second sight about their clients' health.

Well, I have a good look at him, and if he looks a bit anything, out he goes.

This particular bit of professional vanity often coexists a perfectly sound knowledge of the fact that infection is not related to visible signs. She is also afraid of infecting a client's wife, or even his unborn child, a running, uncheckable fear which she may allow to prey on her and to carry other guilts on its back. She is afraid of the sex maniac who may want to kill her; that is why she may keep a dog or, if she can afford it, a maid. If she has no ponce,[5] she may take care to live in a house where the neighbors will accept her and her occupation, then she can shout for them in an emergency. She is afraid of being nicked; however often it has happened (and Mrs. Wilkinson cites a Belgian woman who was arrested 219 times), the appearance at Marlborough Street or Bow Street is always a humiliation. Now, under the new Act, she is afraid of prison.

Above all, she is afraid of old age. The older whores will say quite simply: "There is no way out." The younger ones will keep their chins up and pretend to themselves they're not like the rest. Nobody ever went on the game for keeps.

Of course I'm only in it for five years.
For a few years.
Until I'm bored with it.
For five years.
For five years. I've got it all worked out.
Then I'll—
Buy a shop.
Go into partnership with a friend who has a garage.
Buy house property and let rooms.
Buy a coffee bar.
Buy a restaurant.
Club together with one or two other girls and buy a hotel.
Get some old sucker to marry me.
Put my savings into. Put my savings into.
Put my savings into.

Not one in a hundred can save. The ability to save goes with a retentive personality, with foresight, caution, affective momentum, narrow affections. The whore is all on the surface, mercurial, shortsighted, chaotic, frigid.

What often happens is that they go on and on, into their fifties and even sixties. They pass downward into a class called the four-to-sixers, who go on the streets and into the joints before dawn, when the clients are so drunk they don't care what they're getting. Some become maids to younger women, which is probably the happiest conclusion. Then there is a saying, "End up drinking red biddy in the Docks."

The elderly whore, the old-timer, often has delusions of social grandeur. She has missed the few possible escape lines, and gets attached in a half-light of unreality to the idea of what she might have been. She cannot deny that she is a whore, so she may sideslip into denying that she is something else that she is. If she is Jewish, she may take pleasure in proving that she is not, and in looking down on the Jewish client. If she is poor she may try to prove that she is rich; if Irish, English; and, over and over again, if she is dark she will pretend to be fair. Conversely, she may try to prove that the innocent little woman in the flat above *is* a whore.

One of these old-timers asked me to tea the other day. I went along, and there were just the two of us. She poured out the tea with her little finger crooked and told me how she'd been asked to Buckingham Palace. Afterwards she entertained me by playing Gounod's *Ave Maria* on the piano.

Some whores do get married, or set up what is meant to be a permanent liaison with a man. He may be a former client or not. If he does not even know his wife has been a whore, the situation is emotionally hopeless. If he does know, it may last, conceivably. But if a woman is capable of sustaining a regular relationship, why didn't she do it at first instead of going on the game? They usually come back, the ones who marry; not because of the attractions of whoring, but because the marriages don't work. When they do come back, they are naturally welcomed with open arms; their return justifies the others.

Consider what it is like for a whore to try to construct

a marriage, even in favorable circumstances. Wherever they go together—street, pub, parties, job-hunting, home-hunting—the slightest flicker of interest, of attention, from some man brings back that which has to be forgotten. The man might simply be thinking: "Now where have I seen that girl before?" It might even have been waiting in a movie line. But she knows her husband does not know where it was. If anything goes wrong—some people who are coming to dinner cry off at the last moment, a job falls through—have they found out? There is no defense against the suspicion. Laughter at one's own groundless suspicions is the most mirthless there is.

All right, one may say: London is a great big easygoing metropolis, who cares? Why don't they publish and be damned? Surely so many people would be on their side. . . . But picture turning up at someone's house who *knows.*

I shall probably be the first tart they've ever had in their house. They'll be so damned nice, they'll be curious, with that terrible curiosity of conscious liberalism. They only want to know. They'll observe my dress, my turns of speech, my gait.

That is what the whore who gets married has to face with other people. What she has to face in bed with her husband is easily imagined. It can be done, and it is done, but it's no wonder it is not often done.

The way off the game is feet first.

In 1959 a committee of inquiry chaired by Sir John Wolfenden reported on prostitution in Britain and recommended changes in the law. During the parliamentary debates on the Wolfenden Report, which did in fact lead to the new and more restrictive law, Mr. R. A. Butler, then Home Secretary, promised stiffer penalties against living on immoral earnings as a "consolation." It was not clear what for. Mr. Edwards, the Member for Stepney, a prostitute area, referred to ponces[6] as the "dirtiest, filthiest lot in creation." Another member spoke of "monarchs of the industry." Until 1948, ponces could be flogged. Whenever there is a discussion on prostitution in the press many people write saying this or that about the prostitutes, but end up: ". . . and reserve the really heavy penalties for the ruffians who batten on these unfortunate girls."

The very word *ponce* suggests *pounce;* fifty years ago ponces were called *bullies,* which sounds even fiercer. Try consulting your own feelings about the ponce. There he is, this unspeakably debased male, lurking in doorways and pouncing on his unsuspecting prey, tearing her hard-earned three pounds out of her pathetic clutch, and roaring away in his gangster-type limousine to the next girl, whom he threatens with a razor. He spends the night going round twenty or thirty of his hundred and fifty girls, or perhaps his section of the big syndicate administered by his super-boss, slashing his girls, doling out shots to the junkies, coshing a client or two, and squaring four or five detective inspectors. Toward dawn he goes, surrounded by henchmen, to the girl he has chosen for himself that night and, little recking that her flaccid flesh is still reeking from the forty or fifty slavering lechers who have been before him, enjoys her.

It is quite rare for a London prostitute to have a ponce at all. If she does, it is because she feels she needs someone to kick her out on the street at nightfall, to make sure she has the rent ready on rent day, to keep her off the bottle, to tell her what clothes she looks nice in and, perhaps most important of all, to help her see if she can't build up some sort of a sex life of her own.

The ponce in London today is usually neither more nor less than the whore's husband. He provides stability for her, a bit of discipline, someone to listen to her adventures. He fucks her as much for her sake as for his own, and takes trouble over it. He is also a gauge of her prestige. If she keeps him well in handmade shoes and black silk shirts, then her credit goes up among the whores, and his among the ponces. "Mine's a good earner. Just look at this shirt."

Economically and in prestige values, he corresponds to the wife of the normal citizen, and the fact that he is living on her earnings and not she on his is only of secondary importance to either of them.

It often arises like this. A man is earning ten pounds a week, and he takes up with a girl who is earning a hundred. His self-respect may lead him to keep his own job for a bit, but then one day she is ill, or perhaps her child is ill, or she is picked up and he wants to go to court with her. He stays off work and loses his job. Their earnings drop from a hundred and ten to a hundred a week. So what the hell? He's a ponce: all right, so he's a ponce. There are plenty of others.

Mrs. Wilkinson published figures showing that about forty per cent of those *convicted* of poncing in England have also been convicted of other crimes. It cannot of course be known what proportion of ponces are never convicted either of poncing or of anything else. But the whore is herself usually a criminal—we make her one with our laws—and she develops a modified form of the criminal personality. It is not surprising that she takes up with others for company. Moreover, minorities against whom the majority discriminates will also seek each other out, and this is the main reason for the apparently disproportionate number of colored men among ponces in London.

I used to live in Knightsbridge when I first went on the game. It was terrible. I didn't seem to be real; you know, it was as if nobody could see me. But since I moved over here among the colored people I'm—well, you know—I feel kind of at home. I don't have to pretend any more.

Some share a ponce with another whore, or even with two others, but this arrangement is exceptional in London. It does not arise because the ponce is able to subject two or three reluctant but silly women for his own gain; it arises because in the world of prostitution, as in all other minority worlds which are at once defined and discriminated against by the majority world, like the criminal world proper, the Negro world, the world of the arts and, in former days, the worse-off working class—in such worlds monogamy is not the rule. Add to this that in the world of prostitution chastity is by definition something which does not come in, and that many whores are at least a bit Lesbian, and the multiple ponce becomes comprehensible.

Then there are the call house madams, or switch-bawds. These, in London, are women with a two or three-bedroom flat, and a list of twenty or thirty telephone numbers. The client gives his order; she calls the most suitable girl, he meets her at the flat. He pays the madam, and the madam passes on a proportion—always alleged by the girls to be too low—to the girl. Or she allows the client to go to the girl's flat, and the girl passes on the rake-off. The call house madam is of course just as criminal as the male ponce, but society is not somehow so angry with her. After all, she's a woman, she's probably a superannuated whore herself, and women are never so frightening anyhow.

There has only been one large organization in London since the war, the famous Messina Organization. I cannot vouch for the truth of the following account of it, but it is what is generally believed among the whores.

The five Messina brothers used to buy the best girls out of the, then legal, brothels in France, Belgium and Italy for a down sum, marry them to sailors for fifty pounds, and bring them to London. This was, of course, a white slave traffic, and sounds terrible. But for the girls themselves it was a merciful deliverance. In the closed houses of the Continent, they would be taking fifty men a day and getting anything down to twenty cents a go for it. How they got there is another matter, but once there, there is no doubt that the Messina brothers were so many St. Georges. To come to London was the dream of all of them. In London they were set up two by two in shared flats and provided with "gaffs" (apartments) elsewhere to work in. They were run on Service lines. They paid over their entire earnings each week, and were given spending money. What was left of the earnings after the organization rake-off was then banked for them in a deposit account. They were supplied with an issue of the most destructible clothing, nylons and so on, and with food, and a bottle of wine a day would be sent to their living flats. One of the brothers or their agents would inspect their pitch nightly to see that standards of dress were satisfactory. Other girls who reached this standard were allowed to pitch there too, but anybody who did not was rushed off by the Messina girls themselves. If any girl earned outstandingly well she was given a bonus, typically a mink coat. Medical inspection was provided weekly and hospital treatment when necessary. They were given a return ticket home each year, but, naturally, were not allowed to take any of their savings with them. When they were finally judged unemployable, their savings were released to them and they were sent home. If a girl wanted to get off the game while she was still employable, it was made extremely difficult for her, but she could do it at the expense of a large proportion of her savings. The Messinas would never have English girls in the organization, and the English girls looked at it all between envy and contempt. Envy for the safety and regularity, contempt for the discipline and spoon-feeding; the same mixed feelings that they have for the idea of licensed brothels. The brothers were mostly imprisoned or deported in 1951, but a remnant of their girls remained for some years. Their price dropped from five pounds to three, and badly dressed slacks were no longer hustled off.

Apart from this, allegations in London that so and so is "running a string of girls," generally turn out to mean only that he gives them a cut rate on his string of taxis, or lets rooms to them, but in no sense controls them.

So why then are we so hot against the ponce? To begin an answer to this, we must first ask what we feel about the whore herself. We are all in touch with her, or in touch with her image in our own minds. She has been around for millennia. Every man has thought of going to her, even if he hasn't been. Every woman has thought of her husband or her son going to her. It is enough to ask yourself if you're a man, or your closest man if you're a woman, under what circumstances you would go to her. You go to her when you want a fuck. But if there was a woman by you who loved you and was going to come when you came, you could not possibly go to a whore. Even if there was a woman by you who did not love you, but was still going to come, out of animal spirits and general good will, you could not go to a whore. Even if she was a complete stranger, at a party say, and you didn't know whether it was going to be a good lay or not, you still could not prefer a whore, because if you did you would be paying for the certainty of pretense instead of taking the chance of reality free. By now we are pretty low down the scale, if a complete stranger at a party, whom you think about in terms of "a good lay" is still preferable; we are pretty far away from love. Perhaps the only circumstance in which a man who has experienced love, or even a casual fuck in friendship, could go to a whore would be if he was completely alone in a strange city and had the most terrible stone-ache, like millions of men every day, on military service or traveling one way or another.

So who does go, apart from soldiers and travelers? Kinkies, first. Men who can only come if they're allowed to dress up as this or that, or use the cat, or throw cream buns about; men who have associated the experience of orgasm with something which most people find irrelevant to it. If any moralist wanted to reduce prostitution and the flagellation market in England he could do it by breaking the chain of corporal punishment in the schools. Kicks are infectious; if the teacher likes it, the child will too.

Then the physically deformed; not directly because they are deformed, but because the shyness born of deformity may prevent them ever learning the experience of love. If the whore has a useful social function, as many people say she has, it is with the kinkies and the deformed.

If I have a hunchbacked client, I always keep my eyes on his face while he's undressing. I can't look at his hump, and I can't look away from him; he'd notice it at once and feel it. I keep my eyes fixed on his. I had one the other day, and we turned the light out. Afterwards he said: "Would you mind not turning the light on?" I said: "Of course not, darling. I never do." He said, as quick as lightning: "Why's that?" I said, "I don't like it. I always like to get at least into my bra and pants first."

I had one with an amputated leg, too. There he was unstrapping his wooden leg; I kept my eyes on his face, in the same way. Can you imagine what it's like to feel a man's stump going against your thigh? I don't know what I felt. I think I loved him, or something. I tell you, it takes it out of you.

Then there are the men who want to avoid trouble and

complication, who simply want the "sneeze in the loins" without any responsibility, emotional contact, give-and-take, or indeed any involvement whatever; the duckers.

They know *I'm* not going to ring up and tell them I'm lonely, or write them long letters or go whining to them with this or that.

Lastly there are all the men, all the millions of men in England and America, who feel that sex is something apart from the society they live in, and wrong. They may be simply burning for a blow, or to do it dog-fashion, and daren't turn their wives round. They may be unmarried, and terrified by the thought of having a girl friend. They may never have found out that women come too. All these will end up with the whores, because they have been twisted out of sight of their own natures by the society they grew up in. If once you get to believe it's dirty, regrettable, unmentionable, something you wish to spare a refined woman, then there's not much reason why you shouldn't buy it. And if you've never found out that women come, you may find the whore's pretense of coming quite irresistible, and it may make you feel a hell of a fellow. She hopes it will.

And so back to the ponce. The whore has done her little turn, and you have paid her for it. It probably does not cross your mind that you could have something ten times as good with a real girl if you got up and took it, so you don't worry too much about the money. But the thought that the first thing she does when your back is turned is to hand the money over to someone else, and that someone else a man, and that man fucking her for free, and for all you know sneering with her at your peculiarities—why, it's absolutely revolting. It makes you bust with rage. If ever you laid hands on such a man, you'd beat the life out of him, because he is living proof that what you've had was counterfeit. He is your disillusionment. Into prison with him, and let the illusions flourish. And if two years isn't enough, let him have seven, and that will be some consolation to us all.

In unpublished evidence for the Wolfenden Committee, Mrs. Wilkinson wrote (and kindly allows me to quote):

The society formed by prostitutes and their associates, though not hereditary, is continuous; it has a fairly permanent structure and composition. It exists because it absorbs asocial or antisocial personalities; it is economically dependent on the expression of an antisocial tendency in members of ordinary society. Its cohesion is strengthened by the attitudes of the general public towards the prostitute, her guilt feelings which prevent her return to ordinary life by causing her to exaggerate and anticipate critical attitudes towards her, and by attitudes within the society itself towards its members who try to break away.

The whore world is like a little gearwheel meshing with a big one; it goes round faster, and in the opposite direction. You could see it until recently on the pavements of Piccadilly; the whores standing still and the men pouring past, looking, considering, pausing to haggle, passing on to the next. The countersociety or underworld, like the society or overworld from which it is excluded, is classridden, intolerant, but free from oppression. As to the rest of us, we cherish and pay it with one hand and belabor it with the other. That's how it gets as it is. When we cherish the whore, she feels like a necessary safety valve, warm, trustworthy and useful. When we belabor her, she feels like a criminal.

If that's how it is, I thought, I'll bloody well live up to the image—I'll buy a Rolls and get a Nubian chauffeur in a leopard-skin jockstrap and hustle with all the lights on and a cigarette-holder a mile long. And three Afghan wolfhounds on golden leashes trotting behind. And scythes on the wheels.

The overworld views the whore as a social problem or a social service, according to the amount of use it makes of her. The whore judges the overworld by what she sees. First, she sees the client, whom she holds in contempt for his gullibility and in respect for his purse. Through him she sees his wife who, he inevitably tells her, is cold. To the English whore, England is a country of women as frigid as she is, or more so, but who don't even try to pretend.

Ask me, the only difference between me and some of these wives is that they don't keep the bargain and I do.

The overworld and the underworld depend on each other,

their characters are complementary, and yet ignorance prevails. If it did not, the two worlds would probably fuse, and that would be an end of prostitution. The ignorance itself is preserved by the fear, and the fear is the result of the exclusion of fucking from the realm of the normal. The whore incarnates the Extruded.

I headed this chapter with the whore's catchphrase to sum up her feelings about other women; her bewilderment that they are not whores like her. Let us conclude with a remark made by a girl who had grown up in a prostitute district of London, and who had been much solicited to go on the game because of her looks. To her friends who were whores and ponces, she was "sitting on a fortune." But her answer was: "I don't see how you can, not if you know what love is."

The Self-Image of the Prostitute

NORMAN R. JACKMAN,
RICHARD O'TOOLE,
AND GILBERT GEIS

Unlike Wayland Young, the authors of the following paper focus upon the prostitute's system of values which are part of her psychic equipment which functions to maintain her in the life of prostitution. Drawing their interviews from women

REPRINTED with the permission of the authors and editors from *The Sociological Quarterly*, 4:2:150–161 (April 1963).

The authors are indebted to the Oklahoma City and the Norman Police Departments for their co-operation. Police Inspector E. B. Giddens, Oklahoma City, was extremely helpful in arranging interviews with prostitutes held on vagrancy and disorderly conduct charges. Inspector Giddens clearly expressed to the investigators and the respondents the right of any prisoner to refuse to be interviewed. Our thanks are also extended to the personnel of the vice squad and the matrons of the Oklahoma City jail. Officer Terry Sharp, Norman Police Department, and Robert Bristow contributed as graduate students to this research. Acknowledgment is also due the Faculty Research Fund of the University of Oklahoma for partial financial aid.

who have been in prison (13 of the 15 were in prison at the time), the authors point out the ways in which values are mobilized by the deviants when their behavior is stigmatized by others. Here the focus is on the differences between the value system within the subculture of prostitution and the value system of the larger society. They see, as part of the beginning of a career in prostitution, a general sense of alienation and isolation from the constraints of the larger community. Indeed this sense of alienation may well be central to any career of indiscriminate sexual contacts, whether they are for pay or not. However, over long periods of time an ideology is required that narrows the "conventional" distance from the larger society. One strategy for handling this is to redefine the deviant act to make it less deviant and frequently to "normalize" the motivation to deviance, e.g., the thief says, "All men are thieves at heart." For the prostitute this is forced home in every sexual encounter, since her clients are drawn from predominantly legitimate segments of the society and who, by patronizing the prostitute, are violating the norms of the larger society.

One of the most important points in the authors' discussion is the notion that there are at least two value cultures of prostitution: one which adopts specifically the criminal world's values (the criminal contraculture) and those prostitutes who live in dual worlds with value systems that are related to prostitution but who also have major commitments to conventional values. This latter mode of value adjustment is managed by keeping completely separate the major segments of their lives. What develops from the discussion of these two cultures is the feeling that the career of prostitution cannot be analyzed in any simple way, and that there are many modes of managing careers of prostitution that have very different consequences for the prostitute herself. Thus, we should not allow ourselves to be seduced by the simplicity of the label "prostitute" (nor by the label "homosexual") into thinking that all prostitutes are alike or that they have all become prostitutes for much the same reasons. There is a definite pressure towards this process of simplification which frequently functions to obscure both the complexity of the individual career and the large number of career options that are available.

Sexual behavior represents one of the most sensitive areas in American life. Within this sphere, professional promiscuity on the part of females stands as a striking deviation from what a large segment of the society declares to be acceptable sexual performance. Prostitutes are undoubtedly well aware of the prevailing social attitudes toward their behavior. It would seem, therefore, that these women develop a set of beliefs which counteract the social anathema attached to their way of life. This set of beliefs allows them to continue their behavior and to face and retaliate against persons who share the dominant and negative social values toward them.

Analyses of prostitution have generally employed a socio-economic or a psychological frame of reference. The socioeconomic approach has ranged from Marxist[1] through ecological[2] to sophisticated structural-functional interpretations.[3] Other attempts at causal explanations have stressed mobility[4] and have concentrated on detailed life histories.[5] In addition, there is a wide range of psychoanalytical approaches, including those on frigidity,[6] Oedipal fixation,[7] maternal rejection,[8] homosexuality,[9] "social-existential" castration,[10] and restrictive ego-ideals combined with revenge motives.[11] Nowhere in the literature is there more than a hint of the manner in which the prostitute forms and supports her self-image.[12]

Two questions appear to be central to the problem of the prostitute's self-identity. First, since most Americans scorn prostitutes and these dominant social values travel throughout the society, how are women recruited to prostitution? Second, since a high degree of conformity to the dominant, middle-class American society is considered necessary for the maintenance of self-esteem, how do prostitutes rationalize their violation of a dominant social norm?

INTERVIEW PHASE

Fifteen prostitutes were interviewed for periods averaging two hours each. Thirteen interviews were obtained while these women were held in the city jail awaiting the results of clinical tests. Two other women were interviewed in night clubs.[13]

Open-ended questions were employed for interviewing. The questions were used only to get the respondents to talk: everything they said was recorded and subsequently coded. Standard profile questions were asked (name, age, education, marital status, number, sex, and age of children, religion, etc.) followed by a series of questions organized around certain principal topics. These were (a) account of career, (b) self-conception, (c) group identifications, and (d) role expectations. Specific but unformalized questions were asked in each of these major areas, such as childhood experiences, recruitment to prostitution, attitudes toward clients, police, neighbors, etc., relationships with parents, husbands, children, relatives, other prostitutes, etc., attitudes toward work, future hopes, fears and plans, moods, fantasies, daydreams, and recreation.[14]

ANALYSIS OF THE DATA

The three following propositions concerning the formation and the structure of the self-image of the prostitute emerged from the data.

1. *The more isolated girl in urban society comes to define as acceptable patterns of behavior condemned by general social values more readily than does the less isolated individual.* Evidence indicated that the respondents were alienated from their parents following a break with the father toward whom they all expressed extreme hostility. After their introduction to prostitution, many of them became reconciled with their mothers, though they all maintained that they had kept knowledge of their activities from the mother:

I would go through hell for my mother, but my father is a bastard. Every time my mother got pregnant [respondent has five siblings] my father went out with other women.

My parents were divorced when I was eight. I lived with relatives and in an orphan home until I was thirteen and then I went to live with my mother. . . . My father was cruel to me. . . . I hated my father and stepfather. . . . I was glad when my father died. . . .

My father was a carpenter and a gambler. . . . He always treated me like I was strictly from age two. But I got along good with my mother.

Alienation during the period of entrance into prostitution was indicated by the respondents' statements that they associated with people who meant little to them, or that they had no friends at all. In every case they felt that they stood alone against a hostile or indifferent world, though some of them were introduced to semi-criminal groups with which in time they came to identify themselves.

I ran around with a girl who started and so I started, too. She had a lot of friends. . . . I got to know a lot of people in the hustling racket.

I just been runnin' around with rum-dums all my life, I guess. . . . There was a fellow once in San Antone—I came in off a box car, believe it or not, and I met him in a honky-tonk.

I was hanging 'round bars in Tulsa just looking for kicks. I had no place to go, like. It was strictly from hunger, man.

I figgered it was easy money—prostitution. . . . Nobody cared what I did anyway, and I knew a fellow who would set it up for me.

2. *The general social values, nevertheless, have some impact on the isolated individual. Therefore, the violation of the these values must be rationalized by the individual.* The violation of sexual values is justified in two ways: (*a*) Everyone is rotten. Hence, prostitutes are no worse than other people, and they are less hypocritical. (*b*) Society doesn't really scorn prostitutes. Every prostitute interviewed expressed some degree of

guilt feeling about her activity. This attitude ranged from mild expressions of guilt to statements like the following:

I will rot in hell for what I am doing. If you don't know what you are doing is sinful, then it is not so bad. But it is an unpardonable sin if you know what you are doing is sinful and keep on sinning.

My father told me two things: "Don't ever become a prostitute and don't marry a nigger."

Several respondents reflected in their defensive attitudes their imputation of middle-class disapproval on the part of the interviewers. These responses took the form of an attack on men or women, the world in general, or they reflected the attitude that prostitution did not mean a person was bad.

Men are . . . shrimps. Show me the man that's worth killing and I'll do the job.

Little chippies in bars give it away for a couple of beers.

This business doesn't keep you from having good children. Religion is right. It's a good thing. What we do doesn't affect religious feelings—being a wife, mother, housewife.

Other people look down on you. Deep down inside it hurts, but you ignore it . . . biggest majority are nice people. Several of the vice squad men hold the squad car door open for me [when they arrest her].

3. *The rationalization by prostitutes violating social taboos against commercial sex behavior takes the form of exaggerating other values,[15] particularly those of financial success, and for some the unselfish assumption of the financial burden of people dependent upon them.* Support for these justifications is found through reference groups, real or fictional, whose values the prostitute internalizes and thus is able to act in a consistent and "normal" manner. The behavior of prostitutes is not abnormal given the norms of those groups with which they identify themselves.

We identified two principal types of reference group orientations: one we labeled the *criminal world contraculture* and the other *dual worlds,* the world of prostitution and the middle-class world of American society.

The Criminal World Contraculture

The principal characteristic of this type of prostitute is a strong identification with criminals and with those on the edge of the criminal world—Hobohemians. Yinger argues for the use of the concept *contraculture* for this type of group identification:

> . . . I suggest the use of the term contraculture wherever the normative system of a group contains, as a primary element, a theme of conflict with the values of the total society where personality variables are directly involved in the development and maintenance of the group's values, and wherever its norms can be understood only by reference to the relationships of the group to a surrounding dominant culture.[16]

This group had the greatest contempt for middle-class, "proper" people, whom they felt to be dull, frightened, and hypocritical. On the other hand, they made some attempt to justify their behavior by appealing to such dominant social values as financial success, their ability to move in "big business" circles, and being good mothers.

One respondent in this group said that prostitution was a means to secure money for her husband and herself so that they could lead an exciting life. Her husband is her procurer, and the group with which they associate is composed of people connected with prostitution. They are heavy drinkers, and many of them are addicts. They appear to be carefree and irresponsible, deciding at a moment's notice to go off on trips together. A vice squad officer related an incident wherein this group decided to dig a swimming pool in a back yard. They dug intermittently for several weeks, but finally gave up the project and left on a trip.

Another respondent stated that she liked the easy money. She had gotten tired of working twelve to fourteen hours a day as a waitress.

Another respondent displayed a great deal of satisfaction from claiming to be a big spender, wearing good clothes, and going to expensive restaurants and night clubs. She also associated with a semi-criminal group. She bragged about X,

. . . a very wealthy businessman who pays me twenty-five to thirty dollars an evening just for my company. He takes me to the best places in town for dinner and dancing, and buys me expensive gifts. And I've never been in bed with the man! He told me that I mingled well with the finest people. He said once, "You act like a lady." She also mentioned a boy friend who was in trouble with the Kansas City police.

This respondent, the only one in the criminal subculture who had children, stated that she was "a good mother" who visited her children regularly. However, her account of the break-up of her first marriage indicated that this self-evaluation, as well as the characterization that she acted like a lady, might be questioned.

My husband started running around. I wanted to make him leave so I could keep the children. I cut him off, cursed him, and cut him with a knife, but I couldn't make him go.

Her children lived with her first husband and his second wife. When she visited her children once, she told her ex-husband that his present wife, "had better be good to my kids or I'll stomp her in a mudhole."

The final respondent in this group also stressed the luxurious life she leads as a prostitute and aligned herself with a criminal group. Like the second respondent she stressed her claim to association with the "best" people in the city and her attendance at social functions where such people gather. A vice squad officer said that she had been arrested while they were investigating a tip that she was harboring a criminal who was a known drug peddler.

These four respondents were generally friendly in their feelings toward their clients and middle-class society in general. As indicated above, they maintained with considerable pride that they associated with the best people. Toward their clients they expressed some ambivalence:

Most of my clients are nice guys. . . . Most of them are married. . . . I like older men because younger men look down on you.

Some men take it out on you because they feel guilty about cheating on their wives. . . . I don't hold it against married men for going to prostitutes. Actually, it teaches them the values of affection because prostitutes are so cold. . . . All in all they are pretty nice.

Dual Worlds

The five cases which fell into this category were characterized by a strong identification with their families and a rejection of the world of prostitutes which they were in, but not of. Two of the respondents claimed to be supporting their husbands and children, while the other two lived alone and claimed to be supporting children in other states whom they visited occasionally. The two married prostitutes said that their husbands acted as procurers for them, but for no other women. This group strongly and consistently expressed middle-class values. Unlike those in the criminal subculture, they never swore or used obscene words. They sought constantly to assure the interviewers that they were excellent mothers who made great sacrifices for their husbands, children, and relatives. They professed religious beliefs, and the two married respondents claimed that their associates (with the exception of their husbands) were not prostitutes or criminals. The two single prostitutes said that they associated with no one except their families whom they visited occasionally in another town. They resisted questions about their clients and other aspects of the business of prostitution. In short, they have seemingly dichotomized their world successfully by depersonalizing their prostitute roles and living almost entirely in the dominant world of American middle-class values.

Sherif and Cantril have noted that the ego can be dissociated from the self under certain extreme situations, and they illustrated this concept with a reference to the autobiography of a London prostitute who wrote, "I have moments when I realize that I am a person to no one. . . . The act of sex I could go through because *I hardly seemed to be taking part in it. . . . Indeed, it was scarcely happening even to me: It was happening to something lying on a bed that had a vague connection with me. . . .*"[17]

All of the respondents reported a certain amount of dissociation in their initial commercial experience. What would seem to distinguish the *dual worlds* groups from other groups was that this initial dissociation was continued and strengthened. The other two groups reported varying degrees of dissociation or none at all, some respondents claiming that they occasionally participated emotionally in the sex act and enjoyed it. Because of their middle-class moral values most of the *dual worlds* group avoided the topic of sex completely. The members of this group had successfully repressed their prostitute role and justified it as a self-sacrificing necessity to support those who were helpless and dependent upon them.

One of the married prostitutes in this group said that when she became pregnant her husband left her. She became a prostitute to support herself and her child. Her present husband is an unemployed tile-setter. She apologized for her husband by saying that there isn't too much demand for tile-setters. She claimed that she was supporting six persons and herself.

They don't know what I do for a living, except my husband. I see my little girl often. About once a week. I don't work weekends so I can go see her.

. . . My sister just got a job, but she's not on her feet yet. She has a tiny baby. Her husband is in the penitentiary. [Embarrassed laugh.]

The other married prostitute also claimed to be supporting an unemployed husband, two children, and her mother. Her mother takes care of her children and none of them knows that she is a prostitute.

I think that I am a good mother who takes care of her children. I love my family very much. I have a normal family life other than being a prostitute. I hope that my husband can find a job and gets to working steadily again so I can be an ordinary housewife.

Of the single prostitutes in this group, one had five children by a previous marriage and the other had never been married. The first strongly identified herself with her children, while the second strongly identified herself with her parents. Neither of them associated intimately with other people. Both claimed they had become prostitutes in order to care for their children or their parents.

I am very proud of my family. Even though the mother is a prostitute it doesn't reflect on her family—this business doesn't keep you from having good children. I keep my children in the best private schools and colleges in Texas. One of them married very well. They don't know what I do.

The respondent who identified herself with her parents maintained that her father had given her the best of everything as a child, but she had failed to live up to his expectations because she was too much like him. Nevertheless, she helped both parents financially:

My parents are the most wonderful people alive. I like 'em both but my mother is easier to get along with. Dad and I fight like cats and dogs. Both alike. He thinks I'm two years old. He said, "I knew the day you was born you'd be just like me." He's got suspicious of my work, but not my mother. She had an operation —cancer of the brain. I gave him [father] four hundred dollars and three hundred more after I came back from Chicago. He said, "Myra, I know what you're doing, but for God's sake don't let your mother know."

All four respondents in the *dual worlds* category expressed middle-class values:

I have some friends, some are married women, and some work.

My husband and I run around with other couples where the wife isn't a prostitute.

I got lots of friends not even connected with hustling. Went with a Kansas City dick for a long time.

I don't associate with hustling people. Half their husbands are in McAlester [state penitentiary] or the county jail.

Alienation

The six respondents who fell into this group were characterized by feelings of normlessness, apathy, lack of direction or future goal orientation. They identified themselves with no one and felt their lives to be empty and meaningless. Two of them were young: one an eighteen-year-old who was new to the profession, and the other a nineteen-year-old who had been a prostitute for one year. It is possible that the newest recruit's sense of alienation will become modified as she becomes less a stranger to her environment. The third respondent had been a prostitute for ten years. The length of time in prostitution is evidently not a factor in alienation, however, since the second youngest respondent in this group had been a prostitute for one year, and the prostitute with the longest record (eleven years) seemed to be well integrated in a criminal subculture. As noted above, all of this group dissociated themselves from the sex act.

Their conditions of alienation may be summarized by the following selected quotations:

I been in this racket ten years, I guess it's too late to get out. . . . I got no future; I been married four times and that's enough. . . . I don't care. I spent a hundred and fifty dollars over the weekend on drinking and gambling. I can't save. But I kicked the habit cold turkey. [Another respondent in the *dual worlds* category, who knew this prostitute, said: "Hustling's got the best of Jerry. She's drunk all the time. Girls like that are weak. They got no will power."] I got no friends; everybody's rotten, anymore. Women are as bad as men. Women ain't worth a damn. I'm usually too drunk to know what's going on [sex act].

I live by myself and have no friends. I just sleep and hustle at the night club. No, TV shows and books just bore me. Daydreams? Why daydream when you can't be out doing the things you daydream about? . . . Just before you came in, I was out standing in the rain watching the world cry because it's been so screwed up by all the bastards in it. [This respondent was interviewed in a night club.]

I was drunk when I was arrested—had been drinking for several days. I was too drunk to care. I don't live with anybody. I don't know anyone in this town, except the porter [procurer]. My parents don't care about me, they put me in an Indian boarding school and I ran away from it. Drinking is very bad. I've been so bad I decided I might as well go all the way. I used to walk around town late at night and once a porter from one of the hotels stopped me and tried to get me to start working. He asked me twice. I felt it didn't matter. I was sober when I started, but I had to get drunk to finish it.

SUMMARY AND CONCLUSIONS

The present study is mainly heuristic. We have been concerned with the problem of self-respect. Assuming that commercialized sexual activity is condemned by general social norms in the United States, how do prostitutes maintain a consistent self-image?

The interviews with fifteen prostitutes provided us with data which we feel are related to these questions. The interviews provided support for the following propositions:

1. The more isolated individual in the urban society comes to define as acceptable patterns of behavior condemned by general social values more readily than does the less isolated individual.

2. The general social values have some impact on the isolated individual. Therefore, the violation of these values must be rationalized by the individual.

3. The rationalizations by prostitutes violating sexual taboos against commercial sex behavior take the form of exaggerating other values, particularly those of financial success, and for some the unselfish assumption of the financial burden of people dependent upon them. Two types of reference group orientation important for self-justification were identified: the *criminal world* and the *dual worlds* categories. A third category of alienated individuals was discerned.

We have drawn other tentative conclusions regarding various hypotheses culled from the literature of prostitution. The following hypotheses await further investigations:

1. Prostitution is not a function of ecological factors. Evidence indicates that there exists at the present time a kind of "white collar" prostitution. These are secretaries, stenographers, and file clerks in large corporations who work as call girls in their off-hours in first-class metropolitan hotels.

2. Not all prostitutes are recruited from the economically deprived. The rationalization for prostitution may occur at all occupational and income levels because of urban anonymity

and the weakening of traditional religious and moral values.

3. Most prostitutes have normal intelligence and average educational backgrounds.

4. Personality factors, early socialization, childhood sexual experiences, and adult marital relations are insufficient explanations of recruitment to prostitution. The selection of prostitution as an occupation from available alternatives must be sought in the individual prostitute's interaction with others over a considerable time span.

5. Self-denigration is only one of several alternatives available to the prostitute who is "hooked." Her prostitute's role may be sustained through interaction with others who are important to her, or a fantasy world may sustain a satisfactory self-image.

Further research is planned on a larger scale in view of the results reported in this preliminary study. It is believed that the frame of reference employed here can be useful in a synthesis of existing empirical insights concerning behavior in this area.

Apprenticeships in Prostitution

JAMES H. BRYAN

It is important to note here that prostitution is a world of work, that the sexual activity performed is a form of labor. At the nexus of the relationship between the prostitute and her customer is an exchange of money for sexual services

REPRINTED with the permission of the author and editors from *Social Problems*, 12:3:278–297 (Winter 1965).

This data was collected when the author was at the Neuropsychiatric Institute, UCLA Center for the Health Sciences. I wish to acknowledge the considerable aid of Mrs. Elizabeth Gordon, Miss Carol Kupers, and Mr. Saul Sherter in the preparation and the analysis of this data. I am greatly indebted to Dr. Evelyn Hooker for both her intellectual and moral support, and to Vivian London for her excellent editorial advice. I particularly wish to express my great gratitude to my wife, Virginia, for her tolerance, encouragement, and understanding.

performed. This is one of the reasons why the language of occupational sociology which Bryan uses is so appropriate to a discussion of prostitution. It is this that makes prostitution so different from homosexuality, since for the latter, except in certain circumstances—the homosexual prostitute (see the article by Reiss, pp. 197–228) or the homosexual who makes a living running a gay bar or a clothing store for homosexuals —the commitment to homosexuality does not necessarily organize the rest of a person's life around it.

Bryan's concern in this article is the call girl, a very different case from the prostitutes who were the primary focus in the articles by Young and Jackman et al. The call girl services a very different clientele, primarily middle class in nature, and at considerably higher prices. In the process of serving a clientele for which the activities of the girl may be wider than a purely sexual performance for money, there are greater dilemmas in terms of confusing the contact with a conventional courtship relationship. The function of the apprenticeship period is not only to teach successful management of the customer within the context of the sexual exchange itself, but also to inculcate attitudes toward all customers, and indeed toward the conventional society, that will eventually result in the value climate observed in its fullest form in Jackman et al. Learning values and the management of specifically sexual relationships helps the prostitute cope with the stigma of plying a deviant trade.

One of the dilemmas of the prostitute's life is the aura of mistrust that permeates the occupation in reference not only to customers and the police, but to pimps and other prostitutes as well. The world of prostitution, while providing sources of emotional support and a value system organized to cope with stress, is immensely contaminated with concerns for money and an alienation from conventional society. It is clear from Bryan's discussion that there are great difficulties involved with socialization into prostitution, and the drive to build up a clientele militates against long periods of apprenticeship. Since the prostitute in the call girl situation is predominantly a professional (like the lawyer and unlike the college professor), there are problems in maintaining a col-

lective interest in other persons in the life. Much of the manifest pathology that seems to exist in prostitution is probably a function of its social arrangements and not a necessary attribute of the women prior to the time they entered the life of prostitution.

While theoretical conceptions of deviant behavior range from role strain to psychoanalytic theory, orientations to the study of the prostitute have shown considerable homogeneity. Twentieth century theorizing concerning this occupational group has employed, almost exclusively, a Freudian psychiatric model. The prostitute has thus been variously described as masochistic, of infantile mentality, unable to form mature interpersonal relationships, regressed, emotionally dangerous to males and as normal as the average women.[1] The call girl, the specific focus of this paper, has been accused of being anxious, possessing a confused self-image, excessively dependent, demonstrating gender-role confusion, aggressive, lacking internal controls and masochistic.[2]

The exclusive use of psychoanalytic models in attempting to predict behavior, and the consequent neglect of situational and cognitive processes, has been steadily lessening in the field of psychology. Their inadequacy as models for understanding deviancy has been specifically explicated by Becker, and implied by London.[3] The new look in the conceptualization and study of deviant behavior has focused on the interpersonal processes which help define the deviant role, the surroundings in which the role is learned, and limits upon the enactment of the role. As Hooker has indicated regarding the study of homosexuals, one must not only consider the personality structure of the participants, but also the structure of their community and the pathways and routes into the learning and enactment of the behavior.[4] Such "training periods" have been alluded to by Maurer in his study of the con man, and by Sutherland in his report on professional thieves. More recently, Lindesmith and Becker have conceptualized the development of drug use as a series of learning sequences necessary for the development of steady use.[5]

This paper provides some detailed, albeit preliminary, information concerning induction and training in a particular type of deviant career: prostitution, at the call girl level. It describes the order of events, and their surrounding structure, which future call girls experience in entering their occupation.

The respondents in this study were 33 prostitutes, all currently or previously working in the Los Angeles area. They ranged in age from 18 to 32, most being in their mid-twenties. None of the interviewees were obtained through official law enforcement agencies, but seven were found within the context of a neuropsychiatric hospital. The remaining respondents were gathered primarily through individual referrals from previous participants in the study. There were no obvious differences between the "psychiatric sample" and the other interviewees on the data to be reported.

All subjects in the sample were call girls. That is, they typically obtained their clients by individual referrals, primarily by telephone, and enacted the sexual contract in their own or their clients' place of residence or employment. They did not initiate contact with their customers in bars, streets, or houses of prostitution, although they might meet their customers at any number of locations by pre-arrangement. The minimum fee charged per sexual encounter was $20.00. As an adjunct to the call girl interviews, three pimps and two "call boys" were interviewed as well.[6]

Approximately two thirds of the sample were what are sometimes known as "outlaw broads"; that is, they were not under the supervision of a pimp when interviewed. There is evidence that the majority of pimps who were aware of the study prohibited the girls under their direction from participating in it. It should be noted that many members of the sample belonged to one or another clique; their individually expressed opinions may not be independent.

The interviews strongly suggest that there are marked idiosyncrasies from one geographical area to another in such practices as fee-splitting, involvement with peripheral occupations (e.g., cabbies), and so forth. For example, there appears to be little direct involvement of peripheral occupations with call girl activities in the Los Angeles area, while it has been estimated that up to 10% of the population of Las Vegas is directly involved in activities of prostitutes.[7] What may be typical for a call girl in the Los Angeles area is not necessarily typical for a girl in New York, Chicago, Las Vegas, or Miami.

Since the professional literature (e.g., Greenwald; Pomeroy) concerning this occupation and its participants is so limited in quantity, and is not concerned with training per se, the present data may have some utility for the social sciences.[8]

All but two interviews were tape recorded. All respondents had prior knowledge that the interview would be tape recorded. The interviewing was, for the most part, done at the girls' place of work and/or residence. Occasional interviews were conducted in the investigator's office, and one in a public park. Interviews were semistructured and employed open-ended questions. One part of the interview concerned the apprenticeship period or "turning out" process.

THE ENTRANCE

I had been thinking about it [becoming a call girl] before a lot. . . . Thinking about wanting to do it, but I had no connections. Had I not had a connection, I probably wouldn't have started working. . . . I thought about starting out. . . . Once I tried it [without a contact]. . . . I met this guy at a bar and I tried to make him pay me, but the thing is, you can't do it that way because they are romantically interested in you, and they don't think that it is on that kind of basis You can't all of a sudden come up and want money for it, you have to be known beforehand. . . . I think that is what holds a lot of girls back who might work. I think I might have started a year sooner had I had a connection. You seem to make one contact or another . . . if it's another girl or a pimp or just someone who will set you up and get you a client. . . . You can't just, say, get an apartment and get a phone in and everything and say, "Well, I'm gonna start business," because you gotta get clients from somewhere. There has to be a contact.

Immediately prior to entrance into the occupation, all but one girl had personal contact with someone professionally involved in call girl activities (pimps or other call girls). The one exception had contact with a customer of call girls. While various occupational groups (e.g., photographers) seem to be peripherally involved, often unwittingly, with the call girl, there was no report of individuals involved in such occupations being contacts for new recruits. The novice's initial contact is someone at the level at which she will eventually enter the occupation: not a street-walker, but a call girl; not a pimp who manages girls out of a house of prostitution, but a pimp who manages call girls.

Approximately half of the girls reported that their initial contact for entrance into the profession was another "working girl." The nature of these relationships is quite variable. In some cases, the girls have been long standing friends. Other initial contacts involved sexual relationships between a Lesbian and the novice. Most, however, had known each other less than a year, and did not appear to have a very close relationship, either in the sense of time spent together or of biographical information exchanged. The relationship may begin with the aspiring call girl soliciting the contact. That is, if a professional is known to others as a call girl, she will be sought out and approached by females who are strangers:[9]

I haven't ever gone out and looked for one. All of these have fell right into my hands. . . . They turned themselfs out. . . . They come to me for help.

Whatever their relationship, whenever the professional agrees to aid the beginner, she also, it appears, implicitly assumes responsibility for training her. This is evidenced by the fact that only one such female contact referred the aspirant to another girl for any type of help. Data are not available as to the reason for this unusual referral.

If the original contact was not another call girl but a pimp, a much different relationship is developed and the career follows a somewhat different course. The relationship between pimp and girl is typically one of lovers, not friends:

. . . because I love him very much. Obviously, I'm doing this mostly for him. . . . I'd do anything for him. I'm not just saying I will, I am. . . . [After discussing his affair with another woman] I just decided that I knew what he was when I decided to do this for him and I decided I had two choices—either accept it or not, and I accepted it, and I have no excuse.

Occasionally, however, a strictly business relationship will be formed:

Right now I am buying properties, and as soon as I can afford it, I am buying stocks. . . . It is strictly a business deal. This man and I are friends, our relationship ends there. He handles all the money, he is making all the investments and I trust him. We have a legal document drawn up which states that half the investments are mine, half of them his, so I am protected.

Whether the relationship is love or business, the pimp solicits the new girl.[10] It is usually agreed that the male will have an important managerial role in the course of the girl's career, and that both will enjoy the gains from the girl's activities for an indefinite period:

Actually a pimp has to have complete control or else it's like trouble with him. Because if a pimp doesn't, if she is not madly in love with him or something in some way, a pimp won't keep a girl.

Once the girl agrees to function as a call girl, the male, like his female counterpart, undertakes the training of the girl, or refers the girl to another call girl for training. Either course seems equally probable. Referrals, when employed, are typically to friends and, in some cases, wives or ex-wives.

Although the data are limited, it appears that the pimp retains his dominance over the trainee even when the latter is being trained by a call girl. The girl trainer remains deferential to the pimp's wishes regarding the novice.

APPRENTICESHIP

Once a contact is acquired and the decision to become a call girl made, the recruit moves to the next stage in the career sequence: the apprenticeship period. The structure of the apprenticeship will be described, followed by a description of the content most frequently communicated during this period.

The apprenticeship is typically served under the direction of another call girl, but may occasionally be supervised by a pimp. Twenty-four girls in the sample initially worked under the supervision of other girls. The classroom is, like the future place of work, an apartment. The apprentice typically serves in the trainer's apartment, either temporarily residing with the trainer or commuting there almost daily. The novice rarely serves her apprenticeship in such places as a house of prostitution, motel, or on the street. It is also infrequent that the girl is transported out of her own city to serve an apprenticeship. Although the data are not extensive, the number of girls being trained simultaneously by a particular trainer has rarely been reported to be greater than three. Girls sometimes report spending up to eight months in training, but the average stay seems to be two or three months. The trainer controls all referrals and appointments, novices seemingly not having much control over the type of sexual contract made or the circumstances surrounding the enactment of the contract.

The structure of training under the direction of a pimp seems similar, though information is more limited. The girls are trained in an apartment in the city they intend to work and for a short period of time. There is some evidence that the pimp and the novice often do not share the same apartment as might the novice and the girl trainer. There appear to be two reasons for the separation of pimp and girl. First, it is not uncommonly thought that cues which suggest the presence of other men displease the girl's customers.

Well, I would never let them know that I had a lover, which is something that you never ever let a john know, because this makes them very reticent to give you money, because they think you are going to go and spend it with your lover, which is what usually happens.

(Interestingly, the work of Winick suggests that such prejudices may not actually be held by many customers.)[11] Secondly, the legal repercussions are much greater, of course, for the pimp who lives with his girl than for two girls rooming together. As one pimp of 19 years experience puts it:

It is because of the law. There is a law that is called the illegal cohabitation that they rarely use unless the man becomes big in stature. If he is a big man in the hustling world, the law then employs any means at their command. . . .

Because of the convenience in separation of housing, it is quite likely that the pimp is less directly involved with the day-to-day training of the girls than the call girl trainer.

The content of the training period seems to consist of two broad, interrelated dimensions, one philosophical, the other interpersonal. The former refers to the imparting of a value structure, the latter to "do's" and "don't's" of relating to customers and, secondarily, to other "working girls" and pimps. The latter teaching is perhaps best described by the concept of a short range perspective. That is, most of the "do's" and "don't's" pertain to ideas and actions that the call girl uses in problematic situations.[12] Not all girls absorb these teachings, and those who do incorporate them in varying degrees.

Insofar as a value structure is transmitted it is that of maximizing gains while minimizing effort, even if this requires transgressions of either a legal or moral nature. Frequently, it is postulated that people, particularly men, are corrupt or easily corruptible, that all social relationships are but a reflection of a "con," and that prostitution is simply a more honest or at least no more dishonest act than the everyday behavior of "squares." Furthermore, not only are "johns" basically exploitative, but they are easily exploited; hence they are, in some respects, stupid. As explained by a pimp:

. . . [in the hustling world] the trick or the john is known as a fool . . . this is not the truth. . . . He [the younger pimp] would teach his woman that a trick was a fool.

Since the male is corrupt, or honest only because he lacks the opportunity to be corrupt, then it is only appropriate that he be exploited as he exploits.

Girls first start making their "scores"—say one guy keeps them for a while or maybe she gets, you know, three or four grand out of him, say a car or a coat. These are your scores. . . .

The general assumption that man is corrupt is empirically confirmed when the married male betrays his wife, when the moralist, secular or religious, betrays his publicly stated values, or when the "john" "stiffs" (cheats) the girl. An example of the latter is described by a girl as she reflects upon her disillusionment during her training period.

It is pretty rough when you are starting out. You get stiffed a lot of times. . . . Oh sure. They'll take advantage of you anytime they can. And I'm a trusting soul, I really am. I'll believe anybody till they prove different. I've made a lot of mistakes that way. You get to the point, well, Christ, what the heck can I believe in people, they tell me one thing and here's what they do to me.

Values such as fairness with other working girls, or fidelity to a pimp, may occasionally be taught. To quote a pimp:

So when you ask me if I teach a kind of basic philosophy, I would say that you could say that. Because you try to teach them in an amoral way that there is a right and wrong way as pertains to this game . . . and then you teach them that when working with other girls to try to treat the other girl fairly because a woman's worst enemy in the street [used in both a literal and figurative sense] is the other woman and only by treating the other women decently can she expect to get along. . . . Therefore the basic philosophy I guess would consist of a form of honesty, a form of sincerity and complete fidelity to her man [pimp].

It should be noted, however, that behavior based on enlightened self-interest with concomitant exploitation is not limited to customer relationships. Interviewees frequently mentioned a pervasive feeling of distrust between trainer and trainee, and such incidents as thefts or betrayal of confidences are occasionally reported and chronically guarded against.

Even though there may be considerable pressure upon the girl to accept this value structure, many of them (perhaps the majority of the sample) reject it.

People have told me that I wasn't turned out, but turned loose instead. . . . Someone who is turned out is turned out to believe in a certain code of behavior, and this involves having a pimp, for one thing. It also involves never experiencing anything but hatred or revulsion for "tricks" for another thing. It involves always getting the money in front [before the sexual act] and a million little things that are very strictly adhered to by those in the "in group," which I am not. . . . Never being nice or pleasant to a trick unless you are doing it for the money, getting more money. [How did you learn that?] It was explained to me over a period of about six months. I learned that you were doing it to make money for yourself so that you could have nice things and security. . . . [Who would teach you this?] [The trainer] would teach me this.[13]

It seems reasonable to assume that the value structure serves, in general, to create in-group solidarity and to alienate the girl from "square" society, and that this structure serves the political advantage of the trainer and the economic gains of the trainee more than it allays the personal anxieties of either. In fact, failure to adopt these values at the outset does not appear to be correlated with much personal distress.[14] As one girl describes her education experiences:

Some moral code. We're taught, as a culture . . . it's there and after awhile you live, breathe, and eat it. Now, what makes you go completely against everything that's inside you, everything that you have been taught, and the whole society, to do things like this?

Good empirical evidence, however, concerning the functions and effectiveness of this value structure with regard to subjective comfort is lacking.

A series of deductions derived from the premises indicated above serve to provide, in part, the "rules" of interpersonal contact with the customer. Each customer is to be seen as a "mark," and "pitches" are to be made.

[Did you have a standard pitch?] It's sort of amusing. I used to listen to my girl friend [trainer]. She was the greatest at this telephone type of situation. She would call up and cry and say that people had come to her door. . . . She'd cry and she'd complain and she'd say "I have a bad check at the liquor store, and they sent the police over," and really . . . a girl has a story she tells the man. . . . Anything, you know, so he'll help her out. Either it's the rent or she needs a car, or doctor's bills, or any number of things.

Any unnecessary interaction with the customer is typically frowned upon, and the trainee will receive exhortations to be quick about her business. One girl in her fourth week of work explains:

[What are some of the other don't's that you have learned about?] Don't take so much time. . . . The idea is to get rid of them as quickly as possible.

Other content taught concerns specific information about specific customers.

. . . she would go around the bar and say, now look at that man over there, he's this way and that way, and this is what he would like and these are what his problems are. . . .

. . . she would teach me what the men wanted and how much to get, what to say when I got there . . . just a line to hand them.

Training may also include proprieties concerning consuming alcohol and drugs, when and how to obtain the fee, how to converse with the customers and, occasionally, physical and sexual hygiene. As a girl trainer explains:

First of all, impress cleanliness. Because, on the whole, the majority of girls, I would say, I don't believe there are any cleaner women walking the streets, because they've got to be aware of any type of body odor. . . . You teach them to French [fellatio] and how to talk to men.

[Do they [pimps] teach you during the turning out period how to make a telephone call?] Oh, usually, yes. They don't teach you, they just tell you how to do it and you do it with your good common sense, but if you have trouble, they tell you more about it.

Interestingly, the specific act of telephoning a client is often distressing to the novice and is of importance in her training. Unfortunately for the girl, it is an act she must perform with regularity as she does considerable soliciting.[15] One suspects that such behavior is embarrassing for her because it is an unaccustomed role for her to play—she has so recently come from a culture where young women do *not* telephone men for dates. Inappropriate sex-role behavior seems to produce greater personal distress than does appropriate sex-role behavior even when it is morally reprehensible.

Well, it is rather difficult to get on the telephone, when you've never worked before, and talk to a man about a subject like that, and it is very new to you.

What is omitted from the training should be noted as well. There seems to be little instruction concerning sexual techniques as such, even though the previous sexual experience of the trainee may have been quite limited. What instruction there is typically revolves around the practice of fellatio. There seems to be some encouragement not to experience sexual orgasms with the client, though this may be quite variable with the trainer.

. . . and sometimes, I don't know if it's a set rule or maybe it's an unspoken rule, you don't enjoy your dates.

Yes, he did [teach attitudes]. He taught me to be cold. . . .

It should be stressed that, if the girls originally accepted such instructions and values, many of them, at least at the time of interviewing, verbalized a rejection of these values and reported behavior which departed considerably from the interpersonal rules stipulated as "correct" by their trainers. Some experience orgasms with the customer, some show considerable affect toward "johns," others remain drunk or "high" throughout the contact.[16] While there seems to be general agreement as to what the rules of interpersonal conduct are, there appears to be considerable variation in the adoption of such rules.

A variety of methods is employed to communicate the content described above. The trainer may arrange to eavesdrop on the interactions of girl and client and then discuss the interaction with her. One trainer, for example, listened through a closed door to the interaction of a new girl with a customer, then immediately after he left, discussed, in a rather heated way, methods by which his exit may have been facilitated. A pimp relates:

The best way to do this [teaching conversation] is, in the begin-

ning, when the phone rings, for instance . . . is to listen to what
she says and then check and see how big a trick he is and then
correct her from there.

. . . with everyone of them [trainees] I would make it a point to
see two guys to see how they [the girls] operate.

In one case a girl reported that her pimp left a written
list of rules pertaining to relating to "johns." Direct teaching,
however, seems to be uncommon. The bulk of whatever learning takes place seems to take place through observation.

It's hard to tell you, because we learn through observations.

But I watched her and listened to what her bit was on the
telephone.

To summarize, the structure of the apprenticeship period
seems quite standard. The novice receives her training either
from a pimp or from another more experienced call girl,
more often the latter. She serves her initial two to eight
months of work under the trainer's supervision and often
serves this period in the trainer's apartment. The trainer assumes responsibility for arranging contacts and negotiating
the type and place of the sexual encounter.

The content of the training pertains both to a general
philosophical stance and to some specifics (usually not sexual)
of interpersonal behavior with customers and colleagues. The
philosophy is one of exploiting the exploiters (customers) by
whatever means necessary and defining the colleagues of the
call girl as being intelligent, self-interested and, in certain
important respects, basically honest individuals. The interpersonal techniques addressed during the learning period
consist primarily of "pitches," telephone conversations, personal and occasionally sexual hygiene, prohibitions against
alcohol and dope while with a "john," how and when to
obtain the fee, and specifics concerning the sexual habits of
particular customers. Specific sexual techniques are very
rarely taught. The current sample included a considerable
number of girls who, although capable of articulating this
value structure, were not particularly inclined to adopt it.

CONTACTS AND CONTRACTS

While the imparting of ideologies and proprieties to the prospective call girl is emphasized during the apprenticeship period, it appears that the primary function of the apprenticeship, at least for the trainee, is building a clientele. Since this latter function limits the degree of occupational socialization, the process of developing the clientele and the arrangements made between trainer and trainee will be discussed.

Lists ("books") with the names and telephone numbers of customers are available for purchase from other call girls or pimps, but such books are often considered unreliable. While it is also true that an occasional pimp will refer customers to girls, this does not appear to be a frequent practice. The most frequent method of obtaining such names seems to be through contacts developed during the apprenticeship. The trainer refers customers to the apprentice and oversees the latter in terms of her responsibility and adequacy in dealing with the customer. For referring the customer, the trainer receives forty to fifty per cent of the total price agreed upon in the contract negotiated by the trainer and customer.[17] The trainer and trainees further agree, most often explicitly, on the apprentice's "right" to obtain and to use, on further occasions, information necessary for arranging another sexual contract with the "john" without the obligation of further "kick-back" to the trainer. That is, if she can obtain the name and telephone number of the customer, she can negotiate another contract without fee-splitting. During this period, then, the girl is not only introduced to other working colleagues (pimps and girls alike) but also develops a clientele.

There are two obvious advantages for a call girl in assuming the trainer role. First, since there seems to be an abundant demand for new girls, and since certain service requirements demand more than one girl, even the well established call girl chronically confronts the necessity for making referrals. It is then reasonable to assume that the extra profit derived from the fee-splitting activities, together with the added conveniences of having a girl "on call," allows the trainer to profit considerably from this arrangement. Secondly, contacts with customers are reputedly extremely difficult to maintain if services are not rendered on demand. Thus, the adoption of the trainer role enables the girl to maintain contacts with "fickle" customers under circumstances where she may wish a respite from the sexual encounter without terminating the contacts necessary for re-entry into the call girl role. It is also possible that the financial gains may conceivably be much greater for most trainers than for most call girls, but this is a moot point.

A final aspect of the apprenticeship period that should be noted is the novice's income. It is possible for the novice, under the supervision of a competent and efficient trainer, to earn a great deal of money, or at least to get a favorable glimpse of the great financial possibilities of the occupation and, in effect, be heavily rewarded for her decision to enter it. Even though the novice may be inexperienced in both the sexual and interpersonal techniques of prostitution, her novelty on the market gives her an immediate advantage over her more experienced competitors. It seems quite likely that the new girl, irrespective of her particular physical or mental qualities, has considerable drawing power because she provides new sexual experience to the customer. Early success and financial reward may well provide considerable incentive to continue in the occupation.

A final word is needed regarding the position of the pimp vis-à-vis the call girl during the apprenticeship period. While some pimps assume the responsibility for training the girl personally, as indicated above, as many send the novice to another girl. The most apparent reason for such referral is that it facilitates the development of the "book." Purposes of training appear to be secondary for two reasons: (1) The pimp often lacks direct contact with the customers, so he personally cannot aid directly in the development of the girl's clientele; (2) When the pimp withdraws his girl from the training context, it is rarely because she has obtained adequate knowledge of the profession. This is not to say that all pimps are totally unconcerned with the type of knowledge being imparted to the girl. Rather, the primary concern of the pimp is the girl's developing a clientele, not learning the techniques of sex or conversation.

The apprenticeship period usually ends abruptly, not smoothly. Its termination may be but a reflection of interpersonal difficulties between trainer and trainee, novice and pimp, or between two novices. Occasionally termination of training is brought about through the novice's discovery and subsequent theft of the trainer's "book." Quite frequently the termination is due to the novice's developing a sufficient trade or other business opportunities. The point is, however, that no respondent has reported that the final disruption of the apprenticeship was the result of the completion of adequate training. While disruptions of this relationship may be due to personal or impersonal events, termination is not directly due to the development of sufficient skills.

DISCUSSION AND SUMMARY

On the basis of interviews with 33 call girls in the Los Angeles area, information was obtained about entrance into the call girl occupation and the initial training period or apprenticeship therein.

The novice call girl is acclimated to her new job primarily by being thoroughly immersed in the call girl subculture, where she learns the trade through imitation as much as through explicit tutoring. The outstanding concern at this stage is the development of a sizable and lucrative clientele. The specific skills and values which are acquired during this period are rather simple and quickly learned.

In spite of the girls' protests and their extensive folklore, the art of prostitution, at least at this level, seems to be technically a low-level skill. That is, it seems to be an occupation which requires little formal knowledge or practice for its successful pursuit and appears best categorized as an unskilled job. Evidence for this point comes from two separate sources. First, there seems to be little technical training during this period, and the training seems of little importance to the career progress. Length or type of training does not appear correlated with success (i.e., money earned, lack of subjective distress, minimum fee per "trick," etc.). Secondly, the termination of the apprenticeship period is often brought about for reasons unrelated to training. It seems that the need for an apprenticeship period is created more by the secrecy surrounding the rendering or the utilization of the call girl service than by the complexity of the role. In fact, it is reasonable to assume that the complexity of the job confronting a street-walker may be considerably greater than that confronting a call girl. The tasks of avoiding the police, sampling among strangers for potential customers, and arrangements for the completion of the sexual contract not only require different skills on the part of the street-walker, but are performances requiring a higher degree of professional "know-how" than is generally required of the call girl.[18]

As a pimp who manages both call girls and "high class" street-walkers explains:

The girl that goes out into the street is the sharper of the two, because she is capable of handling herself in the street, getting around the law, picking out the trick that is not absolutely psycho ... and capable of getting along in the street.... The street-walker, as you term her, is really a prima donna of the prostitutes ... her field is unlimited, she goes to all of the top places so she meets the top people....

The fact that the enactment of the call girl role requires little training, and the introduction of the girl to clients and colleagues alike is rather rapid, gives little time or incentive for adequate occupational socialization. It is perhaps for this reason rather than, for example, reasons related to personality factors, that occupational instability is great and cultural homogeneity small.

In closing, while it appears that there is a rather well defined apprenticeship period in the career of the call girl, it seems that it is the secrecy rather than the complexity of the occupation which generates such a period. While there is good evidence that initial contacts, primarily with other "working girls," are necessary for entrance into this career, there seems no reason, at this point, to assume that the primary intent of the participants in training is anything but the development of an adequate clientele.

PART III

Male Homosexuality

The Homosexual Community

EVELYN HOOKER

In this article Dr. Hooker reports on a small part of a major study of homosexuality. Her concern here is the ethnography of the homosexual community, which is defined not in the traditional sense of community, but as an aggregate of persons with a major common commitment. The community consists of a round of activities, places, and people, the latter's lives being interconnected in a specific kind of sexual commitment. Its most public manifestation is the "gay" bar, which is the leisure world of the homosexual, and is, at the same time, the point at which most homosexual behavior is visible to the conventional world. As Hooker notes, it is in the bars that the widest range of persons with homosexual commitments can be observed. In her language (and she notes that it is a metaphor, that is, it describes something in terms which it is not) the bar is a free market into which all persons are admitted and in which sexual selection is centralized.

The bars, as the most public manifestation of the homosexual community, are one of the principal places where

REPRINTED with the permission of the author and publishers from *Perspectives in Psychopathology* Oxford University Press, New York, 1965. This selection first appeared in the *Proceedings of the XIV International Congress of Applied Psychology*, Munksgaard, Copenhagen, 1961, and in its present form was published in *Perspectives in Psychopathology*, Oxford University Press, New York, 1965.

The author is supported in research by a USPHS Research Career Award, No. K6-MH-18,832. Research drawn on for this paper was conducted under Grant No. M-839, and continues under Grant No. MH-06452, the National Institute of Mental Health, The U.S. Public Health Service.

persons who have never recognized their own sexual interests or who have only felt odd and estranged because of their desire for persons of their own sex most often "come out," that is, they discover the nature of their own homosexuality and the homosexuality of others. This period of "coming out" is in a sense similar to the apprenticeship of the prostitute; the individual learns about the rules of the homosexual liaison, the necessity of watching for the police, the places to go, and the things to do that are all part of living a homosexual life.

Behind this public world there exist homosexuals who rarely or never frequent the bars, partially because they have a permanent or quasi-permanent relationship or because they have occupational roles that prevent them from a public expression of their homosexuality. In this other world there are forms of social organization and mutual entertainment patterns that serve the same functions as the bar. These are social groups in which the mask that is worn for the rest of society may be lowered and in which behaviors may be performed that cannot be acted out in other contexts.

This is a community, then, which provides many of the same things that other communities provide for their members. It is a training ground for learning values and behavior, a milieu in which persons already trained may live every day, and a source of social support and information for its members. Seen in this framework, homosexuality loses much of its exotic flavor and can be viewed as a life career composed of many contingencies and crises of identity and personal choice. Once again, as in the case of the prostitute, we move away from a simple category toward the complexity of experience and life as it is lived.

In view of its socially tabooed character, it is not difficult to understand why homosexuality as a collective phenomenon in urban settings has rarely been subjected to scientific investigation.[1] The necessity of escaping the penalties of social or legal recognition impels many homosexuals to lead a highly secret private life. Only when caught by law enforcement agents, or when seeking psychiatric help, are they usually available for study. Gaining access to secret worlds of homosexuals, and maintaining rapport while conducting an ethnographic field study, requires the development of a non-evaluative attitude toward all forms of sexual behavior. Social scientists tend to share the emotional attitudes of their culture, and thus do not find this an easy task. Most psychological studies of homosexuality are clinical in orientation and largely concerned with individual psychodynamics.[2] I know of only one sociological study of a homosexual community in an urban setting (Leznoff & Westley, 1956).

The present investigation of the homosexual community in metropolitan Los Angeles is part of a large project, on which I have been engaged for seven years, which also includes a study of the multiple developmental routes by which males travel to self-identification as homosexuals, and an analysis of adult personality structure and adjustment (Hooker, 1956, 1957, 1958, 1959). It has become increasingly clear that these aspects of the problem must be viewed as functionally interrelated: the homosexual community or world and the kinds of persons who travel those paths and live in that world cannot be treated as independent of each other. The relations between personality variables and homosexual subculture variables in determining the commitment to, and patterns of, adult homosexuality are complex. For many, the stability of the commitment appears to be a function of the interaction of both sets of variables.

My methods for studying the homosexual community are essentially those of an ethnographer: interviewing its members about the institutions and activities and participating in those activities whenever possible, with subsequent recording of my observations. Full participation is impossible for two reasons; my gender—I am studying a male community[3] and my research role. My objective is to see the homosexual world through the eyes of research subjects as the only way in which to know what is really going on; to look with the subject at his world as he knows it. Only if I can achieve and maintain an attitude such that non-evaluation is constant, and that whatsoever I hear or see is simply a matter of sheer interest, will I be able to establish the necessary conditions of trust for complete frankness. The homosexual mask in the presence of a representative of the dominant culture is so firmly set, the expectation of moral disapproval so constant, and the distrust and suspicion of motives so ready-to-be-alerted, that the researcher must prove his trustworthiness again and again. Only if the genuineness of the researcher's interest in simply understanding what he sees and hears is conveyed by his total attitudes of feeling and behavior, is it possible to enlist the full cooperation of the subjects. They must become, in effect, research assistants in the enterprise, seeking to learn as much for themselves about the community in which they live as for the researcher, and to enlist others as well.

My original access to the community was not deliberately sought for research purposes, but developed quite accidentally in the course of normal processes of social interaction with a group of friends to whom I had been introduced by a former student—a highly successful businessman. After a period of testing my capacity to accept their behavior in a non-judgmental way, while divesting themselves of their protective masks, they made an urgent request that I conduct a scientific investigation of 'people like them.' By 'people like them,' they meant homosexuals who did not seek psychiatric help, and who led relatively stable, occupationally successful lives. They had read clinical literature on homosexuality and felt that much of it was irrelevant to an understanding of their condition. With their offer to supply unlimited numbers of research subjects, and to provide entrée into homosexual circles and public gathering places, I accepted the research opportunity. Thus, the original relationship was not that of researcher to research subject, but of friend to friend. With the expansion of contacts through networks of mutual friends, the research role became more clearly defined and separated from its social origin. Independent contacts with official homosexual organizations led to other social strata in the community. Participation in the community and deliberate efforts to locate representative members of varying sectors of it, such as male prostitutes, bisexuals, bartenders and bar owners, adolescents and the aged, produced ultimately a wide cross-section.

There are no unique features of Los Angeles which are necessary conditions for the development of a homosexual community since one exists in every large city in the United States, and indeed, probably in the western world. Only the roughest estimates can be made of the numbers of practicing homosexuals in Los Angeles. The Kinsey estimates of 4% of the white male population as being exclusively homosexual throughout their lives would give an approximate figure of 26,631, age 20 or over, on the basis of the 1960 census. Exclusive homosexuals, however, account for a small proportion of the total. If we accept the Kinsey estimates, the incidence of those having some overt homosexual experience between adolescence and old age reaches 37 percent. The largest proportion will have had heterosexual experiences as well. Thus, the suggested figure does not even begin to encompass the total white homosexual population in Los Angeles—to say nothing of non-Caucasians of whom there are many.

That portion of the homosexual population which forms a loosely organized society, world, or collectivity having a unified character, as distinguished from a mere aggregate of persons, is not a community in the traditional sense of the term, as it has been used by sociologists, in that it lacks a territorial base with primary institutions serving a residential population. If, however, one is permitted to use the term to refer to an aggregate of persons engaging in common activities, sharing common interests, and having a feeling of socio-psychological unity, with variations in the degree to which persons have these characteristics, depending on whether they constitute the core or the periphery,[4] then it is completely germane to homosexuals. Although homosexuals as a total group do not have a bounded territorial base, they are, nevertheless, not randomly distributed throughout the city, nor are the facilities of institutions which provide needed services and functions as focal gathering places. Mapping the residences of persons known to us, or known to subjects who have supplied us with their addresses, and noting the residential areas in the city described by them as having heavy concentrations of homosexuals results in large cluster formations. In these sections, apartment houses on particular streets may be owned by, and rented exclusively to, homosexuals. Single streets of individual dwellings may have only one or two non-homosexual families. The concentrated character of these areas is not generally known except in the homosexual community, and in many instances by the police. The population is also distributed widely throughout the city and its suburbs since other factors than association affect the choice of residence. Buying of tract houses by 'married pairs' has become sufficiently common to be referred to as 'homosexual suburbia,' the term referring to style of living and not the character of the neighborhood.

An adequate description of the 'gay life,' that is, the homosexual community life or 'scene' as the member knows it, depends on whether it satisfies the conditions of our being able to tell a person how to act, think, and feel as the homosexual does as he 'makes the scene.'[5] That scene, as the community member knows it, is essentially a round of activities utilizing a particular set of institutions, facilities, or areas and governed by common expectations, beliefs, and values. It is important to distinguish between the visible, or public community activities in which only a small portion of the total homosexual population appears to participate, and the invisible, private community activities which go on in friendship cliques. A commonplace, but relevant, analogy is the iceberg in which only the top of a very large mass is visible. A stranger to the community may enter it via its public institutions, provided he knows where they are, or its private clique structure, provided he can manage a social introduction. Experienced homosexuals who are strangers to a particular community have no difficulty using either entrance since the community map is fairly standard from one city to another in the United States. The most favorable entrance for the researcher is via the clique structure since it leads inevitably to the public community, whereas the reverse is more difficult.

In the present account of the community, however, I shall begin with the public institutions, facilities and areas used by homosexuals in their round of activities. Because most homosexuals make every effort to conceal their homosexuality at work, and from heterosexuals, the community activities are largely leisure time or recreational activities. The most important of these community gathering places is the 'gay' bar ('gay' is a synonym for homosexual as used by many members of that community), but there are also steam baths catering almost exclusively to homosexuals, 'gay' streets, parks, public toilets, beaches, gyms, coffee houses, and restaurants. Newsstands, bookstores, record shops, clothing stores, barber shops, grocery stores, and launderettes may become preferred establishments for service or for a rendezvous, but they are secondary in importance.

In the Los Angeles area, there are at present count, 60 'gay' bars. Since their continued operation is subject to surveillance by police and alcoholic beverage control authorities, it is difficult to keep the list current. They are not randomly distributed over the city even in areas which permit the licensing of establishments for the dispensing of liquor. A map of the city on which the locations of 'gay' bars is plotted shows that like the residential areas, there is a clustering effect. Bars tend to be grouped in a given area in part because of the bar-going habits of their clientele. An individual seldom spends an entire evening in a particular bar, but usually makes the rounds of bars in a particular area, going from one bar to another, seeking sexual contacts or social partners. There is, therefore, a large turnover of personnel in a given evening. Bars nearby can capitalize on this fact. The areas in which the clusters of bars occur in Los Angeles are characterized by one or more of the following determinants: proximity to 1. residential areas with heavy concentrations of homosexuals, 2. beaches or other places of homosexual group recreation or leisure time activity, 3. public entertainment districts—theatres, etc., 4. areas of high tolerance for and relative permissiveness toward other forms of deviant behavior. In Los Angeles there are five regions

in which 'gay' bars are located. The location of any given
bar, however, within a general region depends on multiple
factors too complex for elaboration in this presentation.

I begin the account of the community life with 'gay' bars
for a number of reasons: 1. In them, the public aspect of 'gay'
life is to be encountered—any stranger may enter. 2. Here,
the 'gay' and 'straight' (heterosexual) worlds intersect: the
'gay' world can become most visible to the 'straight' world or
to representatives of the 'straight' world—the police, newspapers etc. 3. On behalf of these institutions in the 'gay'
world, the legitimacy claim is most often made by protago-
nists such as lawyers in the 'straight' world. 4. Here, one
will find the largest, and widest representation of types, socioeconomic levels, and social strata in the homosexual world—if
one goes from bar to bar, as the homosexual does. It is estimated that on a Saturday night between the hours of 10 and
2 A.M., a thousand men will pass through the doors of one
of the largest and most successful bars. 5. Here, one may
observe one of the most standardized and characteristic patterns of social interaction in the 'gay' world: the meeting of
strangers for the essential purpose of making an agreement to
engage in sexual activity known as the 'one night stand.' 6.
For many homosexuals the 'gay' bar is a social institution,
where friends are met, the news of the homosexual world is
to be heard, gossip exchanged, invitations to parties issued,
and warnings about current danger spots and attitudes of
the police given.

I conceive of homosexual bars as free markets which could
only arise under a market economy in which buyers and sellers
are governed by rules whereby the right to enter in is determined by whether the buyer has the wherewithal. The term
market as applied to bars has two meanings: 1. As a business
enterprise in which leisure is accomplished via the market:
gain from the sale of liquor and entertainment is legitimate.
2. As a metaphor to conceive of transactions between homosexuals, a set of terms relating to the negotiation of an exchange of sexual services.

While individual bars are relatively unstable and may be
short-lived, the bar system is relatively stable, although sub-

ject to the constant surveillance of appropriate authorities of
the repressive agencies. Its stability may be accounted for
by the following facts: 1. Bars are highly lucrative for the
owners and despite harassment and closing of individual bars,
licenses are constantly sought to re-open under new owner-
ship or to establish ones in new locations. 2. They meet the
expectations and needs, and are geared in an integral way
to the behavior patterns of a large homosexual population.
3. Authorities unofficially believe that elimination of the system is both undesirable and impossible: 'that kind of person
has to have someplace to go and at least they are with their
own kind, and you don't lose 'em; you just move 'em around
a little.'

The successful operation of a 'gay' bar is a highly skilled
performance requiring a knowledge of tastes and behavior
of homosexual clientele, and the ability to create the kind of
atmosphere which will attract large numbers, as well as the
ability to successfully control behavior within the limits which
law enforcement officers, behaving as willing objects of the
cruising game, and thus passing as ordinary clientele, cannot
make the subject of legal objection.

I turn now to the second meaning of the term market as
applied to 'gay' bars, that is, as a sexual market: a place
where agreements are made for the potential exchange of
sexual services, for sex without obligation or commitment—
the 'one night stand.' If one watches very carefully, and
knows what to watch for in a 'gay' bar, one observes that
some individuals are apparently communicating with each
other without exchanging words, but simply by exchanging
glances—but not the kind of quick glance which ordinarily
occurs between men. It is said by homosexuals that if another
catches and holds the glance, one need know nothing more
about him to know that he is one of them. The psychological
structure of that meeting of glances is a complex one, involving mutual recognition of social, but not personal, identity,
sexual intent and agreement. Many men in the bar, then, are
not engaged in conversation, but are standing along a wall,
or by themselves at a vantage point in the room so that they
may be seen as well as see, and are scanning faces and bodies.

Occasionally, we may see a glance catch and hold another glance. Later, as if in an accidental meeting, the two holders-of-a-glance may be seen in a brief conversation followed by their leaving together. Or, the conversation may be omitted. Casually and unobtrusively, they may arrive at the door at the same time, and leave. If we followed them, we would discover that they were strangers, who by their exchange of glances had agreed to a sexual exchange. The terms of the exchange remaining to be settled will be the place and the nature of the sexual act. A few minutes, or a few hours later, one or both men may reappear in another bar to begin the same procedure all over again, or they may stay together for the night, and the next night seek a new partner. What I have described is one form of 'cruising.' While the agreements resulting in the 'one night stand' occur in many settings—the bath, the street, the public toilet—and may vary greatly in the elaboration or simplicity of the interaction preceding the culmination in the sexual act, their essential feature is the standardized expectation that sex can be had without obligation or commitment. Irrespective of persons, time, place, and from city to city, in the United States at least, this is a stable, reproducible, standard feature of the interaction.

What stabilizes this pattern of expectation and regularized course of conduct? That is the big question to which I have only partial answers. The promiscuity of the homosexual has been attributed to his psychodynamic structure; among other things, to his primary narcissism. I do not believe that the answer to the question is to be found only in psychodynamic explanations but requires that the system effects of the community be taken into account.

That system, as a sexual market, grows out of the 'market mentality.' Riesman (1954) comments: 'In a market situation pervaded by what Karl Polanyi has termed the "market mentality"... control of the economy will carry with it, to an unusual degree, control of the ethical regime' (p. 60). He suggests that all values are subjected to the market, and are transformed by it; and, further, 'it is not the genuine self that is put on the market... but the "cosmetic" self...' (pp. 59–60). Nothing is more conspicuous in the 'gay' bar market than the emphasis on appearance: on dress, manner, and body build. To furnish a genuine self in the exchange of partners, biography and prospects would be essential. In this meeting of strangers, the disengaged character of activities from any ascriptive characteristics is promoted. The pressures toward maintaining secrecy, with respect to work and personal biography in homosexual encounters, are derived in part from the functional consequences of their being revealed. The legal, occupational, and personal hazards of identification as a homosexual in our society are amply documented. The risk of information leakage from the 'gay' world to the work world is high.

But if the market mentality pervades society, and if it is the cosmetic self that is put on the market, why should sexual exchange in the relations of male to female be exempt from the characteristics of the 'one night stand'—sex without obligation or commitment? The heterosexual world is *not* exempt, but anything other than monogamous, legally sanctioned, obligated relations is a departure from strongly sanctioned norms, whatever the actual practice may be. That these norms are so strongly sanctioned in the heterosexual world, may be in part a function of the fact that sexuality means more to the female than to the male.[6] Women have more to lose by divesting sexuality of rights, obligations, and commitment because their value in the competitive marriage market partly depends on it as bargaining power, and because their role as child-bearers and child-rearers requires psychological and economic support. The relative absence of women in the homosexual world, the negative sanctions of society against homosexual relationships, the pressures toward secrecy and the risks of revealing one's own personal identity as a homosexual, and the market character of the bar setting in which meetings occur, combine to produce the kind of sexual exchange which we have described as a stable feature of the 'gay' world.

'Gay' bars also serve other important functions for the community. It is estimated by bartenders that 50% of the patrons on any given evening will be habitués, who come at least once a week, and, frequently, three or four evenings a week. Every bar has its clusters of friends who gather to exchange gossip, to look over the new faces, and to spend a social evening in an atmosphere congenial to them where the protective mask of the day may be dropped. Bars are, therefore, communication centers for the exchange of news and gossip, and for the discussion of problems and hard luck stories. Practical problems such as finding a job, or a place to live, or a lawyer, may be solved with the help of friends or newly met acquaintances. The opening of the newest bar in town, or a place which has recently become 'hot,' or whether there is a party going on that evening to which one might be invited are topics of conversation. They are also, paradoxically enough, security operations. While arrests are made in bars, and the presence of vice-squad officers or alcoholic beverage control authorities in plain clothes is an ever present possibility, the bartender, or bar owner will, warn the patrons of their presence, if their identity is known—and it frequently is. Warnings will also be passed about particular patrons who are known to be 'dirt,' that is, who are likely to rob or demand money or possessions, or to beat up the sexual partner after the consummation of the sexual act. News travels quickly from bar to bar of harassment activities of the authorities.

Bars also serve as induction and training, and integration centers for the community. These functions are difficult to separate. The young man who may have had a few isolated homosexual experiences in adolescence, or indeed none at all, and who is taken to a 'gay' bar by a group of friends whose homosexuality is only vaguely suspected or unknown to him, may find the excitement and opportunities for sexual gratification appealing and thus begin active participation in the community life. Very often, the debut, referred to by homosexuals as 'coming out,' of a person who believes himself to be homosexual but who has struggled against it, will occur in a bar when he, for the first time, identifies himself publicly as a homosexual in the presence of other homosexuals by his appearance in the situation. If he has thought of himself as unique, or has thought of homosexuals as a strange and unusual lot, he may be agreeably astonished to discover large numbers of men who are physically attractive, personable, and 'masculine' appearing, so that his hesitancy in identifying himself as a homosexual is greatly reduced. Since he may meet a wide cross-section of occupational and socioeconomic levels in the bar, he becomes convinced that far from being a small minority, the 'gay' population is very extensive indeed. Once he has 'come out,' that is, identified himself as a homosexual to himself and to some others, the process of education proceeds with rapid pace. Eager and willing tutors—especially if he is young and attractive—teach him the special language, ways of recognizing vice-squad officers, varieties of sexual acts and social types. They also assist him in providing justifications for the homosexual way of life as legitimate, and help to reduce his feeling of guilt by providing him with new norms of sexual behavior in which monogamous fidelity to the sexual partner is rare.

In the bar world the initiate soon acquires a body of knowledge which includes a set of common understandings[7]—'what everybody knows.' 'Everybody knows' that: sex can be had without obligation or commitment; it is a meeting of strangers, and the too familiar face may not make out in the sexual market; one can't afford to be seen too frequently or one is counted out of the cruising competition—after the initial newcomer phase; preferences for sexual acts may be specialized and congruence of sexual interests between partners is always problematic; discrepancy between expected sexual behavior and appearance is not a surprise; success in the sexual market will be increased by 'masculine' appearance and the appearance of youth; life in the bars for sexual purposes is time limited: older persons (35 or more) may not make out unless they pay for partners; although the potential supply of partners is large, 'making out' may be difficult because everyone in the 'gay' world may be afraid of rejection and the criteria of selection may be highly specific.

Earlier I described the homosexual community with the analogy of the iceberg phenomenon, in which the visible part of the community—visible to those who seek it out—is to be found in a round of activities in public institutions, facilities, and areas. I believe, as do homosexuals I have interviewed, that this is a very small part of the total community, and that submerged or hidden, the secret and private activities of the world of social friendship cliques are fundamental to an understanding of the whole. In this world are to be found persons who have established long-term living relationships with another homosexual, and who rarely if ever go to bars or other public establishments because of their sexually predatory and competitive character. They may have had a period of bar going but now have come to dislike the bar activities or to fear them because of their threat to the stability of an established relationship. Others, especially those of high occupational or socio-economic status, may restrict their community life to private social cliques because of the fear of exposure or arrest. Others may not enjoy drinking, or may find sufficient sexual and social companionship in homosexual groups, whether they are living alone or in an establishment with another homosexual. There are, of course, many homosexuals who are isolates on the margin of both parts of the community.

The organization of the homosexual world outside of the bars, but linked with it by members common to both, is a loosely knit ˉ extended series of overlapping networks of friends. The forms of these networks vary greatly. The three most common are: 1. tightly knit clique structures formed from pairs of homosexually 'married' persons, or singles, many of whom are heterosexually married, 2. larger groups with one or more loose clique structures as sociometrically central and a number of peripheral members; and 3. loose networks of friends who may meet only on the occasion of parties. Clique structures and pairs, as well as loose networks of friends, cut across occupational and socio-economic levels, although particular professions or occupations such as teaching, medicine, interior decoration, and antique dealers may form association in-groups which have social gatherings. Police exposés of homosexual circles or rings frequently reveal the widespread occupational and age ramifications of such groups. Although the networks are overlapping, the population is so large that nothing occurs like the rapid communication in the criminal underground. For example, in comparing two lists of friends, one of 250 names made by a man of 40 and the other of 35 names made by a man of 23, I found only one name common to the two lists although the modal age and range, and the occupations were strikingly similar. The unity of this social world does not consist of close friendship bonds which link person to person throughout the total network, but of common activities, common sexual interests, and a feeling of a common fate which makes them interdependent.

In the cliques, groups, and networks of friends, social occasions, such as evening parties, dinners and cocktail parties are frequent, ranging from the simplest to the most elaborate, and from the most intimate to the large, spur of the moment affairs. 'Wedding' anniversaries, birthdays, and other special occasions, much as in the heterosexual world, call for celebrations. Some groups make special efforts to maintain social relations with heterosexual couples, usually ones who are 'wise,' that is, are aware of and at least partially accept their homosexuality. These, in my experience, are very rare except in literary, other artistic, or highly sophisticated circles. In the main, members feel uncomfortable in the social presence of heterosexuals, and prefer social occasions in which the guest list is made up of homosexuals so that they can, as their phrase puts it, 'let down their hair'—that is take off their protective masks, use their in-group language, discuss intimate details of their sexual lives, and 'camp.' Although the forms of behavior involved and the definitions of camping given by homosexuals vary widely, we shall not distort too greatly, perhaps, by describing it as usually involving some aspect of the feminine, dramatically displayed in gesture or speech—whether in serious or caricatured form. For example, it is a common practice to use feminine nicknames in homosexual circles, and in the diminutive form. An interchange at a party between two homosexual males in which nicknames are used with effeminate gestures would be a form of what the writer, Christopher Isherwood, has called 'low camp.' The social-psychological implications of camping are complex. Some homosexual cliques or groups will not tolerate such behavior, and make every effort to behave in such a way as to

minimize any indication of characteristics which would identify them as homosexual.

As contrasted with the 'one night stand' of the 'gay' bar
world, there is constant seeking for more permanent relationships in the social world outside the bars. Indeed, the hope
of many who engage in the 'one night stand' round of activities is that a particular encounter may lead to a more permanent arrangement. Some long-lasting relationships do begin in
the bars but the total system operates against them, as we
have seen. In these relationships, sometimes called marriages,
complex problems of role management and practical problems of domestic establishments must be solved since they
are subject to the strains of a hostile heterosexual society, as
well as those of the homosexual world. That many do survive
these pressures is well established in my data. Accurate estimates of proportions are impossible since I am not engaged
in a survey. In the limited time, I cannot undertake an adequate description of these relationships; of the variety and
complexity of their patterns. I want to comment only on one
characteristic feature of sex and gender role in relationships
in the homosexual world as I have observed them. Contrary
to a widespread belief, these are not dichotomized in a clear-
cut fashion into masculine and feminine. One does observe
pairs with well-defined differentiation but they appear to be
in the minority. The terms active or passive partner, masculine
or feminine role, as distinguishing members of a pair may
be inapplicable to the greater number of these pairs. Instead,
the variety and form of the sexual acts between pair members,
the distribution of tasks performed, and the character of
their performance do not permit such a differentiation. New
solutions appear for which the old terms are inapplicable. In
part, the emergence of new solutions may be attributed to
the changing culture of the homosexual world. In what appear
to be large sectors of that world, the stereotype of the effeminate is fought. In some, the result is a caricature of masculinity. The motorcycle crowd, or the leather set, with its
affectation of the symbols of tough masculinity, is one form
of caricature. In others, the insistence on being men, despite
the homosexuality, results in a deliberate effort to develop

patterns of behavior which are indistinguishable from the heterosexual, except, of course in the sexual sphere, and here the dominant-submissive pattern is consciously resisted.

One of the important features of homosexual subcultures is the pattern of beliefs, or the justification system. Central to it is the explanation of why they are homosexuals, and involves the question of choice. The majority of those whom I have interviewed believe that they were born as homosexuals, or that familial factors operating very early in their lives determined the outcome. In any case, it is a fate over which they have no control, and in which they have no choice. It follows as a consequence that the possibility of changing to a heterosexual pattern is thought to be extremely limited. To fight against homosexuality is to fight against the inevitable since they are fighting against their own 'nature' in its essential form, as they experience it. They believe that homosexuality is as 'natural' for them, as heterosexuality is for others. Such belief patterns are widely shared by those who identify themselves as members of the community, and who participate in the round of activities we have described. I must reiterate that not all who engage in homosexual practices have accepted this identification, and share these beliefs.

In conclusion, I have attempted to describe some features of a homosexual community in a large urban setting: its ecological distribution; its visible, public institutions which have been conceptualized as market settings for the exchange of sexual services, and as induction, training, and integration centers for the community; its invisible world of friendship cliques and group structures in which more stable patterns of relationships are likely to develop; the common understandings and shared beliefs. In the time allotted I have not been able to discuss other important features of the community, such as the formal leadership structure, the language patterns, the special humor, the management of impressions by community members in interaction with heterosexual society, and the problems of trust and secrecy within the community. I have tried to show that once an individual enters the community, and begins to enter into its round of activities, he is subject to the beliefs, understandings, and norms of that

world. The patterns of behavior which develop, as a consequence, may be as much a function of the system-effects of
the community, as of need-predispositions which play an
important role in shaping the entry routes of some of the
members. It is highly probable that it is at least as accurate
to speak of the homosexual community as a 'deviant community' as to describe it as a 'community of deviants.'

The Homosexual Community

MAURICE LEZNOFF
AND
WILLIAM A. WESTLEY

*In this second look at the homosexual community we are
given a different perspective in another city. This article,
which was written prior to Hooker's, identifies many of the
same features of the homosexual community and finds it serving its members in much the same ways. Leznoff and Westley
present some of the language of the homosexual and the ways
in which language is used as a form of social control over
members of the community.*

*Like Hooker, the authors find a dual world, one composed
of persons who are labeled "overt" in their homosexuality,
that is, those who are willing to reveal themselves as
homosexual to nonhomosexuals, and the other world consisting of those who are secretive about their homosexuality
and who conceal this fact from nearly all others who are not
homosexual and, indeed, from many who are homosexual as
well. This is clearly not a dichotomy but a continuum, with
some people admitting their homosexuality to anyone and*

REPRINTED with the permission of the authors and the editors from
Social Problems 3:4:257–263 (April 1956).

The authors are indebted to the Canadian Social Science Research
Council and to the McGill University Research Fund for grants in
support of this study.

others refusing to have homosexual relations even though they might desire them. What is apparent is that with increasing social mobility and higher occupational rank there is greater pressure to move from overt to secret homosexuality. The same pressure is probably associated with increasing age as well, even when there is no increase in occupational status.

In the secret world of the homosexual, cliques are the basis of social organization. Many of these remain stable over time while others dissolve or experience changes in membership. With changes in membership, or at the dissolution of a clique, the members either search for a new clique or move back into the overt homosexual world. This is frequently a crisis situation, since the covert homosexual must now risk the protected portion of his life as he moves into the overt world.

The significance of homosexuality in our society has been minimized and obscured by the force of social taboo. Yet there is evidence that homosexuals are distributed throughout all geographical areas and socio-economic strata.[1] Furthermore, the subjection of homosexuals to legal punishments and social condemnation has produced a complex structure of concealed social relations which merit sociological investigation. The psychological isolation of the homosexual from society, his dependence upon other deviants for the satisfaction of sexual needs and self-expression, the crystallization of social roles and behavior patterns within the deviant group, the reciprocal obligations and demands within the homosexual community, and their significance for the larger society in which they occur, are but a few of the areas of theoretical interest to the sociologist.

In this paper we shall confine our discussion to the social organization of one homosexual community and its constituent social groups: their function, etiology, and interrelationships.

The report is based upon an intensive study of 60 homosexuals in a large Canadian city. The data consist of four-hour interviews with 40 homosexuals and briefer interviews with 20 others.² In addition, the data include information based on the observation of many homosexual parties and gatherings in bars and restaurants, and a series of 30 letters written by one homosexual to another.

FUNCTIONS OF HOMOSEXUAL GROUPS

The primary function of the homosexual group is psychological in that it provides a social context within which the homosexual can find acceptance as a homosexual and collective support for his deviant tendencies. Most homosexuals fear detection and are often insecure and anxious because of this. The following statement illustrates this:

The thought that you are "gay" is always with you and you know it's there even when other people don't. You also think to yourself that certain of your mannerisms and your ways of expression are liable to give you away. That means that there is always a certain amount of strain. I don't say that it's a relief to get away from normal people, but there isn't the liberty that you feel in a gay crowd. When I associate with normal people I prefer very small groups of them. I don't like large groups and I think I try to avoid them when I can. You know, the only time when I really forget I'm gay is when I'm in a gay crowd.

To relieve this anxiety the deviant seeks collective support and social acceptance. Since the homosexual group provides the only social context in which homosexuality is normal, deviant practices moral, and homosexual responses rewarded, the homosexual develops a deep emotional involvement with his group, tending toward a ready acceptance of its norms and dictates, and subjection to its behavior patterns. The regularity with which he seeks the company of his group is a clear expression of this dependency.

A prohibition against sexual relationships within the group, in a manner suggestive of the incest taboo, indicates the extent to which the group culture is oriented to this function. The quotation which follows is indicative of this taboo:

As far as I know, people who hang around with each other don't have affairs. The people who are friends don't sleep with each other. I can't tell you why that is, but they just don't. Unless you are married[3] you have sex with strangers mostly. I think if you have sex with a friend it will destroy the friendship. I think that in the inner mind we all respect high moral standards, and none of us want to feel low in the eyes of anybody else. It's always easier to get along with your gay friends if there has been no sex. Mind you, you might have sex with somebody you just met and then he might become your friend. But you won't have sex with him any more as soon as he joins the same gang you hang around with.

Within these groups the narration of sexual experiences and gossip about the sexual exploits of others is a major form of recreation. The narration of sexual experiences functions to allocate prestige among the members because of the high evaluation placed upon physical attraction and sexual prowess. Yet it creates hostility and sexual rivalry. The intense involvement of homosexuals in the results of this sexual competition is illustrated in the following statement which was overheard in a restaurant:

Who wouldn't blow up. That bitch is trying to get her[4] clutches into Richard. She can't leave anybody alone. I wouldn't be surprised if she ended up with a knife in her back. I don't mean to say I'm threatening her. But she's not going to get away with that stuff forever . . . playing kneesies under the table all night long. I had to get her away from Richard. That lousy bitch. From now on she better keep away from me.

An additional function is the provision of a social situation in which the members can dramatize their adherence to homosexual values. Thus, the gossip about sex, the adoption and exaggeration of feminine behavior, and the affectation of speech, represent a way of affirming that homosexuality is frankly accepted and has the collective support of the group. The extreme but not uncommon instance of this is the homosexual institution of the "drag" in which the members of the group dress and make themselves up as women. A good description of a drag is contained in the following letter:

Well, doll, last night was one to remember. Raymond of B. (city) gave me a letter of introduction to one of the local belles. He 'phoned yesterday and we arranged to go out in the evening.

Met at my room and proceeded to the Frederick Hotel where I was introduced to my new acquaintances. It was decided to hold a party afterwards, Chez Norman, my new acquaintance. He told me they were supposed to be discontinued but we were going ahead in my honor. And in drag. One queen about 45–50 who is a window dresser brought some materials of fine nylon net, 2 yards wide and changing color across the width from yellow to flaming orange. There must have been about 25 yds. Well, he made his entrance wearing nothing but his shorts and this stuff wound around him and proceeded to do an exotic dance. Included in the costume was a blond wig from one of the store mannequins and artificial tropical fruits. It was something to see. It was very ludicrous to begin with and much more so when you realize that he is by no means graceful and has so much hair on him that I am smooth by comparison. Throughout the evening he kept on making variations of the costume—each becoming briefer until he was down to nothing. Really!

Another one, very slim, put on a pair of falsies, a turban hat to hide short hair, and a dress with a wide flair skirt. Other than hair on the chest which showed, the effect of femininity was so convincing (even his heels) that I promptly lost interest. Actually produced a beautiful effect—the kind of woman I would like if I could. Beautiful dancer, and performed all evening. Later borrowed some of the nylon net of the old queen and did a dance with flowing material and wearing *nothing*, but nothing else.

There were only three of us not in drag, including yrs. truly. But when it came time to leave (not alone, I might add) I couldn't resist flinging about my coat a fox fur which happened to be lying around. Really, my dear, it was quite an affair.

These functions reflect the common needs and problems which homosexuals face in hostile society.

ETIOLOGY: THE EVASION
OF SOCIAL CONTROLS

In our society, homosexuality is defined both legally and socially as a criminal and depraved practice and the homosexual is threatened by powerful legal and social sanctions such as imprisonment, physical violence,[5] social and occupational ostracism, and ridicule. Therefore, all homosexuals face the problem of evading social controls. They do this in two predominant ways.

Some pass for heterosexuals on the job and in most of their social relationships. They mix regularly with heterosexuals for business, entertainment, and other social activities. They avoid situations and persons publicly recognized as homosexual for they fear that discovery will threaten their career and expose them to sanctions. This is illustrated in the following statement of a lawyer:

I know a few people who don't care. They are really pitiful. They are either people who are in very insignificant positions or they are in good positions but are independent. I know of one who is in the retail business. He doesn't care. A lot of the artists don't care. For that reason I have never cultivated the friendship of artists. I just don't get along with anybody who doesn't care. That's why I really can't give you information about those who don't. It's just that I can't afford to get to know them very well, and I try to avoid them. Sometimes personal friends become this way. Then there is a mutual rejection of the friendship. From my point of view I am just no longer interested when they adopt that kind of attitude. From their point of view it means completely living outside of society and they are no longer interested in people who they consider hypocrites.

Others openly admit and practice homosexuality. They usually work in occupations where the homosexual is tolerated, withdraw from uncompromising heterosexual groups, and confine most of their social life to homosexual circles. This attitude is expressed in the following statement by a hairdresser:

Rosenstein can go to hell as far as I care. She works you to the bone if she can get away with it. She told me I run around the place like a regular pansy. So I told her I am a pansy and if she doesn't like it she can get somebody else to do her dirty work for her. I knew she wouldn't fire me. All the ladies ask for me and I don't have to pretend to nobody.

While the problem of evasion is common to all homosexuals, the mechanisms of evasion present various alternatives. Most homosexuals find themselves compelled to conform outwardly to societal demands. They are conscious of their social position within society and seek such satisfactions as occupational mobility and prestige. They endeavor to retain intimate associations within the heterosexual community, and fear recognition as a status threat. Such homosexuals rely upon secrecy and the concealment of their deviant practices. They will therefore be referred to as "secret" homosexuals. A minority retreats from the demands of society and renounces societal goals. Such individuals will be referred to as "overt" homosexuals.

The mode of adaption is largely dependent upon the extent to which identification as a homosexual is a status threat. While economic status cannot be equated with social status, the individual's position within the work world represents the most significant single factor in the prestige scale. Therefore, the extent to which homosexuality is tolerated in various occupations determines to a great extent the mode of evasion chosen by the homosexual. Thus, there are many occupations, of which the professions are an obvious example, where homosexuals are not tolerated. In other areas, the particular occupation may have traditionally accepted homosexual linkages in the popular image or be of such low rank as to permit

TABLE 1. Occupation of 40 Secret and Overt Homosexuals

Occupation[a]	Secret[b]	Overt	Total
Professional & managerial	13	0	13
Clerical & sales	9	4	13
Craftsmen	2	1	3
Operatives	1	1	2
Service	0	6	6
Artists	0	3	3
Totals	25	15	40

[a] Except for artists the categories and ranking are those established by the National Opinion Research Center.[6] Artists have been listed as a separate category because they often represent a group which is apart from the status structure of the community.

[b] The secret homosexuals gave the following reasons for concealment: (a) desire to avoid social ridicule—22 cases; (b) fear of dismissal from the job, or where self-employed, inability to get clients—20 cases; (c) a desire to protect others such as family or friends—18 cases.

homosexuals to function on the job. The artist, the interior decorator, and the hairdresser exemplify the former type; such positions as counter man or bell-hop, the latter. Thus we find a rough relationship between form of evasion and occupation. The overt homosexual tends to fit into an occupation of low status rank; the secret homosexual into an occupation with a relatively high status rank. The relationship is shown in Table 1.

DISTINCTIONS BETWEEN THE SECRET AND OVERT GROUPS

The chief distinctions between homosexual groups correspond to the differences in the general modes of evading social controls which homosexuals have developed. Thus, secret and overt homosexuals form distinctive groups.

The distinctions betwen these groups are maintained by the secret homosexuals who fear identification and refuse to associate with overt homosexuals. This statement by a secret homosexual is illustrative:

If someone who is gay wanted to be spiteful they could say something in the wrong quarter. Nobody who cared about himself would say anything. The trouble is that some don't care. I make it a rule to avoid anybody who is perfectly open about himself. It's easy not to become friendly with those people but it's hard to avoid them entirely. You certainly don't want to snub them because that might make them antagonistic. You just don't call them or see them at social gatherings. But you do meet them at bars and that's where you can be introduced to them. If they remember you and continue to say hello to you on the street, you have to acknowledge them or they might feel that you are trying to snub them.

As a result of this social distance a certain amount of reciprocal hostility has developed between the members of secret and overt groups. This hostility helps maintain the social distance and distinctions between these groups. This is demonstrated in the following statements by an overt and a secret homosexual respectively:

I know some of them because sometimes they stoop down and have an affair with somebody from our gang. They even come to a party over at Robert's once in a while but they never hang around for very long and then you don't see them again. They go over to the Red Room sometimes but we don't have much to say to each other and the same thing happens when we go over to the Burning Flame.[7] We just might say hello. But sometimes they will cruise us and try to take someone home to bed. I think you could say we mix sexually but not socially.

There are some people who I don't like and I wish these people didn't know about me. Then there are the people I don't know too well: people who are obvious or what I uncharitably call the riff-raff. I have always attempted to avoid them and I avoid them now. It is inevitable that you bump into a lot of people you would rather not know. Homosexuals are very democratic people. To achieve their own ends they overlook a lot they wouldn't overlook in other fields. People are bound to each other like a link of a chain. You try to avoid being a link in this chain by carefully choosing.

This poses serious problems for the homosexual who is socially mobile. He is forced to change his primary group affiliations within the homosexual community.

The following statement by the manager of an appliance shop shows how the homosexual tends to change his orientation from "overt" to "secret" as he becomes upwardly mobile.

My promotions have made me more conscious of the gang I hang around with. You see, for the first time in my life I have a job that I would really like to keep and where I can have a pretty secure future. I realize that if word were to get around that I am gay I would probably lose my job. I don't see why that should be, because I know that I'm the same person gay or not. But still that's the way it works. I don't want to hang around with Robert[8] any more or any of the people who are like Robert. I don't mind seeing them once in a while at somebody's house, but I won't be seen with them on the street any more.

Both types of groups were identified and observed in the course of this research. Each group consisted of fourteen members. The descriptions which follow are based on the study of these groups.

Secret Groups

The secret homosexuals form groups which consist of a loose amalgamation of small cliques. Interaction within the cliques is frequent, with members meeting at each other's homes and in bars and restaurants. The clique's structure is a product of the diverse interests and occupations and of the desire to limit homosexual contacts which characterize secret homosexuals. The clique unites its several members in common specialized interests apart from the larger group.

The following chart shows the clique structure and occupational composition of a secret homosexual group.

Clique A	*Clique B*
Lawyer	Clerk-bookkeeper
Personnel manager	Auditing clerk
University student	Assistant office manager
Economist	University student
	Secretary
Clique C	*Clique D*
Stenographer	Accountant
Store manager	Interior decorator
Manager of Statistical dept.	

A secret homosexual group is generally characterized by: (a) informal standards of admission; (b) discretion in the manner in which homosexuality is practiced; (c) an attempt at concealment; (d) partial rather than complete involvement in the homosexual world.

Overt Groups

Overt homosexuals gather in cohesive social groups which become the dominant focus of their lives. These groups are openly homosexual in character. The members make little effort to conceal their deviation, spend almost all their free time with the group, and tend to regard their other activities as peripheral.

These groups generally draw their members from persons

of low socio-economic status who have jobs where concealment is not a prerequisite. Table 2 presents the occupational
composition of the overt group identified in this study.

TABLE 2.   Occupational Composition of an Overt
Homosexual Group

Occupation	Frequency
Manager of appliance shop[a]	1
School teacher	1
Hospital attendant	1
Hairdresser	4
Sales clerk	2
Foundry worker	1
Baker	1
Salesman	1
Waiter	1
Cashier	1
Total	14

[a] This individual had just been promoted and was beginning
to leave the group. Both he and the school teacher retained
for a time their affiliation with an overt group while at the
same time concealing their homosexuality at work.

The members of the group met daily either at a bar, a
restaurant, or at the house of the acknowledged leader or
"queen."[9] They spent their time in endless gossip about the
sexual affairs of the members or other homosexuals known
to them. Often they would go to bars and restaurants in the
attempt to make a "pick-up," or spend the evening "cruising"
individually or in groups of two's and three's.

The queen seems to characterize only "overt" groups. Functionally, the role of the queen is very important in the life
of these groups. He provides a place where the group may
gather and where its individual members may have their
"affairs." He helps finance members in distress, functions as
an intermediary in making sexual contacts, partially controls
the entrance of new members, and warns the members of
hoodlums who would prey upon them. Generally the queen
is an older homosexual who has had wide experience in the
homosexual world.

The following statement about the queen by a member of the overt group provides insight into the functioning of the queen and tells something of the way in which the individuals relate to him.

A queen really means the leader of the group. You see how that is in a small town where there are not many people who are gay and willing to admit it. She knows who's who and what's what. She will know every gay person in town and will arrange things just the way Roberta does.[10] The queen is always somebody pretty old and pretty much out of the game as far as getting anything for herself is concerned. But she doesn't have anything else to do, so she spends all her time on this. I don't know of any queen as commercial as Roberta. But that's because Roberta is so goddam crude. I know the queen in Hillsburg and she was a perfect lady if I ever saw one. She knows everything. She used to make quite a bit but it was always in the form of getting invitations for dinner or as a present. You feel grateful to somebody who does something for you and you pay off. It's like a debt.

Overt groups are characterized by: (a) no particular standards of admission; (b) unselfconscious and unrestrained practice of homosexuality; (c) little or no concealment; (d) high degree of social isolation with little involvement in heterosexual activities; (e) little concern with identification as a status threat or the sanctions of heterosexual society.

THE HOMOSEXUAL COMMUNITY

The diverse secret and overt homosexuals are linked together either through bonds of sex or of friendship. Within the primary group, the emphasis upon friendship rather than sex serves to eliminate excessive sexual competition and preserves group unity. However, this creates a sexual interdependency upon those outside the group with important social consequences.

In the first place, it forces the secret homosexual out into the open in an attempt to solicit sexual partners. He thus frequents the known homosexual meeting places within the city such as specific bars, hotel lobbies, street corners, and lavatories. These activities make him an increasingly familiar figure within the homosexual world.

Secondly, this solicitation leads to the interaction of secret and overt homosexuals on a sexual as opposed to a social basis. While these contacts occur in a spirit of anonymity, an approach to the other often requires an exchange of confidences.

Thirdly, this sexual interdependency increases the anxiety of secret homosexuals since it forces them to contact the overt ones whom they fear as a threat to their security.

Thus, it is the casual and promiscuous sexual contacts between the members of different categories of evasion (i.e., the secret and the overt) which weld the city's homosexuals into a community.

CONCLUSION

The homosexual community thus consists of a large number of distinctive groups within which friendship binds the members together in a strong and relatively enduring bond and between which the members are linked by tenuous but repeated sexual contacts. The result is that homosexuals within the city tend to know or know of each other, to recognize a number of common interests and common moral norms, and to interact on the basis of antagonistic cooperation. This community is in turn linked with other homosexual communities in Canada and the United States, chiefly through the geographical mobility of its members.[11]

The Social Integration of
Queers and Peers

ALBERT J. REISS, JR.

*This article by Professor Reiss is especially instructive (see
the earlier article by Reiss which places this behavior in
larger context) since it deals with norms that structure sexual
relationships between two deviant subcultures. In the search
for sexual partners by a homosexual man who has a particular adjustment, there are often two constraints on the character of sexual partners: youth and masculinity. In this search
there are available to him boys who belong to a delinquent
subculture and who will allow to him sexual access under
very special conditions. The youth of the boys and their
commitment, perhaps excessive in nature, to masculinity,
marks them as especially prized targets for sexual contact.
As Professor Reiss suggests, the homosexual males who are
most prone to contact with the hustler, or with boys who
hustle without defining themselves as such, are frequently
from the secret world of the homosexual outlined by Leznoff
and Westley.*

*There are a number of modes of adjustment to the hustling
life, and the group studied here are males for whom contacts
with homosexuals provide easy money at a low risk. Other
males, who participate in this behavior for longer periods of*

REPRINTED with the permission of the author and editors from *Social
Problems* 9:2:102–120 (Fall 1961).

The word "queer" is of the "straight" and not the "gay" world. In
the "gay" world it has all the qualities of a negative stereotype but
these are not intended in this paper. The paper arose out of the perspective of boys in the "straight" world.

I am particularly indebted to Howard S. Becker, Evelyn Hooker,
Everett Hughes, John Kitsuse, Ned Polsky, H. Laurence Ross and Clark
Vincent for their helpful suggestions and encouragement in publishing
this article.

time, become isolated from the gang culture and move directly into the homosexual world rather than having a tangential economic relationship to it. In a way similar to female prostitution, the sexual act performed must be accompanied by an exchange of money and by a lack of affect. The homosexual who seeks a male giving the appearance of masculinity and heterosexuality is also interested in maintaining these norms since it gives the sexual act a special significance, unlike contacts with males who are openly homosexual themselves.

The activity of these boys is mediated through the local gang culture which places limits on the permitted frequency of the behavior and the contexts in which it may occur. While it is clear that the act is homosexual, that is, occurring between two males, purely sexual gratification is neutralized by the norms controlling the interaction. In this way a homosexual contact can be made without any necessary imputation of homosexual interest on the part of the boy.

This study shows the ways in which acts which are defined objectively as being of a particular class must also be studied from the point of view of the actors involved. Thus, what appears to be a homosexual act is viewed as a purely commercial act by the males involved, and at no time is there any ambivalence about the nature of the experience. Thus, deviant acts that do not carry with them any stigma may be performed by persons as long as they occur in the context of norms and values that label them as contextually conforming.

Sex delinquency is a major form of behavior deviating from the normative prescriptions of American society. A large number of behaviors are classified as sex delinquency—premarital heterosexual intercourse, pederasty, and fellation, for example.

Investigation of sex behavior among males largely focuses on the psychological structure and dynamic qualities of adult persons who are described as "sexual types" or on estimating the incidence, prevalence, or experience rates of sex acts for various social groups in a population. There is little systematic research on the social organization of sexual activity in a complex social system unless one includes descriptive studies of the social organization of female prostitution.

An attempt is made in this paper to describe the sexual relation between "delinquent peers" and "adult queers" and to account for its social organization. This transaction is one form of homosexual prostitution between a young male and an adult male fellator. The adult male client pays a delinquent boy prostitute a sum of money in order to be allowed to act as a fellator. The transaction is limited to fellation and is one in which the boy develops no self-conception as a homosexual person or sexual deviator, although he perceives adult male clients as sexual deviators, "queers" or "gay boys."

There has been little research on social aspects of male homosexual prostitution; hence the exploratory nature of the investigation reported here and the tentative character of the findings. Although there are descriptions of "marriage" and of the "rigid caste system of prison homosexuality"[1] which contribute to our understanding of its social organization in the single sex society of deviators, little is known about how homosexual activity is organized in the nuclear communities of America.

A few recent studies discuss some organizational features of male prostitution.[2] Ross distinguishes three types of male homosexual prostitutes on the basis of the locus of their hustling activity:[3] (1) the *bar-hustler* who usually visits bars on a steady basis in search of queer clients; (2) the *street-hustler*, usually a teen-aged boy who turns "tricks" with older men; (3) and, the *call-boy* who does not solicit in public. The street-hustler has the lowest prestige among hustlers, partly because his is the more hazardous and less profitable form of activity. One might expect their prestige status in the organized "gay world" to be low since they apparently are marginal to its organization. Street-hustlers, therefore, often become bar-hustlers when they are able to pass in bars as of legal age.

The boys interviewed for this study could usually be classified as street-hustlers, given the principal locus of their activity. Yet, the street-hustlers Ross describes are oriented toward careers as bar-hustlers, whereas none of the boys I studied entered hustling as a career. For the latter, hustling is a transitory activity, both in time and space.

There apparently are crucial differences among hustlers, however, in respect to the definition of the hustler role and the self-concept common to occupants in the role. The hustlers Ross studied are distinguished by the fact that they define themselves as both prostitute and homosexual. The boys I studied *do not define themselves either as hustlers or as homosexual.* Most of these boys see themselves as "getting a queer" only as a substitute activity or as part of a versatile pattern of delinquent activity.[4] The absence of a shared definition of one another as hustlers together with shared definitions of when one "gets a queer" serve to insulate these boys from self-definitions either as street-hustlers or as homosexual.

The boys interviewed in this study regard hustling as an acceptable substitute for other delinquent earnings or activity. Although the sexual transaction itself may occur in a two person *or* a larger group setting, the prescribed norms governing this transaction are usually learned from peers in the delinquent gang. Furthermore, in many cases, induction into the queer-peer transaction occurs through participation in the delinquent group. They learn the prescribed form of behavior with adult fellators and are inducted into it as a business transaction by means of membership in a group which carries this knowledge in a common tradition and controls its practices. In particular, it will be shown that the peer group controls the amount of activity and the conditions under which it is permitted. Finally, it is postulated that this is a shared organizational system between peer hustlers and adult fellators.

There apparently exist the other possible types of males who engage in homosexual sex acts based on the elements of self-definition as homosexual and hustler. John Rechy in several vignettes describes a third type who conceive of themselves as hustlers but do not define themselves as homosexual.[5]

... the world of queens and male-hustlers and what they thrive on, the queens being technically men but no one thinks of them that way—always "she"—their "husbands" being the masculine vagrants—"fruithustlers"—fleetingly sharing the queens' pads—never considering they're involved with another man (the queen), and as long as the hustler goes only with queens—and with fruits only for scoring (which is making or taking sexmoney, getting a meal, making a pad) *he is himself not considered queer.* (italics mine)[6]

The importance of being defined as nonhomosexual while acknowledging one's role as a hustler is brought forth in this passage:

"Like the rest of us on that street—who played the male role with other men—Pete was touchy about one subject—his masculinity. In Bickford's one afternoon, a good looking masculine young man walked in, looking at us, walks out again hurriedly. 'That cat's queer,' Pete says, glaring at him. 'I used to see him and I thought he was hustling, and one day he tried to put the make on me in the flix. It bugged me, him thinking I'd make it with him for free. I told him to f . . . off, go find another queer like him.' He was moodily silent for a long while and then he said almost belligerently: 'No matter how many queers a guy goes with, if he goes for money, that don't make him queer. You're still straight. It's when you start going for free, with other young guys, that you start growing wings.' "[7]

The literature on male homosexuality, particularly that written by clinicians, is abundant with reference to the fourth possible type—those who define themselves as homosexual but not as hustlers.

THE DATA

Information on the sexual transaction and its social organization was gathered mostly by interviews, partly by social observation of their meeting places. Though there are limitations to inferring social organization from interview data (particularly when the organization arises through behavior that is negatively sanctioned in the larger society), they provide a convenient basis for exploration.

Sex histories were gathered from 18.6 per cent of the 1008 boys between the ages of 12 and 17 who were interviewed in the Nashville, Tennessee, SMA for an investigation of adolescent conforming and deviating behavior. These represent

TABLE 1. Type of Sex Experience by Conforming-Deviating Type of Boy
(Per Cent by Conforming-Deviating Type)

Type of Sex Experience	Lower Class				Middle Class				All Classes		
	Org. career delinquent	Peer-oriented delinquent	Conforming non-achiever	Conforming achiever	Peer-oriented delinquent	Conforming non-achiever	Conforming achiever	Hyper-conforming former	Non-conforming isolate	Conforming isolate	Total
Total	73	166	250	81	38	86	193	56	24	41	1008
Queers, masturbation and heterosexual	32.5	27.3	5.1	20.0	—	10.0	—	—	37.5	—	17.6
Queers, masturbation, hetero and animal	30.2	4.5	—	—	5.0	—	—	—	—	—	8.5
Heterosexual only	4.7	11.4	—	—	70.0	30.0	—	—	12.5	—	13.4
Heterosexual and masturbation[a]	25.6	34.1	33.3	40.0	15.0	10.0	40.0	—	25.0	—	27.3
Masturbation only	2.3	15.9	48.7	40.0	—	10.0	40.0	57.1	25.0	100.0	21.9
Denies sex experience	4.7	6.8	12.8	—	10.0	40.0	20.0	42.9	0.0	—	11.2
Subtotal	43	44	39	5	20	10	10	7	8	1	187
No sex history	41.1	73.5	84.4	93.8	47.4	88.4	94.8	87.5	66.7	97.6	81.4

[a] Includes 3 cases of heterosexual, masturbation, and animal (2 lower class organized career delinquent and 1 peer-oriented delinquent).

all of the interviews of one of the interviewers during a two-month period, together with interviews with all Nashville boys incarcerated at the Tennessee State Training School for Boys.

As Table 1 discloses, the largest number of interviews was taken with lower-class delinquent boys. There is a reason for this: when it was apparent that delinquents from the lowest social class generally had some contact with adult male fellators, an attempt was made to learn more about how this contact was structured and controlled. Sex histories, therefore, were obtained from all of the white Nashville boys who were resident in the Tennessee State Training School for Boys during the month of June, 1958.

The way sex history information was obtained precludes making reliable estimates about the incidence or prevalence of hustling within the Nashville adolescent boy population. Yet the comparisons among types of conformers and deviators in Table 1 provide an informed guess about their life chances for participation in such an activity.[8]

Only two middle-class boys report experience in the peer-queer transaction. In one case, the boy acquiesced once to solicitation; in the other, the boy had acquired experience and associations in the State Training School for Boys which led to continued participation following his release. Within the lower-class group, it seems clear that the career-oriented delinquent is most likely to report sex experiences with fellators. Roughly three of every five boys report such experiences as contrasted with the peer-oriented delinquent, the type with the next highest relative frequency, where only about one in three report such experiences.

Taking into account the proportional distribution of types of conformers and deviators in a school population of adolescent boys and applying in a very rough way the proportional distribution for type of sex deviation set forth in Table 1, the experience rate with fellators is quite low in a population of all adolescent boys. The peer-queer relationship seems almost exclusively limited to lower-class delinquent boys—particularly career-oriented delinquent boys, where the experience rate is probably very high.

While not of direct concern here, it is of interest that the conformers in Table 1 seem to consist about equally of boys who either report a history of heterosexual and masturbation experience, or masturbation only experience, while hyperconformers either report no sex experience or that they masturbate only.

It might also be inferred from Table 1 that the adolescent conforming boy of lower-class origins in our society is very unlikely to report he never masturbates, though a substantial proportion of middle-class conforming boys maintain they never masturbate and never have masturbated. Although there may be age differences among the class levels in age of onset of masturbation, the class difference may yet be genuine. It is possible, of course, that this difference in masturbation experience reflects only a difference in willingness to report masturbation to a middle-class investigator, i.e., middle-class boys are more likely to hide their sexual experience, even that of masturbation, from others. Nevertheless, there may be class differences in the social organization of sexual experiences, since lower-class boys reported masturbating in groups when they first began to masturbate, while this experience was reported much less frequently by middle-class boys, for whom it is more likely a private matter. The same thing is true for heterosexual experience: lower-class boys, particularly delinquent ones, frequently report they participate in group heterosexual activity in "gang-bangs," while heterosexual experience appears to be a more private experience for the middle-class boy, who does not share his sexual partner with peers. All of this may reflect not only greater versatility in the sex experience of the lower-class male but perhaps a greater willingness to use sex as a means to gratification.

HOW PEERS AND QUEERS MEET

Meetings between adult male fellators and delinquent boys are easily made, because both know how and where to meet within the community space. Those within the common culture know that contact can be established within a relatively short period of time, if it is wished. The fact that meetings between peers and queers can be made easily is mute evidence of the organized understandings which prevail between the two populations.

There are a large number of places where the boys meet their clients, the fellators. Many of these points are known to all boys regardless of where they reside in the metropolitan area. This is particularly true of the central city locations where the largest number of contact points is found within a small territorial area. Each community area of the city, and certain fringe areas, inhabited by substantial numbers of lower-class persons, also have their meeting places, generally known only to the boys residing in the area.

Queers and peers typically establish contact in public or quasi-public places. Major points of contact include street corners, public parks, men's toilets in public or quasi-public places such as those in transportation depots, parks or hotels; and "second" and "third-run" movie houses (open around the clock and permitting sitting through shows). Bars are seldom points of contact, perhaps largely because they are plied by older male hustlers who lie outside the peer culture and groups, and because bar proprietors will not risk the presence of under-age boys.

There are a number of prescribed modes for establishing contact in these situations. They permit the boys and fellators to communicate intent to one another privately despite the public character of the situation. The major form of establishing contact is the "cruise," with the fellator passing "queer-corners" or locations until his effort is recognized by one of the boys. A boy can then signal—usually by nodding his head, a hand gesticulation signifying OK, following, or responding to commonly understood introductions such as "You got the time?"—that he is prepared to undertake the transaction. Entrepreneur and client then move to a place where the sexual activity is consummated, usually a place affording privacy, protection and hasty exit. "Dolly," a three-time loser at the State Training School, describes one of these prescribed forms for making contact:

"Well, like at the bus station, you go to the bathroom and stand there pretendin' like ... and they're standin' there pretendin' like ... and then they motions their head and walks out and you follow them, and you go some place. Either they's got a car, or you go to one of them hotels near the depot or some place like that ... most any place."

Frequently contact between boys and fellators is established when the boy is hitchhiking. This is particularly true for boys' first contacts of this nature. Since lower-class boys are more likely than middle-class ones to hitch rides within a city, particularly at night when such contacts are most frequently made, they perhaps are most often solicited in this manner.

The experienced boy who knows a "lot of queers," may phone known fellators directly from a public phone, and some fellators try to establish continued contact with boys by giving them their phone numbers. However, the boys seldom use this means of contact for reasons inherent in their orientation toward the transactions, as we shall see below.

We shall now examine how the transaction is facilitated by these types of situations and the prescribed modes of contact and communication. One of the characteristics of all these contact situations is that they provide a *rationale* for the presence of *both* peers and queers in the *same* situation or place. This rationale is necessary for both parties, for were there high visibility to the presence of either and no ready explanation for it, contact and communication would be far more difficult. Public and quasi-public facilities provide situations which account for the presence of most persons since there is relatively little social control over the establishment of contacts. There is, of course, some risk to the boys and the fellators in making contact in these situations since they are generally known to the police. The Morals Squad may have "stake-outs," but this is one of the calculated risks and the communication network carries information about their tactics.

A most important element in furnishing a rationale is that these meeting places must account for the presence of delinquent boys of essentially lower-class dress and appearance who make contact with fellators of almost any class level.

This is true despite the fact that the social settings which fellators ordinarily choose to establish contact generally vary according to the class level of the fellators. Fellators of high social class generally make contact by "cruising" past street-corners, in parks, or the men's rooms in "better" hotels, while those from the lower class are likely to select the public bath or transportation depot. There apparently is some general equation of the class position of boys and fellators in the peer-queer transaction. The large majority of fellators in the delinquent peer-queer transaction probably are from the lower class ("apes"). But it is difficult to be certain about the class position of the fellator clients since no study was made of this population.

The absence of data from the fellator population poses difficulties in interpreting the contact relationship. Many fellators involved with delinquent boys do not appear to participate in any overt or covert homosexual groups, such as the organized homosexual community of the "gay world."[9] The "gay world" is the most visible form of organized homosexuality since it is an organized community, but it probably encompasses only a small proportion of all homosexual contact. Even among those in the organized homosexual community, evidence suggests that the homosexual members seek sexual gratification outside their group with persons who are essentially anonymous to them. Excluding homosexual married couples, Leznoff and Westley maintain that there is ". . . a prohibition against sexual relationships within the group . . ."[10] Ross indicates that young male prostitutes are chosen, among other reasons, for the fact that they protect the identity of the client.[11] Both of these factors tend to coerce many male fellators to choose an anonymous contact situation.

It is clear that these contact situations not only provide a rationale for the presence of the parties to the transaction but a guarantee of anonymity. The guarantee does not necessarily restrict social visibility as both the boys and the fellators may recognize cues (including, but not necessarily, those of gesture and dress) which lead to mutual role identification.[12] But anonymity is guaranteed in at least two senses: anonymity of presence is assured in the situation and their personal identity in the community is protected unless disclosed by choice.

There presumably are a variety of reasons for the requirement of anonymity. For many, a homosexual relationship must remain a secret since their other relationships in the community—families, business relationships, etc.—must be protected. Leznoff and Westley refer to these men as the "secret" as contrasted with the "overt" homosexuals,[13] and in the organized "gay world," they are known as "closet fags." For some, there is also a necessity for protecting identity to avoid blackmail.[14] Although none of the peer hustlers reported resorting to blackmail, the adult male fellator may nonetheless hold such an expectation, particularly if he is older or of high social class. Lower-class ones, by contrast, are more likely to face the threat of violence from adolescent boys since they more often frequent situations where they are likely to contact "rough trade."[15] The kind of situation in which the delinquent peer-queer contact is made and the sexual relationship consummated tends to minimize the possibility of violence.

Not all male fellators protect their anonymity; some will let a boy have their phone number and a few "keep a boy." Still, most fellators want to meet boys where they are least likely to be victimized, although boys sometimes roll queers by selecting a meeting place where by prearrangement, their friends can meet them and help roll the queer, steal his car, or commit other acts of violence. Boys generally know that fellators are vulnerable in that they "can't" report their victimization. Parenthetically, it might be mentioned that these boys are not usually aware of their own institutional invulnerability to arrest. An adolescent boy is peculiarly invulnerable to arrest even when found with a fellator since the mores define the boy as exploited.[16]

Situations of personal contact between adolescent boys and adult male fellators also provide important ways to *communicate intent* or to carry out the transaction *without* making the contact particularly visible to others. The wall writings in many of these places are not without their primitive communication value, e.g., "show it hard," and places such as a public restroom provide a modus operandi. The entrepreneur and his customer in fact can meet with little more than an exchange of non-verbal gestures, transact their business with a minimum of verbal communication and part without a knowledge of one another's identity. In most cases, boys report "almost nothing" was said. The sexual transaction may occur with the only formal transaction being payment to the boy.

INDUCTION INTO THE
PEER-QUEER TRANSACTION

The peer-queer culture operates through a delinquent peer society. Every boy interviewed in this study who voluntarily established contacts with fellators was also delinquent in many other respects. The evidence shows that contact with fellators is an institutionalized aspect of the organization of lower-class delinquency oriented groups. This is not to say that boys outside these groups never experience relationships with adult male fellators: some do, but they are not participants in groups which sanction the activity according to the prescribed group standards described below. Nor is it to say that all delinquent groups positively sanction the peer-queer transaction since its distribution is unknown.

How, then, do lower-class delinquent boys get to meet fellators? Most boys from the lowest socioeconomic level in large cities are prepared for this through membership in a delinquent group which has a knowledge of how to make contact with fellators and relate to them. This is part of their common culture. Often, too, the peer group socializes the boy in his first experiences or continuing ones with fellators. The behavior is apparently learned within the framework of differential association.

The peer group actually serves as a school of induction for some of its members. The uninitiated boy goes with one or more members of his peer group for indoctrination and his first experience. Doy L., a lower-class boy at a lower-class school and a two-time loser at the State Training School, explains how he got started:

I went along with these older boys down to the bus station, and they took me along and showed me how it was done . . . they'd go in, get a queer, get blowed and get paid . . . if it didn't work right, they'd knock him in the head and get their money . . . they showed me how to do it, so I went in too.

In any case, boys are socialized in the subcultural definitions of peer-queer relations by members of their group and many apply this knowledge when an opportunity arises. Within the group, boys hear reports of experiences which supply the cultural definitions: how contacts are made, how you get money if the queer resists, how much one should expect to get, what kind of behavior is acceptable from the queer, which is to be rejected and how. Boys know all this *before* they have any contact with a fellator. In the case of street gangs, the fellators often pass the neighborhood corner; hence, even the preadolescent boy learns about the activity as the older boys get picked up. As the boy enters adolescence and a gang of his own which takes over the corner, he is psychologically and socially prepared for his first experience, which generally occurs when the first opportunity presents itself. Lester H. illustrates this; his first experience came when he went to one of the common points of convergence of boys and fellators—The Empress Theatre—to see a movie. Lester relates:

I was down in the Empress Theatre and this gay came over and felt me up and asked me if I'd go out . . . I said I would if he'd give me the money as I'd heard they did, and I was gettin' low on it . . . so he took me down by the river and blowed me.

In a substantial number of cases, a brother introduces the boy to his first experience, much as he introduces him to other first experiences. Jimmie M. illustrates this pattern. Jimmie describes how he was led into his first heterosexual experience:

When I was almost 14, my younger brother said he'd screwed this woman and he told me about it, so I went down there and she let me screw her too.

His induction into the peer-queer transaction also occurred through his younger brother:

Well, my younger brother came home and told me this gay'd blowed him and he told me where he lived ... And, I was scared to do it, but I figured I'd want to see what it was like since the other guys talked about it and my brother'd done it. So I went down there and he blowed me.

Not all boys belonging to groups which sanction peer hustling accept the practice. Some boys reject the peer-queer transaction while retaining membership in the group. It is not too surprising that such exceptions occur. Although in most delinquent groups some forms of sex activity confer status, it is rarely an absolute requisite for participation in such groups. Some boys in gangs which frequently gang shag, for example, refuse to participate in these activities. "I don't like my meat that raw" appears to be an acceptable "out." Exemption appears possible so long as the boy is acceptable in all, if not most, other respects. A lower-class delinquent boy apparently doesn't "chicken-out" or lose his "rep" if he doesn't want to engage in sex behaviors which most of his peers practice. (The same condition may hold for other practices, such as the use of narcotics.) Jerry P. from a lower-class school is in a group where all the other boys go with fellators; but he refuses to become involved, though he goes so far as to ride in the car with one of the gang's "regular queers." Jerry is in a gang which often gets picked up by a well known "local gay," a David B. Jerry admits: "I ride with B. a lot, but he's never done anything to me; I just can't go for that." When asked how he knew B. was a queer, he replied, "Oh, all the guys say so and talk about doin' it with him. ... I could, but I just don't want to." Joe C., at a school which crosscuts the class structure, was asked if he had any other kind of sex experiences. His reply shows his rejection of his peer group's pattern of behavior with fellators. "You mean with queers?" "Uh huh." "I don't go with any. Most of my friends queer-bait, but I don't." A friend of his, Roy P., also rejects the activity: "Ain't no sense in queer-baitin'; I don't need the money that bad."

The impression should not be gained that most lower-class boys who are solicited by fellators accept the solicitation. A majority of all solicitations are probably refused when the initial contact is made unless several other conditions prevail. The first is that the boy must be a member of a group which permits this form of transaction, indoctrinates the boy with its codes and sanctions his participation in it. Almost all lower-class boys reported they were solicited by a queer at least once. A majority refused the solicitation. Refusal is apparently easy since boys report that queers are seldom insistent. There apparently is a mutual willingness to forego the transaction in such cases, perhaps because the queer cannot afford the risk of exposure, but perhaps also because the probability of his establishing contact on his next try is sufficiently high so that he can "afford" to accept the refusal. Looked at another way, there must be a set of mutual gains and expectations for the solicitation to be accepted and the transaction to proceed. Boys who refuse to be solicited are not vulnerable for another reason: they usually are members of groups which negatively sanction the activity. Such groups generally "bug" boys who go out with fellators and use other techniques of isolation to discourage the transaction. There also are gangs which look upon queers as "fair game" for their aggressive activity. They beat them, roll, and otherwise put upon them. A third condition that must prevail is that the boy who accepts or seeks solicitation from fellators must view the offer as instrumental gain, particularly monetary gain (discussed below).

There are boys, however, particularly those who are quite young, who report a solicitation from a man which they were unable to refuse but which they subsequently rejected as neither gratifying nor instrumentally acceptable. It is these boys who can be said to be "exploited" by adult fellators in the sense that they are either forced into the act against their will, or are at least without any awareness of how to cope with the situation. One such instance is found in the following report:

This guy picked me up down at Fourth and Union and said he was going over to East Nashville, so I got in . . . but he drove me out on Dickerson Pike. [What'd he do?] . . . Well, he blowed me and it made me feel real bad inside . . . but I know how to deal

with queers now . . . ain't one of 'em gonna do that to me again
. . . I hate queers. . . . They're crazy.

There is an important admission in the statement, "But I know
how to deal with 'em now." The lower-class boy as he grows
older learns how to deal with sexual advances from fellators.
Boys exchange experiences on how they deal with them and
it becomes quite difficult to "exploit" a lower-class boy who
is socialized in a peer group. It is perhaps largely the very
young boy, such as the one in the case above, or those isolated from peer groups, who are most vulnerable to solicitation without previous preparation for it.

Lower-class boys, as we have seen, have the highest probability of being in situations where they will be solicited by
fellators. But, *the lower-class boy who is a member of a career-
oriented gang which positively sanctions instrumental relationships with adult male fellators and which initiates members
into these practices, and a boy who at the same time perceives
himself as "needing" the income which the transaction provides, is most likely to establish personal contact with adult
male fellators on a continuing basis.*

It is suggested that the peer-queer transaction is behavior
learned through differential association in delinquent gangs.
This cannot be demonstrated without resort to a more specific
test of the hypothesis. But, as Sutherland has pointed out,
"Criminal behavior is partially a function of opportunities
to commit special classes of crimes. . . . It is axiomatic that
persons who commit a specific crime have the opportunity to
commit that crime. . . . While opportunity may be partially a
function of association with criminal patterns and of the specialized techniques thus acquired, it is not entirely determined
in this manner, and consequently differential association is not
a sufficient cause of criminal behavior."[17] Middle-class boys
are perhaps excluded from the peer-queer transaction as much
through lack of opportunity to commit this special class of
crime in their community of exposure as through any criterion
of differential association. The structure of the middle-class
area is incompatible with the situational requirements for the
peer-queer transaction.

NORMS GOVERNING THE TRANSACTION

Does the peer society have any norms about personal relations with fellators? Or, does it simply induct a boy into a
relationship by teaching him how to effect the transaction?
The answer is that there appear to be several clear-cut norms
about the relations between peers and queers, even though
there is some deviation from them.

The first major norm is that *a boy must undertake the relationship with a queer solely as a way of making money;
sexual gratification cannot be actively sought as a goal in
the relationship.* This norm does not preclude a boy from
sexual gratification by the act; he simply must not seek this
as a goal. Put another way, a boy cannot admit that he failed
to get money from the transaction unless he used violence
toward the fellator and he cannot admit that he sought it as
a means of sexual gratification.

The importance of making money in motivating a boy to
the peer-queer transaction is succinctly stated by Dewey H.:

This guy in the Rex Theatre came over and sat down next to me
when I was 11 or 12, and he started to fool with me. I got over
and sat down another place and he came over, and asked me,
didn't I want to and he'd pay me five bucks. I figured it was *easy
money* so I went with him . . . I didn't do it before that. That
wasn't too long after I'd moved to South Nashville. I was a pretty
good boy before that . . . not real good, but I never ran with a
crowd that got into trouble before that. But, I met a lot of 'em
there. [Why do you run with queers?] It's *easy money* . . . like I
could go out and break into a place when I'm broke and get money
that way . . . but that's harder and *you take a bigger risk* . . . with
a queer it's *easy money.*

Dewey's comments reveal two important motivating factors
in getting money from queers, both suggested by the expression, "easy money." First, the money is easy in that it can
be made quickly. Some boys reported that when they needed
money for a date or a night out, they obtained it within an
hour through the sexual transaction with a queer. All a boy
has to do is go to a place where he will be contacted, wait

around, get picked up, carried to a place where the sexual transaction occurs, and in a relatively short period of time he obtains the money for his service.

It is easy money in another and more important sense for many of these boys. Boys who undertake the peer-queer transaction are generally members of career-oriented delinquent groups. Rejecting the limited opportunities for making money by legitimate means or finding them inaccessible, their opportunities to make money by illegitimate means may also be limited or the risk may be great. Theft is an available means, but it is more difficult and involves greater risk than the peer-queer transaction. Delinquent boys are not unaware of the risks they take. Under most circumstances, delinquents may calculate an act of stealing as "worth the risk." There are occasions, however, when the risk is calculated as too great. These occasions occur when the "heat" is on the boy or when he can least afford to run the risk of being picked up by the police, as is the case following a pick-up by the police, being put on probation or parole, or being warned that incarceration will follow the next violation At such times, boys particularly calculate whether they can afford to take the risk. Gerald L., describing a continuing relationship with a fellator who gave him his phone number, reflects Dewey's attitude toward minimizing risk in the peer-queer transaction: "So twic'd after that when I was gettin' real low and couldn't risk stealin' and gettin' caught, I called him and he took me out and blowed me." Here is profit with no investment of capital and a minimum of risk in social, if not in psychological, terms.

The element of risk coupled with the wish for "easy money" enters into our understanding of the peer-queer relationship in another way. From a sociological point of view, the peer-queer sexual transaction occurs between two major types of deviators—"delinquents" and "queers." Both types of deviators risk negative sanctions for their deviant acts. The more often one has been arrested or incarcerated, the more punitive the sanctions from the larger social system for both types of deviators. At some point, therefore, both calculate risks and seek to minimize them, at least in the very short-run. Each then becomes a means for the other to minimize risk.

When the delinquent boy is confronted with a situation in which he wants money and risks little in getting it, how is he to get it without working? Illegitimate activities frequently provide the "best" opportunity for easy money. These activities often are restricted in kind and number for adolescents and the risk of negative sanctions is high. Under such circumstances, the service offered a queer is a chance to make easy money with a minimum of risk.

Opportunities for sexual gratification are limited for the adult male fellator, particularly if he wishes to minimize the risk of detection in locating patrons, to avoid personal involvement and to get his gratification when he wishes it. The choice of a lower-class male, precisely because of his class position, somewhat reduces the risk. If the lower-class male also is a delinquent, the risk is minimized to an even greater degree.

This is not to say that the parties take equal risks in the situation. Of the two, the fellator perhaps is less able to minimize his risk since he still risks violence from his patron, but much less so if a set of expectations arise which control the use of violence as well. The boy is most able to minimize his risk since he is likely to be defined as "exploited" in the situation if caught.

Under special circumstances, boys may substitute other gratifications for the goal of money, provided that these gratifications do not include sexual gratification as a major goal. These special circumstances are the case where an entire gang will "make a night (or time) of it" with one or more adult male fellators. Under these circumstances, everyone is excepted from the subcultural expectations about making money from the fellator because everyone participates and there is no reason for everyone (or anyone) to make money. For the group to substitute being given a "good time" by a "queer" for the prescribed financial transaction is, of course, the exception which proves the rule.

Several examples of group exemption from the prescribed norm of a financial gain were discovered. Danny S., leader of the Black Aces, tells of his gang's group experiences with queers:

There's this one gay who takes us to the Colonial Motel out on Dickerson Pike . . . usually it's a bunch of us boys and we all get drunk and get blowed by this queer . . . we don't get any money then . . . it's more a drinking party.

The Black Aces are a fighting gang and place great stress on physical prowess, particularly boxing. All of its members have done time more than once at the State Training School. During one of these periods, the school employed a boxing instructor whom the boys identified as "a queer," but the boys had great respect for him since he taught them how to box and was a game fighter. Danny refers to him in accepting terms:

He's a real good guy. He's fought with us once or twice and we drink with him when we run into him. . . . He's taken us up to Miter Dam a coupla times; he's got a cabin up there on the creek and he blows us. . . . But mostly we just drink and have a real good time.

These examples illustrate the instrumental orientation of the gang members. If the expense of the gang members getting drunk and having a good time is borne by a "queer," each member is released from the obligation to receive cash. The relationship in this case represents an exchange of services rather than that of money for a service.

The second major norm operating in the relationship is that *the sexual transaction must be limited to mouth-genital fellation. No other sexual acts are generally tolerated.*[18] The adult male fellator must deport himself in such a way as to re-enforce the instrumental aspects of the role relationship and to insure affective neutrality.[19] For the adult male fellator to violate the boy's expectation of "getting blowed," as the boys refer to the act, is to risk violence and loss of service. Whether or not the boys actually use violent means as often as they say they do when expectations are violated, there is no way of knowing with precision. Nevertheless, whenever boys reported they used violent means, they always reported some violation of the subcultural expectations. Likewise, they never reported a violation of the subcultural expectations which was not followed by the use of violent means, unless it was clearly held up as an exception. Bobby A. expresses the boys' point of view on the use of violent means in the following exchange: "How much did you usually get?" "Around five dollars; if they didn't give that much, I'd beat their head in." "Did they ever want you to do anything besides blow you?" "Yeh, sometimes . . . Like they want me to blow them, but I'd tell them to go to hell and maybe beat them up."

Boys are very averse to being thought of in a queer role or engaging in acts of fellation. The act of fellation is defined as a "queer" act. Most boys were asked whether they would engage in such behavior. All but those who had the status of "punks" denied they had engaged in behavior associated with the queer role. Asking a boy whether he is a fellator meets with strong denial and often with open hostility. This could be interpreted as defensive behavior against latent homosexuality. Whether or not this is the case, strong denial could be expected because the question goes counter to the subcultural definitions of the peer role in the transaction.

A few boys on occasion apparently permit the fellator to perform other sexual acts. These boys, it is guessed, are quite infrequent in a delinquent peer population. Were their acts known to the members of the group, they would soon be defined as outside the delinquent peer society. Despite the limitation of the peer-queer sexual transaction to mouth-genital fellation, there are other sexual transactions which the peer group permits members to perform under special circumstances. They are, for example, permitted to perform the *male* roles in "crimes against nature," such as in pederasty ("cornholing" to the boys), bestiality (sometimes referred to as buggery) and carnal copulation with a man involving no orifice (referred to as "slick-legging" among the boys) provided that the partner is roughly of the same age and not a member of the group and provided also that the boys are confined to the single-sex society of incarcerated delinquent boys. Under no circumstances, however, is the female role in carnal copulation acceptable in any form. It is taboo. Boys who accept the female role in sexual transactions occupy the lowest status position among delinquents. They are "punks."

The third major norm operating on the relationship is that *both peers and queers, as participants, should remain affectively neutral during the transaction.* Boys within the peer society define the ideal form of the role with the fellator as one in which the boy is the entrepreneur and the queer is viewed as purchasing a service. The service is a business deal where a sexual transaction is purchased for an agreed upon amount of money. In the typical case, the boy is neither expected to enjoy or be repulsed by the sexual transaction; mouth-genital fellation is accepted as a service offered in exchange for a fee. It should be kept in mind that self-gratification is permitted in the sexual act. Only the motivation to sexual gratification in the transaction is tabooed. But self-gratification must occur without displaying either positive or negative affect toward the queer. In the prescribed form of the role relationship, the boy sells a service for profit and the queer is to accept it without show of emotion.

The case of Thurman L., one of three brothers who are usually in trouble with the law, illustrates some aspects of the expected pattern of affective neutrality. Thurman has had a continuing relationship with a queer, a type of relationship in which it would be anticipated that affective neutrality would be difficult to maintain. This relationship continued, in fact, with a 21-year-old "gay" until the man was "sent to the pen." When queried about his relationship with this man and why he went with him, Thurman replied:

Don't know . . . money and stuff like that I guess. [What do you mean? . . . stuff like that?] Oh, clothes. . . . [He ever bought you any clothes?] Sure, by this one gay. . . . [You mind being blowed?] No. [You like it?] Don't care one way or the other. I don't like it, and I don't not like it. [You like this one gay?] Nope, can't say that I liked anythin' about him. [How come you do it then?] Well, the money for one thing. . . . I need that. [You enjoy it some?] Can't say I do or don't.

More typical than Thurman's expression of affective neutrality is the boy who accepts it as "OK" or, "It's all right; I don't mind it." Most frequent of all is some variant of the statement: "It's OK, but I like the money best of all." The definition of affective neutrality fundamentally requires only that there be no positive emotional commitment to the queer *as a person*. The relationship must be essentially an impersonal one, even though the pure form of the business relationship may seldom be attained. Thus, it is possible for a boy to admit self-gratification without admitting any emotional commitment to the homosexual partner.

Although the peer group prescribes affective neutrality toward the queer in the peer-queer transaction, queers must be regarded as low prestige persons, held in low esteem, and the queer role is taboo. The queer is most commonly regarded as "crazy, I guess." Some boys take a more rationalistic view "They're just like that, I guess" or "They're just born that way." While there are circumstances under which one is permitted to like a particular fellator, as in the case of all prejudices attached to devalued status, the person who is liked must be the exception which states the rule. Though in many cases both the boy and the fellator are of very low class origins, and in many cases both are altogether repulsive in appearance, cleanliness and dress by middle-class standards, these are not the standards of comparison used by the boys. The deviation of the queers from the boy's norms of masculine behavior places the fellator in the lowest possible status, even "beneath contempt." If the fellator violates the expected affective relationship in the transaction, he may be treated not only with violence but with contempt as well. The seller of the service ultimately reserves the right to set the conditions for his patrons.

Some boys find it difficult to be emotionally neutral toward the queer role and its occupants; they are either personally offended or affronted by the behavior of queers. JDC is an instance of a boy who is personally offended by their behavior; yet he is unable to use violence even when expectations governing the transaction are violated. He does not rely very much on the peer-queer relationship as a source of income. JDC expresses his view: "I don't really go for that like some guys; I just do it when I go along with the crowd. . . . You know. . . . That, and when I do it for money. . . . And I go along. . . . But . . . I hate queers. They embarrass me."

"How?" "Well, like you'll be in the lobby at the theatre, and they'll come up and pat your ass or your prick right in front of everybody. I just can't go for that—not me." Most of the boys wouldn't either, but they would have resorted to violent means in this situation.

Two principal types of boys maintain a continuing relationship with a known queer. A few boys develop such relationships to insure a steady income. While this is permitted within peer society for a short period of time, boys who undertake it for extended periods of time do so with some risk, since in the words of the boys, "queers can be got too easy." The boy who is affectively involved with a queer or his role is downgraded in status to a position, "Ain't no better'n a queer." There are also a few boys affectively committed to a continuing relationship with an adult male homosexual. Such boys usually form a strong dependency relationship with him and are kept much as the cabin boys of old. This type of boy is clearly outside the peer society of delinquents and is isolated from participation in gang activity. The sociometric pattern for such boys is one of choice into more than one gang, none of which is reciprocated.

Street-hustlers are also downgraded within the peer society, generally having reputations as "punk kids." The street-hustler pretty much "goes it alone." Only a few street-hustlers were interviewed for this study. None of them was a member of an organized delinquent group. The sociometric pattern for each, together with his history of delinquent activity, placed them in the classification of nonconforming isolates.

A fourth major norm operating on the peer-queer relationship serves as a primary factor in stabilizing the system. This norm holds that *violence must not be used so long as the relationship conforms to the shared set of expectations between queers and peers.* So long as the fellator conforms to the norms governing the transaction in the peer-queer society, he runs little risk of violence from the boys.

The main reason, perhaps, for this norm is that uncontrolled violence is potentially disruptive of any organized system. All organized social systems must control violence. If the fellator clients were repeatedly the objects of violence, the system as it has been described could not exist. Most boys who share the common expectations of the peer-queer relationship do not use violent means unless the expectations are violated. To use violence, of course, is to become affectively involved and therefore another prescription of the relationship is violated.

It is not known whether adult male fellators who are the clients of delinquent entrepreneurs share the boys' definition of the norm regarding the use of violence. They may, therefore, violate expectations of the peer society through ignorance of the system rather than from any attempt to go beyond the set of shared expectations.

There are several ways the fellator can violate the expectations of boys. The first concerns money: refusal to pay or paying too little may bring violence from most boys. Fellators may also violate peer expectations by attempting to go beyond the mouth-genital sexual act. If such an attempt is made, he is usually made an object of aggression as in the following excerpt from Dolly's sex history:

[You like it?] It's OK. I don't mind it. It feels OK. [They ever try anything else on you?] They usually just blow and that's all. [Any ever try anything else on you?] Oh sure, but we really fix 'em. I just hit 'em on the head or roll 'em . . . throw 'em out of the car. . . . Once a gay tried that and we rolled him and threw him out of the car. Then we took the car and stripped it [laughs with glee].

Another way the fellator violates a boy's expectations is to introduce considerable affect into the relationship. It appears that affect is least acceptable in two forms, both of which could be seen as "attacks on his masculinity." In one form, the queer violates the affective neutrality requirement by treating the adolescent boy as if he were a girl or in a girl's role during the sexual transaction, as for example, by speaking to him in affectionate terms such as "sweetie." There are many reasons why the feminine sex role is unacceptable to these lower-class boys, including the fact that such boys place considerable emphasis on being "tough" and masculine. Walter Miller, for example, observes that:

. . . The almost compulsive lower class concern with "masculinity" derives from a type of compulsive reaction-formation. A concern over homosexuality runs like a persistent thread through lower class culture—manifested by the institutionalized practice of "baiting queers," often accompanied by violent physical attacks, an expressed contempt for "softness" or frills, and the use of the local term for "homosexual" as a general pejorative epithet [e.g., higher class individuals or upwardly mobile peers are frequently characterized as "fags" or "queers"].[20]

Miller sees violence as part of a reaction-formation against the matriarchal lower-class household where the father often is absent. For this reason, he suggests, many lower-class boys find it difficult to identify with a male role, and the "collective" reaction-formation is a cultural emphasis on masculinity. Violence toward queers is seen as a consequence of this conflict. Data from our interviews suggests that among career-oriented delinquents, violation of the affective-neutrality requirement in the peer-queer relationship is at least as important in precipitating violence toward "queers." There are, of course, gangs which were not studied in this investigation which "queer-bait" for the express purpose of "rolling the queer."

The other form in which the fellator may violate the affective neutrality requirement is to approach the boy and make suggestive advances to him when he is with his agemates, either with girls or with his peer group when he is not located for "business." In either case, the sexual advances suggest that the boy is not engaged in a business relationship within the normative expectations of the system, but that he has sexual motivation as well. The delinquent boy is expected to control the relationship with his customers. He is the entrepreneur "looking" for easy money or at the very least he must appear as being merely receptive to business; this means that he is receptive only in certain situations and under certain circumstances. He is not in business when he is with girls and he is not a businessman when he is cast in a female role. To be cast in a female role before peers is highly unacceptable, as the following account suggests:

This gay comes up to me in the lobby of the Empress when we

was standin' around and starts feelin' me up and callin' me
Sweetie and like that . . . and, I just couldn't take none of that
there . . . what was he makin' out like I was a queer or some-
thin'. . . so I jumps him right then and there and we like to of
knocked his teeth out.

The sexual advance is even less acceptable when a girl is
involved:

I was walkin' down the street with my steady girl when this
gay drives by that I'd been with once before and he whistles at me
and calls, "hi Sweetie.". . . And, was I mad . . . so I went down to
where the boys was and we laid for him and beat on him 'til he
like to a never come to . . . ain't gonna take nothin' like that off'n
a queer.

In both of these instances, not only is the boys' masculinity
under attack, but the affective neutrality requirement of the
business transaction is violated. The queer's behavior is particularly unacceptable, however, because it occurs in a peer
setting where the crucial condition is the maintenance of
the boy's status within the group. A lower-class boy cannot
afford to be cast in less than a highly masculine role before
lower-class girls nor risk definition as a queer before peers.
His role within his peer group is under threat even if he suffers
no anxiety about masculinity. Not only the boy himself but
his peers perceive such behavior as violating role expectations
and join him in violent acts toward the fellator to protect
the group's integrity and status.

If violence generally occurs only when one of the major
peer norms has been violated, it would also seem to follow
that *violence is a means of enforcing the peer entrepreneurial
norms of the system.* Violence or the threat of violence is thus
used to keep adult male fellators in line with the boys' expectations in his customer role. It represents social control,
a punishment meted out to the fellator who violates the
cultural expectation. Only so long as the fellator seeks
gratification from lower-class boys in a casual pick-up or
continuing relationship where he pays money for a "blow-job,"
is he reasonably free from acts of violence.

There is another, and perhaps more important, reason for the use of violence when the peer defined norms of the peer-queer relationship are violated. The formally prescribed roles for peers and queers are basically the roles involved in all institutionalized forms of prostitution, the prostitute and the client. But in most forms of prostitution, whether male or female, the hustlers perceive of themselves in hustler roles, and furthermore the male hustlers also develop a conception of themselves as homosexual whereas *the peer hustler in the peer-queer relationship develops no conception of himself either as prostitute or as homosexual.*

The fellator risks violence, therefore, if he threatens the boy's self-conception by suggesting that the boy may be homosexual and treats him as if he were.

Violence seems to function, then, in two basic ways for the peers. On the one hand, it integrates their norms and expectations by controlling and combatting behavior which violates them. On the other hand, it protects the boy's self-identity as nonhomosexual and reinforces his self-conception as "masculine."

The other norms of the peer society governing the peer-queer transaction also function to prevent boys in the peer-queer society from defining themselves as homosexual. The prescriptions that the goal is money, that sexual gratification is not to be sought as an end in the relationship, that affective neutrality be maintained toward the fellator and that only mouth-genital fellation is permitted, all tend to insulate the boy from a homosexual self-definition. So long as he conforms to these expectations, his *"significant others" will not define him as homosexual;* and this is perhaps the most crucial factor in his own self-definition. The peers define one as homosexual not on the basis of homosexual *behavior* as such, but on the basis of participation in the homosexual *role,* the "queer" role. The reactions of the larger society, in defining the *behavior* as homosexual, are unimportant in their own self-definition. What is important to them are the reactions of their peers to violation of peer group norms which define roles in the peer-queer transaction.

TERMINATING THE ROLE BEHAVIOR

Under what circumstances does a boy give up earning money in the peer-queer transaction? Is it altogether an individual matter, or are there group bases for abandoning the practice? We have little information on these questions since interviews were conducted largely with boys who were still participants in the peer-queer culture. But a few interviews, either with boys who had terminated the relationship or spoke of those who had, provide information on how such role behavior is terminated.

Among lower-class adolescent boys, the new roles one assumes with increasing age are important in terminating participation in the peer-queer relationship. Thus older boys are more likely to have given up the transaction as 'a source of income. Several boys gave as their reason, "I got a job and don't need that kind of money now." An older boy, who recently married, said that he had quit when he was married. Another responded to the question, "When do you think you'll quit?" with, "When I quit school, I reckon. . . . I don't know a better way to make money afore then." A few boys simply said that they didn't care to make money that way any more, or that since they got a steady girl, they had quit.

The reasons older boys have for giving up the peer-queer transaction as a means of making money are perhaps different for the career-oriented than for the peer-oriented delinquent boy. As career-oriented delinquents get older, the more serious crimes direct their activity and the group is more actively involved in activities which confer status. The boy has a "rep" to maintain. The peer hustler role clearly contributes nothing to developing or maintaining a reputation, and the longer one gets money this way, the more one may risk it. The older career-oriented delinquent boy perhaps gives up peer hustling activity, then, just as he often gives up petty theft and malicious destruction of property. These are activities for younger boys.

As peer-oriented delinquents get older, they enter adult

groups where a job becomes one of the acceptable ways of behaving. Many of them may also move out of the "tight little island" of the peer group which inducted them into the activity. If one gets enough money from a job, there is no socially acceptable reason for getting money in the peer-queer transaction. One risks loss of status if one solicits at this age, for this is the age to move from one steady girl to another and perhaps even settle on one and get married, as often one "has to."

Regardless of the reasons for moving out, it seems clear that most boys do move out of their roles as peer hustlers and do not go on to other hustling careers. The main reason perhaps that most boys do not move on in hustling careers is that they never conceived of themselves in a hustling role or as participants in a career where there was a status gradation among hustlers. Hustling, to the peer hustler, is simply another one of the activities which characterize a rather versatile pattern of deviating acts. It is easier, too, to move out when one has never defined oneself as homosexual. It is in this sense, perhaps, that we have reason to conclude that these boys are not involved in the activity primarily for its homosexual basis. Peer hustlers are primarily oriented toward either delinquent, and later criminal, careers, or toward conventional conformity in lower-class society. They become neither hustlers nor queers.

SUMMARY

This paper explores a special form of male prostitution in American society, a homosexual relationship between adult male fellators and delinquents. It is seen as a financial transaction between boys and fellators which is governed by delinquent peer norms. These norms integrate the two types of deviators into an institutionalized form of prostitution and protect the boys from self-definitions either as prostitutes or as homosexuals.

The conclusions offered in this paper must be regarded as tentative, because of limitations inherent in the data. Study

of the fellator population might substantially change the
conclusions. Cross-cultural studies also are necessary. Discussion of these findings with criminologists in Denmark and
Sweden and exploratory investigations in several larger American cities, however, suggest that the description and explanation offered in this paper will hold for other American
cities and for some other social systems.

The Development of the Homosexual
Bar as an Institution

NANCY ACHILLES

*The bar is the primary and necessary locus for the male
homosexual community. Its importance derives from the requirement that people who live in a subculture have the
opportunity to get together. Since homosexuality for the
most part occurs during leisure hours, the bar meets all the
requirements of an institution that can service the community.
There are many kinds of bars, and they service both general
and specialized homosexual populations, depending on the
interests of the owner as well as the neighborhood location
of the bar. What is significant is the special case of the San
Francisco homosexual community where the bars, while not
approved by the conventional community, are not regulated
through either systematic harassment or illegal taxation
(bribes) by local law enforcement officials. In most metropolitan centers bars are not operated by their true owners
and the opportunity for corruption is much higher. As
Achilles points out, less sexual activity occurs in locally owned
bars—where the owner is personally running a risk—than
occurs in bars in cities where the operation of the establish-*

REPRINTED with the permission of the author from an unpublished
M.A. thesis, Committee on Human Development, University of Chicago,
1964.

ment depends upon the corruption of local law enforcement representatives. In this case, a more permissive environment results in less public sexual activity even though the homosexual community is itself more manifest.

In addition, the variety of bars available is a function of the size of the city. Once the size of the local homosexual community is large enough, bars appear to deal with particular homosexual populations. In smaller communities there is not nearly the differentiation of bar types, and they tend to serve more general populations. This may have some impact on the development of individual homosexual career styles since in a large metropolis a desire may be acted out because there are available both institutions and others who have already so behaved. Thus, a particular kind of homosexual commitment (such as sado-masochism) may be inhibited from expression in a small community, while in a larger community institutions are available to provide the necessary opportunity structure for the behavior.

An institution must arise from a particular social situation, when the individuals concerned feel that there is a need for a change in the existing order or a need for the creation of a new order. Thus it may be that all institutions have their origins in deviance.

When an individual experiences strain in the social system, he may become motivated toward deviance. When this occurs, three basic alternatives are available to the potential deviate. He may continue to participate in his environment, finding conformance to its norms frustrating, but less painful than deviance and separation. He may alter his environment through an alliance with others who share his dissatisfaction, in the formation of a subculture, or in joining an already existing subculture. The final choice open to him is to alienate himself from his environment altogether and attempt to chart his own life course.

If the second alternative is adopted, and the individual becomes a participant in a subculture, he may find moral legitimatization for his deviance and satisfaction of his socio-emotional needs. Socio-emotional gratification, however, is not sufficient. When the individual pulls away from his former reference group, he is also apt to pull away from the established system of goods and services with which his former institutionalized group was connected. According to Cohen:

> The important point is that the consequences of an act in terms of want satisfaction depend upon the way in which it articulates with the established systems of interaction through which goods and services are produced and distributed. Families, businesses, fraternal organizations, churches . . . are such systems. To obtain the goods and services they offer, the individual must participate in them on their own terms.[1]

The act of joining a deviant group may force the individual to break away from these systems, wholly or in part. A new reference group may satisfy his social wants and needs, but not his nonsocial ones. For this an institution must be created, a system which can supply goods and services as well as social interaction. When such an institution is established, the individual may remain completely and comfortably within his subculture, maintaining only minimal ties with the larger society.

The goods and services provided by the bar are well adapted to the needs of the homosexual Community. Its most important service is the provision of a setting in which social interaction may occur; without such a place to congregate, the group would cease to be a group. The milieu of this institution is both permissive and protective, necessary conditions for the continued functioning of the group. It provides the social stimulus and diversion of alcohol and entertainment especially created for the homosexual. Articulating with various commercial and political institutions in the larger society, the bar may obtain legitimate and illegitimate goods and services for its clientele. As each bar develops a "personality" of its own and becomes an institution in its own right, it fulfills more specialized social and nonsocial functions. A particular bar, for example, may serve as a loan office, restaurant, message reception center, telephone exchange, and so forth.

The bar was naturally adopted as the institution serving the homosexual Community for several reasons. For the most part, participation in the Community is a leisure time activity, albeit the participants' most important activity. Therefore, the institution serving the Community must be one adapted to sociability and leisure. Homosexuals, subject to pressure from law enforcement agencies, require a gathering place which is as mobile and flexible as possible, that is, a place which can open, close, and open again without great alteration or loss. The bar is sufficiently flexible, as it can be situated almost anywhere, and requires little space and few material embellishments. The Community's main institution must be one which provides some degree of anonymity and segregation from the larger society. The bar renders this service well, because it is such a common type of establishment that there is no great pressure from members of the larger society to gain access to any particular bar. Bars located in the outlying districts of the city, with inconspicuous façades, may appear quite innocent and unenticing to all but the cognoscenti.

An essential service which this institution must render is to permit, yet control, the formation of sexual relationships. Sexual contacts may be made on the street, in the park, or on the bench, but as Cory states:

From the gay street to the gay bar may be but a few steps, or several miles, but an aura of respectability is to be found at the latter that is lacking at the former. . . . in the final analysis, it may be that the bar provides a superstructure behind which the libidinous impulses can hide, whereas on the street the passions are denuded, deprived of an aura of romance and culture. In one place it is fun, in the other it is lust. . . . the drinks, the music and the atmosphere of friendliness give a far less outlawed aspect to sex. . . .[2]

The bar is the only place where these contacts, necessary to those concerned and illegal according to the law, can be made with a reasonable degree of safety and respectability. The individual may feel much less anxiety and guilt if he is able to carry on this aspect of his life in an organized framework of social norms and values. The bar is the homosexual equivalent of the USO or the youth club, where the rating and dating process may unfold in a controlled and acceptable manner.

Despite the efforts of management and clientele alike, the bar cannot, by its very nature, remain a totally private and segregated institution. It must be open to the public, and if outsiders choose to enter, they may do so. The bar, therefore, becomes both the center of the private activities of the Community and its liaison with the larger society.

Perhaps the most frequent, and certainly the most frequently discussed, contact between the bar and its surroundings occurs via the police force. While the bar generally protects its patrons from the hazards of "going it alone," it exposes them to the risk of becoming involved in a police action directed against the bar itself. "Disorderly conduct," "lewd and obscene behavior," and "running a disorderly house" are the most common charges brought against the gay bars, and encompass behavior ranging from homosexual dancing to brief and incidental physical contact. Should the owner of the bar be found guilty of these charges, which is usually the case, the bar may be closed or the liquor license revoked.

The fear of a "raid" is always present in a gay bar, and stories of past raids on now defunct bars are part of the group tradition. It becomes rather a badge of honor to have been involved in such an escapade and have survived. Stories of what one did and how one escaped identification and/or arrest are passed on in full detail to newcomers to the group, accompanied by advice as to what one should do in such situations. The owners and employees, however, are fully aware of the consequences of such police action, and take great care to see that their customers toe the mark. A few bars have the extra precaution of warning lights or bells which signal an approaching officer, at which sign all customers are to make certain that no one is standing too close to his neighbor.

The question of "payoff" always arises in such situations, with many rumors and few substantiations. It is unlikely, however, that such arrangements occur frequently in San

Francisco for several reasons. The "gay life" in San Francisco is more visible and more a matter of public knowledge than it is in many other cities. As the president of the LCE [a homophile reform group—eds.] described it:

Another thing that makes San Francisco unique is that the gay life is very open—everyone knows it goes on, where a lot of the bars are, and so on. But the practices are closed—nobody can get away with anything, anyone trying to make propositions or making out or even dancing in most places gets thrown out. The owners stick together on this, they're a pretty close group. This makes people from out of town make mistakes sometimes, they think that because the gay life is so evident they can just cut loose and have a ball—and they find out they can't. Bars in Chicago and LA, for example, are hard to find, but once you get in you can do almost anything.

This openness makes the gay bars less subject to underworld control and, therefore, less likely to be involved in police bribery. Secrecy is almost impossible, as the homosexual communication network reaches almost every corner of the city, and the homosexual "problem" receives considerable attention from the press. Furthermore, most of the bars are owned by residents of the city and represent their entire business investment. There is seldom enough capital to make bribery practical. The bar owners, as the preceding quote indicates, are a cohesive group, and are generally opposed to illegitimate dealings with the law. It is interesting to note, however, that only three of the thirty-seven San Francisco bars considered in this study were owned by persons who were not residents of the city. These three were all large, successful, and inclined to be rather lax in enforcing behavioral stand-ards. Although all three have been in existence for an unusual length of time, according to gay bar standards, none has ever been troubled by the police.

Several respondents in this study reported having had direct experience with the method of "entrapment" used by law officers in gathering evidence against the homosexual collectivity, the gay bars, and their patrons. Entrapment is a system whereby an officer learns the language, behavior, and dress of the homosexual group, enters a bar or walks down a street frequented by homosexuals, and pretends he is one of them in order to elicit a sexual "pass." He may then use the behavior he calls forth as evidence against the individual or against the owner of the bar in which it occurred. Needless to say, the reaction against this method as expressed by the homosexual organizations and by individuals is rather strong. One respondent recalled his experience as follows:

I remember I was sitting in the —— one night, a week night, and it was quiet. Only about five other people there. I was by myself, having a beer and about to go home. A young guy with a crew cut comes up and sits next to me. He had on a bright shirt and slacks and tennis shoes, the whole bit. He started a conversation and was real friendly and all, and kind of cute, so I talked to him. Then he started pressing his knee against mine, which you don't do in a bar with only five people in it unless you're asking to get 86'd.[3] I should have known, but hell, you can't suspect everybody! He went out after me when I left, and walked with me to my apartment. So what the hell, naturally I invited him up, and then I find out he's a cop. He took me downtown and said I should be booked for a sex crime.

Another respondent:

I was walking down the street and a man started to follow me. I went faster, and he kept pace, right behind me. Then he came up to me and mumbled something that sounded like he was asking me what I liked to do. I wasn't going to have any part of that, so I kept on walking. He went with me about two more blocks, until he saw he wasn't going to get to add me to his arrest quota. Then he said, "I'm a police officer, and you'd better stop wandering around the streets or I'll arrest you for vagrancy."

If there is one particular issue which calls forth a unified protest from the homosexual Community, it is that of police activity. Many homosexuals remain passive until a favorite bar or a close friend is threatened by the police; then all the latent hostility is fully expressed. A manifestation of hostility from the representative of the larger society calls forth a similar response from the homosexual Community.

It's a police state, I'm telling you. They make me so goddamn mad sometimes. Like the ——, no one had made any trouble there and it was a nice place. But they wanted to get something on it, just for the record, so they parked a police car in front of the door every night for two weeks. That usually scares people off, but it didn't this time. So they put a cop in uniform right inside the door every night, with a dog yet! It got to be kind of a kick after a while, people would come in and bring things to feed the dog, and pet him and everything. It got so the dog was friends with everyone in the place. Not the cop, just the dog.

The cops are fantastic, really. Before they finally closed ——'s, there was one that used to come in every night for a drink. But he wouldn't drink out of the same glasses that all those dirty fairies used, he had to keep his own glass under the bar!

The greatest sense of group cohesion in the homosexual Community is expressed in reaction to the police. The homosexual organizations, apparently aware of this fact and seeking to further develop a sense of unity, give police activity maximum coverage in their publications. The homosexual's relationship to the law and the police, however, may be viewed as latently functional for the group, and this may explain why the group is often reluctant to express its resentment in action as well as words. The homosexual's legal status enables him to see himself as wronged and persecuted, which relieves his own feeling of guilt. The police are a target upon which he may center his hostility; they are the enemy and he is the underdog. It is in large part due to the police that the homosexual can, and often does, regard himself as a member of an unfairly treated minority group.

In addition to the latent functions they provide for the homosexual group, police "brutality" and "persecution" rally some support from the larger society on behalf of the group. Reports of brutality against any group, even if they are exaggerated, tend to stimulate the traditional American spirit of "rooting for the underdog."

It is often the bars themselves which make the most salient plea for the homosexual's civil rights, for it is most often the bars which undertake a defense in cases involving the law. The attorneys hired to defend the bars serve as intermediaries between the institutions of the homosexual group and those of the larger society.

The case of the Black Cat in San Francisco illustrates both the arousal of some degree of public support for the homosexual collectivity and the attempt to legalize it through institutionalized channels. The Black Cat has long been a part of San Francisco tradition, and is well known to the city's inhabitants. It began as a meeting place for literary Bohemia, and developed into one of the few places in the city where homosexuals, tourists, bohemians, and socialites congregated together. Its reputation, however, was as a "gay" bar.

Over a period of fifteen years, the Alcoholic Beverage Control Board brought various complaints against the owner of the Black Cat, who hired one of the city's most renowned civil rights lawyers in his defense. The case went to the California Supreme Court in 1954, with the ruling that homosexuals, if properly behaved, had the legal right to congregate. However, a change in the administration of the liquor control board and a charge of "lewd and indecent acts" ended the bar's career in October of 1963.

The state liquor agents elected to close the Black Cat on Halloween, the night of the traditional costume party at the bar. This brought a response of protest from many quarters, so the agents altered their plans and revoked the license on the preceding evening. The Black Cat, however, remained open on Halloween, serving only coffee and soft drinks. The party that evening was attended by a crowd of some 2000 persons, including a large representation from the homosexual Community, and "college students, business men, matrons with mink coats and jewelry, tee-shirted men in boots, and couples who looked as if they had just come to town for a big night out."[4] The crowd lined the sidewalks, and television cameras were present to record the entrance of the costumed "drag queens." Toward the end of the evening, the bartender led the entire congregation in a rendition of "God Save the Nellie Queen."

The coverage accorded the occasion by the press included three feature columns and several articles. One article quoted the partner of the Black Cat's attorney as saying, "That place is like an institution. This is like closing the cable cars or the Golden Gate Bridge." The same story presented the views of the bar's owner: "I know it's an unpopular cause. The Black Cat has been the symbol of a fight that has benefited the gay people to a degree. That's why they want to knock us out. . . . "5

The public response, while it manifested more amusement and curiosity than actual sympathy, seemed an illustration of the sophisticated and liberal attitude upon which San Franciscans base their city's image. As a bystander proudly remarked, "It could only happen here." This self-conscious liberalism may be one reason why San Francisco has attracted such a large homosexual population and why the gay life in the city is unusually visible. San Franciscans seem rather ambivalent toward the homosexual collectivity, at times defending it as something of a tourist attraction, and at other times demanding that "something be done about the problem." What effect this type of attitude has had in making the San Francisco homosexual collectivity different from that of other cities cannot be determined without comparative data, which are not yet available.

It is through the bars that members of the larger society may become acquainted with the homosexual Community. The tourist, the reporter, the researcher, the heterosexual who enters a bar by mistake or out of curiosity, and the straight person with friends in the gay Community, all are potential means of interchange between the world of the homosexual and that of the heterosexual.

The official attitude of the larger society toward any deviant group is determined to a great extent by what is contained in the statutes, and the law is often the last institution to adapt to changes in public opinion. Although homosexuality may be considered a form of mental disorder in some quarters and a fashionable peccadillo in others, legally it remains a crime. The police, as the society's official agents, are required to apprehend anyone committing a homosexual act, in private or in public. In practice, however, such legalities are difficult to enforce. A police officer described the situation as follows:

We can't get rid of them, there's too many of them. You close one bar and another one opens somewhere else. As long as they behave themselves you might as well have the bars, at least it keeps them

off the streets. People complain about so many bars for that kind of
people in the city, but they'd probably complain a lot more if they
were all running around in public. All we can do is keep an eye on
them, try to keep them in line.

Police relations with the gay bars are closely linked to the
politics of city government. When a change of administration
is due or there are reports in the press about sex crimes or
the increasing crime rate, the pressure on the homosexual
bars is intensified. The closing of a bar tends to pacify the
public demand for action, and makes it appear that the administration is doing a fine job of cleaning up the city. Much
of the evidence gathered in the constant police surveillance
of the bars is held in abeyance until political expediency requires it. The bar owners, aware of the shifting patterns of
police pressure, often have a fairly good idea of when the
"heat" will be most intense.

In the final analysis, little is resolved in the contest between
the gay bars and the police, but important latent functions
emerge from the situation. The homosexual collectivity develops a greater unity, its societal position is brought to
public attention, and it gains support and sympathy from
some sectors of the larger society. On the other hand, those
so inclined may vicariously vent their feelings of hostility
toward the homosexual group.

OPENING AND CLOSING OF THE BARS

A gay bar does not develop by accident; it is the result of
careful and systematic planning. Homosexuals rarely infiltrate
an already established bar and make it their own; a gay
bar is gay from the beginning. Opening such a bar is a
calculated risk; the owner is virtually assured of many
customers and a good income, but his successful enterprise is
apt to be short-lived.

The most important factor to be considered in opening a
gay bar is attracting the type of clientele desired. This again
is not a matter of chance. The location of the bar determines

its clientele to some extent, but the personal characteristics of the owner and his employees are most significant.

The gay bars of San Francisco comprise a closely knit social system. The individual bars may open and close rapidly and regularly, but the system and its participants remain the same. As familiar bars close and new ones replace them, the employees and customers move in a steady flow from one to another. In this shifting system, a particular owner may have operated several bars, and a particular bartender may have been employed in a dozen. These individuals become well known in the Community and acquire personal "followings." The character of a bar often reflects the personality of its owner, and will attract a certain type of customer as a result. According to the president of the LCE:

> I think the owner's personality makes a lot of difference. That's another thing about San Francisco gay bars that's different from anywhere else in the country. The owner is always around, and everyone who goes to the bar knows him by name. That really puts a stamp on a place, and you either like it or you don't. There are only three major bars whose owners live out of town, and any gay person could tell you which ones they are. Take Bill out at the ——, for example, he puts everything he has into that bar, and he's a wonderful guy. They only serve beer there, but it's packed every night. It's a matter of the owner's personality, Bill never lets anyone feel he doesn't belong.

The personality of the bartender is even more important than that of the owner in drawing a particular group or type of customer. A successful bartender attracts a personal following, a large number of people who come to a bar because he is employed there. It may be his personality, his looks, his wit, or his style that brings the customers, but whatever it is, he becomes the bar's most valuable asset. If a bartender with a large following leaves one bar and goes to work in another, his retinue usually accompanies him. The services of the most popular bartenders, known to everyone in the homosexual Community, are sought by many owners. A classified advertisement to this effect appeared in the *LCE News:* "Bartender—Liquor bar, must be experienced and either have a following or the personality to build a follow-ing."[6]

The gay world is one marked by a galaxy of social types, each one comprising a sub-group within the Community. Often a bar will cater to one particular sub-group, and the bartender will be representative of its social type. For example, one bar will be known as a "leather bar,"[7] where the customers are the exaggeratedly masculine type, sporting motorcycle jackets and boots. Another bar may be popular with the effeminate "queens." The bartender has an important symbolic function, serving as a mark of identification. One swift glance at the bartender, and the initiate knows what kind of a bar he is in and what kind of people he is likely to find there. The bartender in the leather bar will be a rough looking individual, dressed accordingly; in the "faggot"[8] bar, the person mixing the drinks does so with a limp wrist. A female behind the bar indicates a primarily Lesbian clientele. The same applies to more subtle distinctions; in the discreet gilt and mahogany bars of the financial district, the bartenders wear black ties and speak with Oxford accents; in the neighborhood bars, slacks and sport shirts are the rule.

Someone who intends to open a gay bar may intentionally try to attract a particular sub-group, hoping to reduce competition by catering to those other bars exclude. This goal is accomplished by hiring a bartender who personifies the sub-group's social type.

There aren't many faggot bars in town, really, mainly because no one can stand to have them around. Also because most of them aren't old enough to drink. So Carl opened the ——, as a coffee place. It's full of them, running around like a bunch of crazy parrots. That bartender has got fingernails long enough to reach across the bar. I don't know if it'll stay that way long though, it's so near ——'s that that crowd, the general gay crowd, may start going there for coffee after closing time.

Once a bar's character has been established and a suitable bartender installed, a regular clientele builds up and becomes its own attraction. One goes to a particular bar because his friends meet there, or because he is "cruising" that night and wants a "butch"[9] bar.

Occasionally the process of invasion and succession occurs, and one group begins to frequent a bar which was the stronghold of another or which was merely "gay" and catered to no particular sub-group. In this case, the owner may make it clear that he does not care for the new patronage or he may change the "identity" of the bar. The latter is done quite simply; he hires a new bartender. A respondent outlined the history of a bar with a distinctly protean character.

It's in transition now, I guess it always has been. They've had more trouble down there, and none of it their fault. It was a leather bar, and then somebody started pushing pills, which always seems to bring Hell's Angels.[10] They're not very popular anywhere, so the owner hired a real faggot. That got the motorcycle boys out, and for a while it was all swish. Then the hustlers moved in, and there was a lot of that going on, so they closed for a while. A new owner has it now, and it's a nice place. Some of the girls are going there now, it's mostly a mixed crowd.

A grand opening almost always launches a new bar into the gay world. This usually means a party, with gifts and prizes, entertainment, and food and drinks either gratis or greatly reduced in price. Members of the Community are advised of the event through various channels. If the owner is well known, it is likely that his future plans are also, and the opening of his new bar will be eagerly anticipated. If a popular bartender is to be employed at a new bar, his following will certainly be present at the opening, and his friends will bring their friends. In some instances, the owner will send announcements of the opening to members of the Community, a procedure described by the president of the Mattachine Society as follows:

Someone may decide to open a bar, and he sends out announcements to everyone on a gay mailing list. There are several of these around, I have one—not the Mattachine membership list; that's confidential, but one of people I know who go to the bars. The owners get them by having guest books where people sign, or by selling tickets to things, on which people put their names and addresses, or just by knowing a lot of people. Often people ask to be put on mailing lists. I have about 900 names on mine. Then the bar sends printed announcements, and offers a party or a special price on drinks, or something similar to attract customers.

Ecological Factors

The location of a bar is another important factor in determining the nature of its clientele. The bar situated in one of the residential areas will almost always be a neighborhood bar, which those who live nearby use as a social meeting place. Unless the owner or bartender is particularly well known or the bar has a unique attraction, its business will be limited primarily to those who live within a short distance. It is this type of neighborhood bar which most often performs extra services for its patrons, such as taking messages, lending money, or providing a bottle of milk for the cat.

Bars in the outlying areas of the city, away from the main business and entertainment districts, are not as unified in character. For the most part, however, they too have a club-like atmosphere, and often cater to those who come to the city from other parts of the Bay Area or to a particular group of city residents who have adopted it as their own.

Several bars are located in the Tenderloin district of San Francisco, and several others in the industrial section and its adjacent waterfront. The nature of these bars varies widely, and they include some which serve the sub-groups within the Community. In general, they tend to be large and rather impersonal places, where people come for entertainment, to "cruise," or for a change of scenery.

Bars are often intentionally situated in a particular area or type of area, in order to draw a desired clientele.

It's not going to have any alcohol at all, just dinners and short-orders, from eight until four in the morning. It's near the —— and ——, so it'll get those people after the bars close. What she [the owner] wants most are the bartenders, after they get off work. I think they'll come, they want a clean place where they can unwind after work. They're a particular group, and if they like it, it'll go.

I'm going to have it out along the avenues, not near the downtown area. A nice quiet bar, just beer and wine and maybe some games and singing. I don't want anyone there who might make trouble. If it's out there, I think the Sausalito crowd will come.

Patrons go to a specific bar for a specific purpose, and a bar's locale may be an important factor in determining the purpose for which it is used.

Bars where everyone knows everyone else are hard to cruise in, so if that's what you have in mind, you don't go to the neighborhood bar. You want to see some new faces, and you don't want your sisters[11] coming up and slapping you on the back and saying "Hi Mary"[12] when you're trying to make an impression.

A big shift happens right before the bars close. If all you want is a bed partner, there's no use hanging around a bar all night waiting, so you sit around in the early hours with your friends, and maybe go find someone later on at ——'s or the ——. The big bars are always jammed right before closing time, especially on weekends. If someone doesn't make it then, maybe you'll find him in one of the coffee places that stay open all night.

The purely physical characteristics of an area also influence the nature of a bar's patronage.

A lot of how a bar gets to be a certain way or draws a certain crowd depends on the area. People with cars like to go away from around where they live, and it can depend on whether the roads between their homes and the bars are hilly, or whether there's a lot of stoplights, or if there's parking. The bars in the industrial area off Market have acres of parking after five o'clock, and the streets are empty then too, so people don't have to worry about being seen.

The internal layout of the bar is an additional factor.

The actual layout of the bar may have something to do with who goes to it, depending on what they're looking for. A well-lit place will get a different crowd than a dark place. Some of the bars in the Tenderloin have johns arranged so that there's a lot of traffic by them. A dark bar like ——'s, with long narrow passages is a paradise for the hustlers and such.

Economic Factors

In a city with a homosexual population the size of San Francisco's, a gay bar is a lucrative enterprise. To operate such an establishment is a gamble, as no gay bar lives for long, but the income one produces far exceeds that usually obtained from a "straight" bar. According to one bartender:

——'s brings in more money than any bar in the city. The only place that sells more beer is the Red Garter, and beer's all they sell there. On a week night there will always be at least 75 guys in there, and on a weekend it always reaches 250 capacity.

The probability of financial success often means that an owner will receive some assistance in opening a gay bar and need invest less of his own capital at the outset.

The gay bars are so sure to be a success that the juke box company or the beer supplier will give an owner all he needs to begin, if they know he's opening a gay bar. Or they'll pay his expenses if he gets in trouble, just so he keeps buying from them.

Thus the gay bar articulates with commercial institutions in the larger society, to the profit of both. These economic factors often outweigh the dangers inherent in an operation which borders on illegality.

Closing of the Bars

Due to its inimical relations with the police force, the gay bar has a brief life expectancy. A bar may be closed or its license revoked for any one of the many reasons previously discussed, and these legal complaints account for the highest percentage of the mortality rate. Other pressures may be brought to bear, however; the gay bar is in the path of an urban renewal project, or the Health Department finds a leaky pipe, or the neighbors complain of the noise.

The bars come and go, like a chain of lights blinking on and off over a map of the city, but the system remains constant. When a bar closes, its patrons shift their activities elsewhere. In the new bar, the same music comes out of the jukebox, the same bartenders mix drinks, the same faces appear, and the conversation repeats the same themes. And often, the same policeman is standing by the door.

PART IV

Female Homosexuality

The Lesbians: A Preliminary Overview

WILLIAM SIMON AND
JOHN H. GAGNON

All roles which are expressive of sexual activity are complex. As one might expect of any set of roles for which there is (1) little available public language, (2) a constraint upon private language, and (3) little basis for a mutual evaluation of performance even among those who are involved with each other, sexual roles lend themselves to processes of privatization more easily than do most other roles. Our imagery of what appear to be sexually active roles is heavily invested with elements of anxiety and fantasy. In contrast to roles in which sexuality appears salient, it would appear that for most conventional roles—even those for which an assumption of sexual activity can safely be made—the constraint is to view the role incumbents in largely nonsexual terms. In such roles as, for example, husband and wife, the individual's sexual commitments and activities are typically not a highly significant or remarkable feature of his public identity. However, where sexual activity is identified with a role, our sense of the dimensions of this sexual component is often widely exaggerated.

The two elements most commonly associated with the imputation of a sexually active status are apparent sexual availability and sexual deviance. To most people, the lower class, certain minority groups, a number of occupational

THIS PAPER was written especially for this book.

roles, and the female who is not linked to a conventional family role are seen as differentially available sexually and, consequently, as more sexually active. Such persons are seen as having greater sexual appetites and less self-control over these capacities. Similarly, and perhaps more understandably, persons engaging in sexually deviant practices are particularly vulnerable to creating an appearance of more extreme or intense sexuality than, in fact, is the case. Many such persons do have high rates of sexual activity or do engage in specific sexual practices that are unconventional; however, the prevailing image of such persons is less rooted in a knowledge of these actual practices than in the elements of fantasy and anxiety encouraged both by limited individual experience with, and vague or inaccurate societal definitions about, unconventional sexual behavior. This may be observed dramatically in the contrast between a popular picture of the rapist as a person who is particularly intense and deliberate in his sexuality, and the image that emerges from recent research on sex offenders reported by the staff of the Institute for Sex Research. In this research the rapist is seen as a person extending his general incompetence into the sexual area, and one who is amazingly unself-conscious and nondeliberate in his opportunism.[1]

Homosexuality, either male or female, is obviously vulnerable to such extensive complication and "enrichment" by the general public. As in the case of the rapist, homosexuals are popularly viewed as being excessively sexual. They are seen as people who willingly organize their lives to facilitate their sexuality, at least more readily than do most persons with heterosexual preferences. Finally, the homosexual is seen as indulging in a wider variety of sexual activity and this more frequently than the nonhomosexual. Much of the general apprehensiveness about the homosexual rests on what is usually a faulty assumption: that homosexuals have a lower capability in controlling their impulses than do heterosexuals. Stated differently, heterosexuals often assume that homosexuals are prepared to take greater "risks" to gain sexual gratification than are heterosexuals.

In a contrast between male and female homosexuals, it is

probable that the former perhaps have a less complicated stereotype. For male homosexuality the severity of sanctions is sufficiently strong to organize and limit the content of the general social image. The broader society is manifestly more concerned with repressing and sanctioning male homo- sexuality than with repressing and sanctioning female homo- sexuality. It is possible that the level of anxiety in the general population evoked by male homosexuality is sufficiently high to place a constraint on the direct imputation of fantasy ele- ments. The image of the female homosexual, however, is less likely to be organized by a single, strong theme; it may be more easily complicated by unmediated mixtures of anxiety and fantasy. The lesbian, despite the general negative value attached to homosexual actors, remains a potentially erotic object to heterosexual males in a way or to a degree that the male homosexual is unlikely to be defined.[2]

Thus, as we begin our consideration of aspects of female homosexuality, it is important that we be sensitive to the complexities and distortions that tend to occur in such discus- sions, even in scientific work. One potential corrective to such distortions is the refusal to make judgments about the mean- ing of specific sexual activities in isolation from the larger context of the social life of a deviant actor. This means that we must take into account the problems of managing relations with family and friends, of earning a living, of finding emo- tional and social support, and, possibly of greatest importance, of struggling (as we all do) to accept our constantly changing selves. It is possible that a broader perspective will aid us in seeing deviant behavior as less exotic, that is, in viewing it in terms of the realities of everyday existence and in ways that discourage expressions of both anxiety and fantasy.

A second corrective is to break through the simplifying process that is present whenever a human population is cate- gorized by a brief label, to treat with suspicion all presenta- tions that offer to provide us with a description and/or analy- sis of *the* homosexual or *the* lesbian. It requires no great familiarity with this topic to appreciate that a similarity in the gender of sexual object choices masks a vast amount of variation in other dimensions that are crucial to living. This is not to suggest that developing a homosexual commitment does not, by definition, have a profound impact upon behavior. Very clearly, to be a homosexual automatically places most homosexuals in a special relationship to the larger society and to the conventional patterns of moving through life cycles that characterize that society. Thus, for example, only some persons with extensive homosexual commitments will establish and maintain conventional families. However, it is clear there are many different ways of expressing homosexuality, many different ways of organizing a life and identity that include this commitment, and many different kinds of consequences of being homosexual. Indeed, there may be as many ways for a homosexual to organize his life as there are for a heterosexual, and the overlap between the two populations may be greater, in many respects, than many of us are prepared to admit.

The present paper is strongly committed to both of these corrective perspectives: viewing homosexuality in the context of general patterns of social and personal adjustment, and being sensitive to possible variety in the ways of being a female homosexual (a lesbian). At the same time, however, the paper does not pretend to be definitive or, in a strict sense, systematic in its coverage of the topic. To attempt either would require the availability of a quality of data that the scientific community does not presently possess. The best that can be meaningfully offered at this juncture is a sense of the lesbian experience, a sense of the variety of forms and styles female homosexuality may take, and a tentative attempt to seek out what might be general themes.

For the purposes of this essay a small number of female homosexuals were interviewed at considerable length. The interviewing was unstructured; the aim was not to procure quantifiable data but rather the language of some part of the experience. Though this small group was quite varied in age, social position, and social background, we can be very sure that they represent only a small part of the actual range. Thus, it is probably safe to assume that, to the degree the present effort provides a sense of diversity, it is only part of a larger diversity. In the same sense, any attempt at generalization should be taken as extremely tentative.

ON BECOMING A LESBIAN

One note that ran through all the interviews was a sense of how totally feminine was the mode of discovery or entry into a homosexual career. One of the strongest findings to emerge from the initial research of Kinsey and his associates was the relatively early development of sexuality among males and the striking contrast this had to the experience of females.[3] Clearly, the organizing event in male sexuality is puberty, while the organizing event for females is that period of romantic involvement that culminates for most in marriage. For males, then, a commitment to sexuality, or at a minimum, the reinforcing experience of orgasm, occurs early in adolescence and for females late in adolescence or in the early adult years. One might say that for females the "discovery" of love relations precedes the "discovery" of sexuality while the reverse is generally true for males. For the lesbians we interviewed this appears as a rather consistent pattern. The discovery of their homosexuality usually occurred very late in adolescence, often even in the years of young adulthood, and the actual commencement of overt sexual behavior frequently came as a late stage of an intense emotional involvement. Indeed, in many instances their first emotional attachment, which began to generate in them a recognition of their special sexual inclination, involved only the most preliminary forms of sexual activity, unmarked by anything as unambiguously sexual as genital contact.

This romantic drift into sexual behavior was typified by one lesbian who described the beginning of her first homosexual affair in the following way:

The fall after graduation from high school I started at [a residential school]. I met a girl there who was extremely attractive. She had a good sense of humor and I was drawn to her because I liked to laugh. Many of the girls used to sit around in the evenings and talk. As our friendship grew, our circle narrowed and narrowed until it got to be three or four of us who would get together at night and talk. Then there was only three. Then two— us. And maybe after a couple of months of this our relationship developed into something more. Starting out by simply kissing. Later petting. That type of thing. It didn't actually involve overt sexuality [genital contact] until February.

Clearly, for the woman in question there was only a vague sense of what was associated with such behavior. There was little awareness of what a lesbian is and what she does.

[When was the first time you began to talk about yourself using terms like "lesbian" or "homosexual"?] Even when I was involved with her for five or six months, we didn't talk about it. We didn't give ourselves names. We spoke about how much we cared for one another. But we didn't discuss it. I may have thought it, but I don't know.

A second lesbian described a situation that was very similar. In this case there actually was some mild homosexual play during mid-adolescence, though with no apparent recognition of a homosexual inclination.

It was at home with my cousin. It was like a game we played in bed at night. It really wasn't, to the fullest extent, sex. It was caressing, fondling. It was, as I said, something we did last night . . . we never talked about it.

However, her strongest emotional attachment was to come several years later. Between the first relation with the cousin and this second attachment, there was no sexual involvement, and the second "affair" was itself overtly sexual only to a limited degree.

We met at the [a residential hotel for women]. We started out just being friends and then it became something special. She taught me a lot of things. I love music and she taught me how to listen to it and appreciate it. She liked things I liked, like walking. We read a lot together. We read the Bible, we read verses to each other. We shared things together. We caressed each other and kissed. I think it was a need to have someone there. And I was there and she was there and we just held on to each other. *[Did you ever become sexually involved on a more physical level?]* Not to the fullest and when I say not to the fullest extent I mean we didn't take off our clothes and lie in the nude with each other. I enjoyed being with her. I got something from her without going through the actions of sex.

Yet, although the young woman in question went on to become involved in several overt homosexual affairs, the above-described relationship and the woman involved became, for her, a model of what an ideal relationship and love object should be like.

It is not uncommon for lesbians to report that the realization of their own homosexuality appeared early in adolescence or even during childhood. Typically, one lesbian reported an acute "shock of recognition" upon encountering a dictionary definition of homosexuality during very early adolescence. Another reported a sense of tentative recognition in childhood.

I always had this fantasy about being a cowboy or Robin Hood. And then I realized they always had a girl friend, a Maid Marian. So in my fantasies I began to have my girl friends.

However, the amount of existential distortion in such recall remains an unknown quantity. One must remember that such retrospection occurs after an identity has been refashioned to contain an active homosexual component, and that it is not uncolored by an understandable desire to establish a sense of continuity with the past.

What is interesting in both these cases of early recognition (as was true for others like them) is that active involvement in sexual behavior did not occur until the subjects were in their early twenties. For them, apparently, a commitment to a socially deviant choice of sexual objects was not a necessary, immediate stimulus to alienation from other socially ordered aspects of sexual career management. Most lesbians, apparently, are not exempt from the constraints and norms that regulate the development of female sexuality in general. This appears to be particularly true of the timing or phasing of entry into active sexual roles, as well as of the quality of relationships required to facilitate that entry.

While the pattern described above has the suggestion of modality, in this—as in most things—human behavior is complex and tends to present itself as a range. One does encounter modes of entry that were immediately sexual and that occurred earlier in adolescence. In one case, though there are surely numerous others, early homosexual activity was associated with sexually segregated, institutional arrangements. Such environments have historically been charged with generating unusually high proportions of homosexuals. One might keep in mind, however, that the operating mechanism may involve more than little opportunity for heterosexual activity; a question to be considered is the alienative effects of the process that brings the adolescent girl to this type of institution in the first place.

Our limited number of interviews yielded only one example of a young woman who actively sought a test of her lesbian impulses.

I've had these tendencies ever since I can remember. In high school I'd look at this or that girl and I'd have the desire to talk to her, get to know her better. I was never aroused by just any girl, I always had to have a special attraction to her. I just didn't want her, I'd want her to want me. I didn't want to be the aggressive one. . . . I started dating boys when I was twelve and a half and just stopped a month ago. I had light petting when I was thirteen or fourteen, I had intercourse when I was sixteen or seventeen. I'm not a tramp or anything. I don't like having sex with a guy, I just did it to cooperate when they got too pushy. I've never enjoyed it, I never had an orgasm with a guy. [How did your homosexuality become sexual?] Through this guy I was going with. He wasn't satisfying me and so I told him how I felt. That I had this attraction for girls. I heard that there were lesbian bars and I told him I wanted him to take me to one so I could find out if this was what I wanted. And he went along with it thinking that after I found out I might go back to guys. So he asked a friend who knew about these things and got an address. He took me there and left me. I met a girl there and went home with her.

The number of homosexual careers characterized by an experience comparable to this is hard to determine. We suspect that the proportion may not be too large, perhaps no larger than the proportion who have as extensive a history of sexual activity during adolescence as did this girl. What might be necessary, in order to be able to articulate a sexual need as this young woman did, is the deinhibition that often follows extensive sexual activity.

Curiously, the experiences that follow for this respondent fell into an essentially feminine pattern despite the seemingly "masculine" and detached character of her pursuit of the lesbian experience. In short succession she had brief contact with three females, all of whom left her as unsatisfied as did her previous encounters with men. It was only the fourth contact, which had a more extended and intense emotional content, that provided the respondent with her first, positive sociosexual experience as well as her first orgasm. Possibly, the process of development that constrains the female in our society to become trained in the rhetoric of love prior to the rhetoric of sex can be discarded only with a more total rejection of feminine identification than most lesbians are capable of.

What was missing in the interviews was one of the most popular representations of the introduction into homosexuality provided us by modern fiction: seduction by an older woman. While there were some instances in which the initial partner was an older woman, in most cases there was advance evidence of movement away from conventional heterosexual patterns. In several of these cases the older woman was the object of seduction rather than the seductress. This is not to say that this cannot occur. There is the likely possibility that we missed lesbians for whom seduction by an older woman was the mode of entry into homosexuality and, more importantly, the cause of detachment from more conventional patterns, but the size of such a group is probably not very large. The real social importance of the image of the older seductress, an imagery providing the basis for many popular "explanations" of the "causes" of homosexual behavior, lies in its function of reducing a sense of guilt and shame. Suddenly, as the image of the corrupt and corrupting seducer appears on the scene, the need to examine relationships and processes closer to home is considerably reduced.

THE ROOTS OF FEMALE HOMOSEXUALITY

As has already been suggested, a great concern to identify and label the sources that supposedly induce homosexuality is reinforced by its guilt- and anxiety-reducing function. Such explanations allow the homosexual to counter societal rejection and the inevitable and terribly cruel sense of self-rejection with an "it's not my fault" posture. Explanations postulating a biological accident or a seduction allow parents of homosexuals to avoid the unanswerable question—"What did I do wrong?" In a society in which the repression of the homosexual is most commonly punitive and nonrational, there is a requirement to view the behavior as pathological, and out of this interest in causation arise a number of proposed pseudorational cures and preventatives.

Clearly, understanding the sources of homosexual behavior is possible on some ultimate level, and it is surely very important, if only for what might be learned about general human behavior in the process. However, it is our feeling that a better understanding of these behavior sources will reveal a complex, multivariate process in which there is great variation in the combination of attributes that produce similar outcomes. What is most important is to avoid the frequently made assumption that even extensive knowledge of the processes that initiate a homosexual commitment will provide substantial knowledge about how a homosexual career will be enacted. Implicit in such an assumption is the belief that subsequent homosexual behavior will represent, to a significant degree, a reenactment of the originating circumstances. Such assumptions seem to be unwarranted, for the factors that initiate a homosexual career, indeed any career, remain only a part of a series of elements in a dynamic and variable process. This is a theme which will be returned to later.

Much of the literature on the lesbian, particularly the psychiatric literature, emphasizes the quality of life in childhood when crucial sex-role distinctions are learned, and places a special emphasis upon the significance of parent-child and/or parent-parent relations which appear to impinge upon this development.[4] In this small group of lesbian interviews two factors emerged with noteworthy consistency. First, about half of the women reported that their parental homes were broken either by death, divorce, or separation. Second, although our discussion of group attributes should not be interpreted as hard statistics based upon an unbiased sample, it was particularly impressive that in almost every case there was a strongly expressed preference toward one of the parents, and attitudes toward the other parent or substitute parent ranged from condescending neutrality to open hostility. However, the preference for the male or female parent was almost equally divided.

Thus, some described their parents in the following way:

If I never had to see him [father] again, I wouldn't mind one bit. . . . I remember when I was a kid I caught my parents fooling around. It made me sick. I hated my father for touching my mother.

Another described her stepfather as follows:

I was five when my mother asked me if I cared if she married him. He wasn't a threat to me. I ruled the roost when I was five and I have since. It wasn't because I was spoiled. If I did something wrong, I was spanked for it by my mother. And when I was young, by my uncles. But I never thought much of him as a man and neither did my mother. My mother couldn't look to him to do the things other men did. She'd either do it or have me do it. There was nothing wrong with my stepfather, but she wouldn't think of asking him because he always whined or cried if she asked him. *[Discussing her stepfather's reaction to the disclosure of her homosexuality.]* My father, I don't know, you could call him dense, but homosexuality—or almost anything—they don't seem to register.

On the other hand, others' descriptions of relations with parental figures took a totally different cast:

I lived with my grandmother 'til I was ten and then I went to live with my father. My mother was a surgical nurse and was constantly on call and couldn't take care of the kids. I feel pretty close to my father. We liked to go fishing together, build things like bookcases. We get along, but we both have tempers.

Or:

Mother was sick a lot of the time. She was just there. Someone to be taken care of.

While it is evident that extreme relations with parental figures in any direction appear to predispose individuals to deviant patterns, the same predisposing factors are equally evident in many families that do not produce homosexuals. Clearly, the term to be underscored is "predisposing." The question simply stated then becomes: such predisposing factors, plus what, lead to lesbian commitments? And this is a question that is not likely to be answered in any comprehensive way in the near future.

A second approach to the roots of homosexuality is found in a listing of physical, genetic, or hormonal "faults." Within the limits of currently available research findings, there is little to suggest that homosexual populations can be differentiated from heterosexual ones on these characteristics.[5] The only marked biological difference for the lesbian group interviewed was that a large number began menstruation earlier or later than most girls with whom they were growing up. None reported difficulty with menstruation. Among those who felt they were late in arriving at menarche, most reported a sense of relief at now sharing the experience of their peers. Like unconventional family situations or attachments, the out-of-phase onset of menstruation appears not to link specifically with a homosexual adaptation, but rather to a tendency to experience alienation from modal development and socialization processes.

Linked to this interest in physical explanation is another argument about the sources of female homosexuality, one that is difficult to take seriously. This argument states that female homosexuals are really heterosexual rejects; more simply stated, the lesbian becomes such because she is not sufficiently attractive to "make out" as a woman. Our own experience runs contrary to this. Few of the women interviewed were in any sense obviously homosexual (whatever that might mean), over-masculine, or physically ugly. Though there is a great deal of subjectivity involved, the interviewers' opinion was that, as a group, the women tended to appear feminine.

Another line of explanation involves social rejection and holds that the crucial factor involved is an inability to manage conventional social relationships successfully, a kind of social ineptitude that leads individuals to seek a more supportive social milieu. Experiences exemplifying this possibility were noticeable in several of the interviews. One, for example, described herself in adolescence in the following way:

I was unhappy, unsure of myself socially, though not intellectually. I wore braces and had acne. My sister, who was ten years older, was quite beautiful. I was always the other daughter. Following behind her in school, I got used to the expression of disbelief that followed when teachers realized that I was her sister.

Or in another case:

I was the original clumsy dolt. If there was anything to break, I would break it. I was too large to manage. I couldn't say the right things. After a while, I was just scared all the time. And that just made it worse.

On the other hand, another lesbian reported:

My high school years were very happy simply because I was active in so many things. President of this and a member of that. I went to many parties. I was in charge of many functions. Being active, having lots of friends, being smiled upon by the gods because I was also an honor student, which wasn't difficult for me, and I was happy.

However, this latter kind of report was relatively rare. Most described some moderate amount of social activity during school; very few could be described as isolates. The essential factor that appeared to be emerging was an estrangement from conventional heterosexual social involvement which was beginning to flower among their peers.

Almost all the women reported some heterosexual dating and mild sex play during their high school years. Only two carried it to the extent of intercourse, although a larger

number indicated that they had experimented with heterosexual coitus after homosexual experiences. The sense of difference seemed in most cases to precede their withdrawal from
conventional social life rather than the reverse. The young
woman who reported such a happy period during her high
school years, in describing dating activity during that same
period, already begins to foreshadow an eventual departure
from that happy world.

It was when I was fifteen or so, the sophomore or junior year.
That's when everyone really started dating. I had a very close
friend. It was very traumatic for me at the time. We had gone to
junior high and through the freshman year together very intimately.
We shared everything, did everything together. And then, in our
sophomore year, she began going steady with this boy. And then
it hit me. You know, all of a sudden she wasn't around anymore.
This boy friend was a good friend of mine and he said to me this
buddy of his wanted me to go out, the four of us to go out. I didn't
particularly want to go, but I'd just go so I could be with my
friend. After a while I did go out. I dated as much, if not more,
than the other girls. I enjoyed going out to an athletic thing or to
dances because I like to dance. But as far as the boys were concerned, I wasn't interested like the other girls were interested. You
know, looking for someone to care for or marry. At that time, they
were thinking about things like that.

Lastly, we might consider the causal explanation that attributes a corrupting influence to literary representations of
deviant behavior. Generally, there is scant evidence that literature serves as a crucial triggering mechanism for deviant
sexual tendencies. In only two cases did respondents report
reading about lesbian behavior prior to becoming overtly
homosexual. For one young lady such reading apparently had
little consequence, since her homosexual experiences were not
to begin for some five or more years; she remembered it as
merely "a trashy sex novel where the beautiful girl is rescued
from an evil lesbian by being made love to by a 'real' man."
In the second case, *The Well of Loneliness* was read by one
lesbian while in her late teens.

As I look back now, it really is a silly book. But then . . . it was like an explosion. I had had these strange feelings for a long time and then to discover that I wasn't the only one in the world like that.

Even though extensive reading is absent from the early histories of the lesbians interviewed, almost all had later read extensively in the available "lesbian literature." But once again the pattern of general adult reading resembles that reported by Kinsey for females as a group, that is, relatively limited sexual arousal from literature.[6]

ON BEING IN THE "COMMUNITY"

For both male and female homosexuals one can talk about the existence of a community, at least in most relatively large cities. As for many ethnic or occupational groups, which also can be said to have a community, this subcommunity does not require a formal character or even a specific geographical location. It is, rather, a continuing collectivity of individuals who share some significant activity and who, out of a history of continuing interaction based on that activity, begin to generate a sense of a bounded group possessing special norms and a particular argot. Through extensive use such a homosexual aggregate may identify a particular location as "theirs," and in almost all large cities this includes one or more taverns that cater exclusively to a particular homosexual group. In these bars the homosexual may more freely act out his self-definition as compared with less segregated situations. Recently, several homophile social and service organizations have appeared, which offer a more public image of the homosexual. These various kinds of social activity reinforce a feeling of identity and provide for the homosexual a way of institutionalizing the experience, wisdom, and mythology of the collectivity. A synonym for this community, one not untouched by a sense of the ironic, is the "gay life."

For the individual homosexual the community provides many functions. A major function is the facilitation of sexual union; the lesbian who finds her way to the community can now select from a population that, while differing in other attributes, has the minimum qualification of sharing a lesbian commitment. This greatly reduces what is for the isolated lesbian the common risk of "falling for a straight girl," i.e., a heterosexual. The community provides a source of social support; it is a place where the lesbian can express her feelings or describe her experiences because there are others available who have had feelings and experiences very much like them. It is an environment in which one can socialize one's sexuality and find ways of deriving sexual gratification by being admired, envied, or desired, while not necessarily engaging in sexual behavior. Lastly, the community includes a language and an ideology which provide each individual lesbian with already developed attitudes that help her resist the societal claim that she is diseased, depraved, or shameful.

While all the lesbians interviewed were part of a community to one degree or other, a larger proportion of lesbians avoid such communities than is the case for male homosexuals. This possibly occurs because the lesbian has less need for the community, since her homosexuality is not as immediately alienating from the conventional society. The lesbian may mask her sexual deviance behind a socially prepared asexuality. Not all categories of women in our society are necessarily defined as sexually active, as, for example, the spinster. In line with this, the image of two spinsters living together does not immediately suggest sexual activity between them, even when considerable affection is displayed. The same is not true for men. The bachelor is presumed to be even more sexually active than the married man, and the idea of two males past young adulthood rooming together strikes one as strange indeed. It is possible that the same techniques of repression that lead to differences between males and females in age of initiating sexual activity also allow the female to handle later sexual deprivation more easily. More female homosexuals than male homosexuals, then, should be able to resist quasi-public homosexual behavior that increases the risk of disclosure, as well as resist relations that involve only sexual exchange without any emotional investment.

One lesbian, who had previously avoided the community

(during a long period of heterosexual marriage followed by a period of no sexual activity) and now was involved with the community only on a fairly marginal basis, expressed resistance to "the gay life" and its tendency to reinforce lesbian commitments at the expense of greater alienation from conventional society.

No, I didn't consider myself part of the gay world and I consider myself fortunate. *[Why?]* From what I've seen of the gay world, not the elite, but kids who hang around the bars get too . . . involved. Particularly the young girls. It drains all of her energy, all of her time, and her money. I see an awful lot of girls who have a lot of potential and ability which has never been used and will probably never be used because they waste all those good years. They hang around the bars and just because they're homosexual the gay life becomes everything.

Another lesbian, who had spent eight years defining herself as a homosexual and had experienced three fairly long homosexual affairs before she encountered the homosexual community, represented one of the positive aspects of the community. She came initially from a working-class background and had previously worked at a fairly low status, semiskilled occupation. Her affairs, initiated largely on the basis of adventitious meetings, were conducted with the most limited awareness of other lesbians and with lovers who were drawn essentially from similar social backgrounds. Entry into the gay world for this young woman provided her the first sustained interaction across social-class lines. The very salience of sexuality provided a basis for her transcending many social barriers in this community. In rather short order her aspirations in many other areas of life began to rise. She became dissatisfied with her present occupation and started training for one that paid more, possessed higher prestige, and required greater skill. Her commitments to art, music, and eating, and the very style of her life began a rapid transformation. Clearly, for some persons the homosexual community represents a new kind of opportunity structure, while for others it is a resource that is paid for by withdrawal from the larger community.

WOMEN WITHOUT MEN

The most common image of the lesbian is probably that of a pseudomale, a female who, in her biological inability to be a male, is a caricature of maleness. This is the denotation that stands behind that hackneyed word "dyke." There are a few lesbians for whom a masculine identification is terribly important, and for some it manifests itself as transvestism (wearing of male clothing). This need for adopting a masculine self-image or playing a masculine role emerges from very shadowy origins, and, if little is known about the etiology of homosexuality in general, still less is known about this phenomenon. Where transvestism appears, it is associated with a feeling of alienation that leaves few viable connections with conventional social life, although the language of cause and effect somehow seems out of place. A great intensity of feeling and a quality of overdetermination are other distinguishing characteristics of this commitment, both of which may justify labeling the behavior compulsive in a way that is not justified in describing most lesbians.

The polarity of sexual roles, which is part of the content of sexual learning for the lesbian as well as everyone else in our society, has fundamental consequences for such a woman who is now involved in homosexuality. It is this tendency of the lesbian to model her experiences on heterosexuality that produces such role categories as "butch" (the supposed male-husband surrogate in the lesbian relationship who is the more aggressive, controlling, managerial, money-making, etc.) and the "fem" (the female-wife surrogate with an attendant attention to feminine attributes and activities). The very existence of these role categories in the homosexual community's argot results in an uncritical acceptance of their validity both by the homosexual world and by heterosexual outsiders. Indeed, the importance of the continuing value of the terms may lie more in their clarification of the structure of interaction in the community than in guiding any of the members of the community itself as they interact with persons they already know.

While, as suggested, few lesbians become committed to this totally masculine role as a near-permanent life style, many more lesbians may experiment with this kind of strategy for a short period, particularly during the identity crisis that occurs at the time of the first self-admission of a deviant sexual commitment or at entry into the culture of the homosexual community. During this early phase of career development, it is not unlikely that many lesbians overreact because they are still imbued with the essentially heterosexual language of their earlier socialization and think of themselves as an accident of nature: a man trapped in a woman's body. Such a self-conception surely helps in reducing uncertainty and in creating the necessary distance from previous and less viable identities. At this extremely crucial moment of transition overidentification with masculinity helps the deviant to reduce dissonance.

Another reason that this role style may be attractive for short periods is the obviousness of the style. This obviousness becomes helpful to the newly "turned out" lesbian, who may not yet have become adept at other styles of handling sociosexual relations. One young lesbian commented:

For instance, when I first got into the gay world with the first girl, there was no butch or fem. We didn't know, though I was slightly more aggressive. *[In making love?]* No, I mean in taking care of things, managing, planning. When we made love, there was a kind of flow, a sharing. So I eventually came out in the gay world as kind of butch. Mostly because I felt you had to be somewhere. Later, if someone asked, I said I was butch, but mostly because I didn't want any of these bull dykes coming to me.

Almost all of the women we interviewed saw themselves as women who wanted to become emotionally and sexually attached to another woman who would, in turn, respond to them as a woman. This was expressed rather clearly by a lesbian who thought of herself as being classified as a "fem."

[Do you have a preference as to active or passive role?] For me it would be reciprocal. But among the gay people I know, I guess I am classified as fem. Probably because I'm not the aggressive type. I don't go around asking girls to dance—I can't lead

for one thing. *[Do you prefer girls who are butch or fem?]* That's
hard to say. I think that most of the girls that I have been attracted
to were also attractive to men, some of them very much so. Also,
there has to be some community of interests so that there is
something to talk about. A way of seeing things the same way.

Another young woman, whose first two lesbian contacts were
both "butch" types, commented:

They didn't like me to touch them, or anything. They had to
do everything. Just like most men, but if that's what you want, you
might as well go "straight."

Despite what we feel to be an essentially feminine quality
that pervades the sexual commitments of most lesbians, there
is often a distinct masculine aspect to lesbian life. What is
deceptive is that many of these masculine elements arise from
nonsexual sources and have nonsexual roots that are missed
because one is dealing with a specifically homosexual population. One such partial, nonsexual explanation is offered by
Simone de Beauvoir in her discussion of the lesbian in *The
Second Sex*.[7] There she observes that the descriptive phrase
"women without men" has a literal meaning beyond just
describing sexual behavior. When they abandon the social
route that for the majority of women culminates in heterosexual marriage, most lesbians must take responsibility for a
whole range of activities and skills that ordinarily fall to the
male in the family.

A quasi-masculine appearance also insulates the lesbian
from the relations that create demands she either cannot or
does not desire to accept. One young lesbian, who is both
feminine and attractive in appearance, described the dysfunc-
tions of her femininity at work in the following way:

At work all the people are "straight" [heterosexual], and I have
to put on this big scene of being heterosexual. And I don't like
putting on fronts. But the men who come in like to flirt and expect
me to flirt back. If I could just tell everyone that I'm homosexual,
I wouldn't have to put on this big front, but everyone won't accept
it.

In considering this insulation function of a nonfeminine presentation of self, it is important to remember that it need not

be considered by all persons as indicative of homosexuality; it can also be defined merely as asexuality.

Another aspect of this question of the style of self-presentation involves the lesbian community. For lesbians who are involved in the community, there may exist a constraint to appear less feminine than many of them might individually be in a free choice situation. In the community context, uniform or recognizable styles of dress or presentation quickly establish group membership and heighten the sense of group solidarity.

UNIVERSAL PROBLEMS

Family

One thing of which we may be fairly certain is that parents do not deliberately raise their children to be homosexuals, for in all known societies adult homosexuality is an undesirable outcome of the child-rearing process. Nonetheless, homosexuals do emerge from families, and no matter how unusual or strained the family may have been, the homosexual is confronted with the same problem that everyone faces upon becoming an adult, that is, working out some relationship with his parental family so that his new self-definition may be expressed. The mere fact that a commitment has been made to a deviant sexual pattern that limits the possibilities of realizing some of the conventional parental expectations, such as getting married and having children, makes this transition more difficult for the lesbian. However, there is no indication that the distribution of solutions to this dilemma for the lesbian population differs substantially from those adopted by heterosexuals. At the same time it must be acknowledged that substantial strains on more specific levels do occur.

For a small proportion of the lesbians we talked to, family connections were minimal. This severing of family ties varied between rejection of the lesbian by the family, rejection of the family by the lesbian, or a mutual rejection. But this was the case for few, and in most instances some partial family ties were maintained, if only through one sympathetic

member. This was typified by one lesbian who described her
family relations in the following way:

> The only one I see is my brother and his wife. At least once a
> month I will go and have dinner with them. Their children are
> always glad to see me and I am very fond of them. They know,
> but we don't talk about it. Once I brought a girl friend along,
> but it seemed to create too much embarrassment. I am sure,
> though, if I were ever in trouble, they would come through for
> me. We don't talk about them [parents and another brother] often.
> Even though it's been a long time, it still hurts.

So, while cases like this one appear and while it is evident
that homosexuality played an important role in the rupturing
of family ties, there are numerous instances in a general population where family ties are ruptured over factors having
nothing to do with sexual deviance.

Some larger proportion of lesbians manage this problem
by masking their homosexual activity from all or almost all
family members and seem to cope with family relations fairly
well. One commented:

> Once mother accepted the fact that I didn't want to live at home
> and that I wasn't going to get married, it worked out very well.
> I talk to them about once a week and go out every few weeks.
> My girl friend comes along and she gets along very well with
> the family. Mother, particularly, is pleased that I have such a
> well-educated and refined roommate. I am sure that she doesn't
> know. I don't think mother or father can conceive of something
> like homosexuality.

Frequently, parents suspect, or even know, but decide to
ignore the possibility or the fact of lesbianism. In one case
it was quite clear that the mother was fully cognizant of her
daughter's sexual preference, since it was the reason for the
daughter's expulsion from a school. However, following that
event no further reference was made to lesbian activity. Indeed, in most families where there is knowledge or partial
knowledge there is avoidance of the issue. In relatively few
cases, perhaps as few as those involving complete rejection,
there is full knowledge and an open, casual acceptance.

What should be clear is that there is no one pattern of

family adjustment for the lesbian, particularly not one predicated exclusively around the fact of lesbianism. There are satisfying family relations and unsatisfying ones, relations that are disruptive for the individual lesbian and those which are highly supportive, relations of intimacy and of distance, and relations where the family simply is not a very significant factor. The tendency for strain is evident. For example, in a large number of cases the disclosure to parents of her homosexual commitment was made by the lesbian as a manifestly aggressive and hostile act directed toward one or both parents. The pattern of alienation that we commented upon in our earlier discussion suggests that in many instances disordered family patterns can be observed; however, these family problems might be best understood in terms of general approaches to the study of the family rather than in terms of a special theory organized around the concept of homosexuality.

Earning a Living

Most lesbians are confronted with the problem of earning a living. When a woman foregoes the conventional path where her husband would perform this role, labor-force participation becomes much more salient. In some cases it is this more serious involvement with work that adds to the public misconception of the masculine character of lesbians, for, in our society, work still predominantly remains in the masculine sphere. There is, of course, a problem that all women who take work seriously, homosexual and heterosexual alike, must face, for too often the assumption is made that working women are imperfect females.

One lesbian who worked at a fairly skilled job wrote in a British lesbian publication describing her sense of frustration at constantly being passed over for promotion by men who she felt were no more competent than she. This woman understood that the judgment was being made that most women are only temporarily involved in the world of work, and that there is little point in training them for higher positions, since they ultimately marry and withdraw from full labor-force participation. She commented that she wants to tell her superiors that she is a lesbian and unlikely to marry, but her desire to do so is curbed by her anticipation of the firm's reaction to her sexual preference.

Most lesbians, then, appear to be more seriously committed to work than most women. Reflecting this, they tend to have relatively stable work histories. Most movement between jobs is associated with an upgrading of jobs. Some lesbians, to be sure, display extremely erratic work histories, and this is frequently associated with difficulties in managing personal and sexual relations. One commented:

> When I broke up with ——, things just went to hell. I must have had six different jobs in less than a year. Just when things were settling down, I met ——. Off on the merry-go-round I went. Nothing seemed to matter, just being with her. Then I realized that she was supporting me and that was a drain on the relationship.

Other lesbians are persons with a very limited commitment to the world of work, who might be termed highly dependent. Such lesbians, however, may not differ in many respects from their heterosexual counterparts who find in marriage many of the supports for their dependency needs. Parenthetically, this relatively small proportion of highly dependent lesbians may be "overrepresented" in both lay and professional views because these women are among the most likely to seek therapy and the most likely to participate in the visible part of the homosexual community. As a consequence, they help sustain the "fem" motif in the "butch-fem" polarization of female homosexuality; such a view is, of course, a caricature of heterosexual relations. It would appear that, for whatever reasons, lesbians with disordered work patterns constitute a minority of all female homosexuals. Knowing what we do about the problems associated with adopting a deviant social role, we should not be surprised to observe that some part of a lesbian population has this kind of difficulty; rather we might better be surprised at the number who appear to function well in the world of work.

A significant factor in the work adjustment of the lesbian is obviously the character of the occupation or profession that she selects. For some occupations aspects of a lesbian commitment may actually prove helpful, for her sexual commitment frees her from many of the normal demands of family life and particularly from the demands of childbearing and rearing. In other occupations this same sexual commitment may prove difficult to manage or at least may constrain the lesbian either to restrict her occupational activity or to limit her sexual activity. Also important is the degree to which work can be separated from other spheres of life. Many jobs place demands on aspects of the individual's conduct that would be considered private activity in other occupations. For example, the job requirements of the public school teacher or employment with the federal government set severe limits on the conduct of one's personal life. And, while lesbians are employed as teachers and government workers, they must either learn to conduct their sexual relations with greater discretion than many other lesbians (and conduct these relations in an atmosphere of greater fear and anxiety) or be prepared to have their careers suffer. One lesbian occupying a high-paying position with private industry commented on just this:

My company advertises me as one of the features of our service. My name is on the letterhead. It has been hard work and it has taken years to arrive at this position, this reputation. The hardest thing is knowing that all of this can be wiped out at any moment because of some publicity. I don't think the people with the company would object, but the customers? Who knows? —— [her girl friend and roommate] likes to go to the gay bars. I do too, but not as much. So we go, but I keep waiting for someone who knows me at work to come walking in. It's like living under a sword or with a time bomb.

Another factor which is important in understanding homosexuals' work problems is the degree of involvement with other people that the occupation requires. Many people have very strong feelings about homosexuality, and many more feel uneasy in its presence. One lesbian who worked at a routine office job for several years said:

I work very hard at not letting people at the office know. I don't think I would get fired or anything. It's just the nervousness I know it would start. The other girls look at you curiously. Any touching, even accidental, is taken for a pass. I've had it happen before, when I got careless and let someone know who talked. I got so that I'd wait for the john to be empty before I'd go in. I don't want to go through that again.

Another woman observed:

You can't get too close to people at work. It gets too complicated. You start going out and they want to know too much about you. One girl tried to fix me up with her brother. It is really better to be a little standoffish.

Still another factor is the amount of interest the lesbian takes in her job, that is, the degree to which work itself is rewarding or engaging. For many people work is merely a way of earning a living. For others, however, it is an important and gratifying activity. In the latter case, work not only becomes a constraint on, but also an important substitute for, many of the relations and gratifications that the lesbian, almost by definition, is denied. The potentialities that work offers the lesbian obviously differ widely, and the fate of the professional woman is different from that of the shop clerk or waitress.

Friends

None of us has an opportunity to select our parental family, although as adults, even with the pressure of social expectations, we can modify the degree and extent of our involvement. But part of growing up means that it is frequently very difficult to share new experiences or tastes with parents who are, by definition, a generation away in experience or even to share such things with sibs with whom one has had a prolonged, diffuse, and complex relationship. This fact makes friendship so very important; friendships tend not only to be supportive and reinforcing, but also to be more specific and controlled than familial attachments. So the lesbian must count available friendships as an important resource in the process of coping with the contingencies of her existence. Perhaps more than in the other areas of social life we have considered, the homosexuality of the lesbian becomes a highly salient factor in her friendship selection.

None of the lesbians we interviewed could be considered isolates, although it is probable there are some who had been, particularly during various transitional states. For most, the inclination to speak aloud their feelings and desires becomes something of a constraint in forming friendships with other lesbians. Although it is interesting to note that almost all the lesbians we interviewed included some male homosexuals among their friends, for some of the lesbians male homosexuals constituted their only close male friends. This need for the socialization of deviance is one of the major foundations of a homosexual community. One relatively isolated lesbian, who was very critical of certain aspects of the homosexual community, described the importance of her few lesbian friends in the following way:

There are two or three girls here I think I could talk to, to get some sympathy. I don't think it would be a matter of seeking advice so much as letting off steam. As a matter of fact, that did happen last spring. One of the girls, we both cried on each others' shoulders for awhile.

However, while a homosexual commitment endows friendship with a special significance, it may also be the factor that makes friendship less stable. This instability arises partially from the fact that the population from which the individual lesbian is likely to select her friends is the same population from which she also is likely to select her lovers and sexual partners. As a result, most discussions of friendship were filled with a sense of anticipated impermanence. The fact that friends are often ex-lovers or are current or recent rivals appears to foster an ultimate reserve or, in some extreme cases, a constant mistrust. Almost paradoxically the instability of many lesbian alliances, a fact that contributes to making friendships among female homosexuals so important, also tends to limit the quality of friendships that develop. However, despite this reservation, most of the lesbians interviewed reported managing their friendships fairly well, at least in the sense of having friends with whom they could spend their leisure time and to whom they could turn in moments of stress.

Many of the women also reported having close friends who were not homosexual and who had knowledge of their homosexuality. The existence of such friends obviously facilitates adjustment. This seemed particularly true for those lesbians who had made the best occupational adjustments, i.e., those who had jobs they enjoyed and/or had relatively stable work histories. Both of these—nonhomosexual friendship ties and work adjustment—may well be linked, however, to the somewhat elusive elements that are associated with meeting the conventional world on its own terms. Friendship with knowing nonhomosexuals often appeared to have a limited quality, indicating something like a separate worlds phenomenon. Indicative was the fact that very few lesbians can handle an attempt to bring their two worlds together, but, of course, this would be characteristic of virtually all deviant subcultures.

Another large proportion of the lesbians reported having nonhomosexual friends who did not know they were homosexual. Such friends play a role in filling the lesbian's social life with people, but to the extent that these friends do become an important resource in a lesbian's life, they also become a source of considerable anxiety. One lesbian described her situation in the following way:

Some [friends] may suspect. I don't know. Normally I just don't tell people unless there is a reason for it. You know, where the question comes up, where I might have to explain some peculiar behavior. Once or twice it came out when I had too much to drink. I try to watch it, but you can't be on your guard all the time. Normally, my practice is not to tell people unless I'm pretty sure what the reaction will be.

The lesbian population observed represents, then, differing basic styles of handling the question of friendship. For some, it meant living in almost exclusively homosexual social circles, while others lived in homosexual and nonhomosexual social worlds simultaneously. There were also different styles of living in the nonhomosexual world. Little is known systematically about the determinants of these alternative patterns, although the ways they relate to work and family are surely involved. And perhaps here, more clearly than elsewhere, it is evident that the content of social life for lesbians can be more adequately grasped by understanding the social response to homosexuality than by understanding the psychodynamics involved.

Finding Love

Romantic love, like children, is an invention of the modern world.[8] As such, it plays a peculiarly important role in stabilizing social life. This is particularly true for that form of love that embodies, and is partially expressed through, sexuality. Few people grow up in our society without an understanding of the desirability of love, even fewer do not feel that its absence represents a crucial personal impoverishment, and extremely few fail to respond to the rhetoric that emerges from it. The lesbian is no exception to this. The difference here, as in many other spheres of life, is that for her the establishment of an enduring love relation is more problematic.

Almost without exception, the lesbians we interviewed expressed a significant commitment to finding such an enduring love relationship. Perhaps because their alienation from the larger society is centered in the sexual area and, as a result, they are more conscious of its role, their sense of its importance appears to be even greater than it would be for other populations. What is apparently involved is an almost nineteenth-century commitment to romantic ideals. Their aspirations were fundamentally those embodied in "the American dream": a comfortable home, an interesting job, access to enjoyable leisure activities, and, above all, a sustaining and loving partner. This may rest in the fact that love, as a social value, becomes a way of overriding the inevitable uneasiness accompanying a deviant commitment.

Unfortunately, as frequently occurs with goals that are extremely important, the very enormity of the importance of love often frustrates success. This frustration may take several forms. One is the endowment of casual relations with a greater intensity of feeling than the relationship can sustain. One older lesbian observed:

This falling in and out of love is something that the younger girls do. They turn on to each other and it fulfills a certain psychological need of the moment. They think they're in love. And, of course, it breaks up after a while. What would you expect? Sometimes they've only known each other two weeks.

Another form of frustration stems from the tendency to develop impossible expectations regarding the performances of their partners. This was expressed with considerable clarity by one young woman:

Maybe it will pass, but right now love is very important to me. Being very near someone all the time. Wanting to love them and having them love you back. It's like being on a high and not wanting to come down. Maybe it's my fault. Maybe I've just had bad luck in the lovers I've known. They seem to come down too quickly and then it becomes ugly and sordid.

Still another tendency is a balancing, and frequently self-defeating, reserve that derives from an understandable anticipation of instability in relationships, and is a way of self-protection against a very likely unhappy ending. One lesbian, whose commitment to a substantial emotional investment was strong, described her reluctance to share living quarters with her current lover in the following way:

I guess I feel a sense of security with her. It's not just sexual attraction. I don't know how to explain it. I can talk to her; she understands me. If it broke up, I'd be crushed. There's something there that I've never had before. It's just like I can't let her go. The only happiness I find in life right now is her. [Would you like to live with her?] I don't want to live with anyone. I've been stuck with too many lemons. I find living by myself very enjoyable. She can come over whenever she likes. But if she's living with me . . . I just feel crowded. I want to know that whatever happens, this place will be me . . . mine.

So, as with friendship, the lesbian appears to have both a greater need for love and, out of that greater need, a greater probability for frustration.

It also should be remembered that some lesbians do manage long, enduring relationships. Still others have difficulty managing even temporary affairs. In this, as in other areas of life, there is considerable variation in the capacities between lesbians at any given point in time and for given lesbians during different phases of the life cycle. The differences emerge as the need for, and meaning of, love change. Moreover, while the quest for love is problematic for the lesbian, it is not totally lacking in its problematic aspects for heterosexuals, who, after all, have at their disposal a larger number of substitute rewards and formal constraints which function to bolster a love relationship.

Acceptance of Self

Perhaps the single, most important variable in understanding the adjustment of the lesbian is the process by which, or the degree to which, she comes to accept herself, that is, to manage her feelings about her emotions and preferences and to bring into some balance what she is and what she wants to be. Put into its simplest terms, this is her ability to like herself. Much, of course, depends upon the outcome of many of the things we have discussed: relations to family, extent and quality of friendships, utilization of and role in a homosexual community, work adjustment, and success in the quest for love. These, of course, function in a complex, interactive system about which we know relatively little, primarily because of the scarcity of inquiry into these areas of life. How much success or failure in any of these specific areas of life leads to more general effects remains an important, but unanswered, question. However, it is clear that the most crucial expression occurs in the area of existential self-consciousness, for it is here that these more abstract judgments of success or failure are translated into the alternatives of contentment, happiness, confidence or despair, demoralization, and self-hatred.

Once again, what may be problematic for most heterosexuals becomes more problematic for the lesbian. While most individuals can expect positive confirmation from the surrounding social world for the roles they strive to maintain, the lesbian, except in the most exceptional circumstances, can only expect disapproval and rejection. For most people there is little public discourse about personal sexual activity, and they are usually protected from the consequences of sexual failure or mismanagement by the relative nonsalience of sex to other social roles. What little public language there is for the lesbian is predominantly negative, and her sexuality is certainly more salient for her other social roles. It is perhaps not surprising, then, that many lesbians appear to have difficulty at this level and that most talk about it at one time or another. Nor is it surprising that the search for an effective basis for self-acceptance is fairly costly and most typically involves learning to deny the importance of certain activities, relationships, and statuses that the society defines as eminently desirable and part of the "natural" course of life.

Several of our respondents indicated just how costly this process can be. One lesbian fled her homosexual commitment by entering an unsuccessful marriage that endured for six or seven years. This was followed by a period of sexual inactivity and later by involvement in homosexual activity. She commented:

> Sex is not very important to me now, in spite of the fact that there is greater sex activity. It is not as important as it was when I was in my twenties by any means. I've had too many years of conditioning; having lived without it, I made a conscious effort at psychologically conditioning myself not to think about sex. And I was fairly successful. *[Are you happier now?]* Yes I have . . . well, I don't know about happier. I was happiest when I decided not to live a "straight" life. In other words, I wasn't going to try to look for another man or to get married again. I'm not sure I am happier now that I made a second decision to live as if I were a lesbian. But there was a great deal of . . . peace is not the word, I felt I was reconciled with myself.

Decisions for this lesbian were problematic, but are not entirely exceptional. A majority of the lesbians we talked to had experimented with the possibility of heterosexual relations, and a good proportion of these had seriously considered marriage. One described her situation as follows:

The first fellow was the dashing type, involved in everything. He was part owner of ——. I was serious because I enjoyed being with him; I found him interesting, even fascinating. But he didn't excite me physically; as a person he excited me. I enjoyed doing things with him. But physically, for instance, when he touched me I said I felt nothing, absolutely nothing. So if he made any attempt or made any suggestions, I put him down and said I didn't want it. And if he argued, I'd get sick to my stomach and think: my God, is he going to force me? But he never did. He wasn't pushy about it. I guess he thought it would be all right after we got married, so he proposed. I cared for him, but I didn't love him. It got to a point where every time he took me out, he proposed, so I broke it off. [*Did you ever feel the temptation to try to fake it?*] Of course I thought about it at the time. He really was a nice boy and I thought . . . Well, maybe it won't be such a bad idea. I might even be surprised. But then I realized I couldn't; it would be too much a lie.

The temptation is clearly to sacrifice the sexual gratification for significant gains in the availability of conventional rewards and statuses, such as the approval of friends and family, a recognized position in the general community, a family of one's own, and so on. Another young lesbian, repeating an almost identical occurrence, added:

For a while we all thought I would get married; my parents were happier than I can recall. One of my mother's big disappointments was the fact that there would be no grandchildren. I love both of my parents a great deal, and I would do almost anything for their happiness, but I couldn't do that. I think I was saddened, too, when I broke it off. Then I knew that I wasn't ever going to have children. And I would like to have some . . . for myself.

For the lesbian who learns to accept herself, this surrender of access to major cultural goals may be among her most difficult tasks. Moreover, we suspect that this surrender is never final but tends to reemerge at different points in a life history with differing degrees of intensity.

The need to see oneself as conforming to the moral order of the society also creates problems. The entry into a deviant career does not automatically bring release from moral constraints; to the contrary, the need to deal with conventional morality may loom more sharply for deviants than for persons following conventional and conforming patterns who can readily assume universality of their moral commitments. More specifically, religiosity plays an important role, and nearly all of our society's organized religions take hostile positions with respect to homosexuality, defining it as wicked and sinful. This frequently creates a great problem for the lesbian who must somehow attempt to reconcile her religious commitment with her sexual identity. For one lesbian this was the greatest obstacle to her self-admission of her sexual preferences. She observed:

I just felt that it had to be unnatural. I knew how men and women made love. It was present in the very biology. I didn't have the slightest idea of how women might; I didn't know what I could do to provide pleasure for another woman. I somehow decided that if God had intended women to love one another, He would have made it more obvious, like He did for men and women in love.

For most lesbians there is a movement away from religious involvement, particularly from the conventional communions. For some this involves a kind of agnosticism or merely an avoidance of religious subjects and thoughts. For others, however, the roots of religious training and conviction run too deeply. Some part of these manage by rearranging their religious beliefs, and they develop a personal style of religion and a personal image of God. One very religious woman described her feelings by saying:

I stopped going to church when my minister told me that if I couldn't control the feelings, I could control acting on them. That it was a challenge. I just knew that God would not have given me these feelings if they were so bad. Somehow I know He understands.

Other lesbians, unfortunately, can't make this kind of transformation in their belief systems, and for them the resultant sense of self-rejection and self-hatred becomes severe. In a way that introduces disorder in many spheres of life, a number of such lesbians attempt to anticipate divine punishment by self-punishment. One such lesbian accounted for her refusal to follow up many encouraging prospects in her field of work by saying: "I didn't because I felt I didn't have the right; I was too unworthy." However, the role of the church may change as an increasing number of the major religious bodies are now in the process of rethinking their original position on the question of homosexuality, particularly the question of whether it is, by definition, sinful and is a sufficient basis for exclusion from the religious community.

Psychiatry and the growing use of the language of mental health increasingly play a role in this process of self-acceptance. A large number of the women interviewed had been in one kind of psychological therapy or other. A large number of them displayed considerable familiarity with the literature of psychology and psychiatry. The effects of such experiences and reading appear to be mixed. On the one hand, it should create problems for full self-acceptance, since the prevailing clinical view of homosexuality is that it is an expression of pathology. On the other hand, use of the language of psychotherapy lessens the risks of self-hatred, as it permits the lesbian to see herself as the outcome of a process over which she had little control.

CONCLUSIONS

The major shortcoming of many previous discussions of the lesbian was one of omission rather than commission; the lesbian was described almost exclusively from the perspective of what appeared to be her distinguishing characteristic: her sexual conduct. What was missing in these discussions was the rest of the activity that fills the daily round of her life. Even when such aspects of life were considered, they were used to show the way her sexuality expressed itself in this nonsexual activity. Rarely, for example, was her sexual activity viewed as something that might express other forms of social activity. In this present tentative, unsystematic, and incomplete essay, we have attempted to alter this perspective somewhat—to impose a sense of this complexity upon the study of female homosexuality.

A second goal of the present discussion has been to present a sense of the diversity of forms that female homosexuality may take and to relate this diversity to a number of different dynamic factors and contingencies. While this view may be inaccurate in its selection or recognition of these factors and contingencies, we feel confident in the assertion of the need for this kind of complex view. More than anything else, the success of this paper rests upon its ability to help move consideration of this problem away from dangerously simplified notions of *the* lesbian or *the* causes of female homosexuality. We are *not* trying to argue that female homosexuality is natural. To the contrary, we are arguing that it is unnatural, but unnatural in the way that all human behavior is unnatural; that is, it is without an absolutely predetermined and fixed shape and content, and it is a complex condition which derives from man's unique abilities to think, act, and remember and his need to live with other humans.

Notes

[1] In those cases in which the deviant experience had some duration or frequency, they were acts of low social visibility and/or were inherently part of certain nondeviant life styles. Often such more frequently committed deviant acts represent behavior that the community has learned to tolerate while still resisting the acceptance of it as legitimate. Equally often, it is not the immediate consequence of the act or its intrinsic character that requires it to be defined as deviant, but rather the problems involved in defining such behavior as proper when it is opposed to already existing definitions of proper behavior. In the sexual realm, masturbation and premarital coitus and petting, under certain circumstances, are examples of this problem of integrating certain forms of deviance with the prohibitions against them. In addition to this problem there are kinds of situations and particular social attributes of actors, both of which constrain community agencies to redefine the act to exclude it from the deviant category. An example of the former condition is premarital coitus between an engaged couple (which is therefore at least quasi-legitimate), and of the latter, a car theft by middle-class youths (which becomes a "boyish prank").

[2] A certain amount of informal group reinforcement of the behavior, and attitudes relating to it, does occur, especially with reference to premarital coitus. This may be observed in some of the values expressed by males and females who are involved in the "youth culture," but these do not represent, except in some very unusual cases, long-term commitments to values expressed in the peer groups. Such talk as does occur reinforces conventional ambivalent male attitudes towards coitus in male peer groups and reinforces female caution among female peer groups. In addition to this factor, however, there is coming into existence a new ideological literature reinforcing acting in certain deviant patterns. This trend undoubtedly reflects the easing of constraints toward such behavior. Contemporary works on sex education generally make a self-conscious attempt to reduce feelings of guilt about masturbation: the traditional warnings about masturbation saying that it results in either ill health or insanity now give way to cautions about social isolation or social maladjustment. Masturbation is not positively valued, but it is no longer seen as the root cause of serious adult pathology. Similarly, marriage counselors, moralists, and theologians publicly debate the justifications for premarital sexual relations; and marriage manuals—including those sponsored by religious organizations—describe mouth-genital contact as one of several standard sexual techniques.

Sexuality and Sexual Learning in the Child
JOHN H. GAGNON

[1] An analysis of this historical change, particularly in France, is the work by Phillipe Ariès, *Centuries of Childhood;* New York, Knopf, 1962. For changes in attitudes toward sexuality see especially pp. 100–127. A remarkably original work tracing from an existentialist point of view the general implications of this change in consciousness is Jan H. van den Berg, *The Changing Nature of Man;* New York, Dell, 1964

[2] Steven Marcus, "Mr. Acton of Queen Anne Street, or, The Wisdom of Our Ancestors," *Partisan Review* (1964) 31:201–230.

³ An example of the confused thought that results from this dilemma
—that children should know about sex but not act out their knowledge
—is provided by the following paragraph in a relatively sensible popular work on the sexual development of children. "Shielding children
from the awareness of adult sex conduct goes without saying. Much
more injurious than any play among themselves would be the observation of adult behavior and loose significant talk. As in the case of vul-
garities—the greater the prudery the greater the pornography—so the
greater the freedom among adults the greater the freedom among children. Also, the greater the denial of legitimate understanding among
them, the greater the exploration. Far from being an abnormal or
perverted or precocious entrance into heterosexuality, sex play in children is a normal, if socially unacceptable instance of sex interest, an
expression of a normal developmental need. If they are not to provide
an answer to that need themselves, we must provide it for them, not
only in knowledge of the life processes, but in legitimate though vicarious participation in those processes. Words alone do not satisfy." Fran-
cis Bruce Strain, The Normal Sex Interests of Children; New York,
Appleton-Century-Crofts, 1948; p. 139.

⁴ It may, in fact, be a myth of the intellectualizing classes that value
consensus as an outcome of rational deliberation exists to any extent in
lower-class populations. There is a strong tendency among those to
whom ideas and language are important to impute the same significance
to others for whom words are inadequate or unimportant.

⁵ Alfred C. Kinsey, Wardell B. Pomeroy, and Clyde E. Martin, Sexual
Behavior in the Human Male; Philadelphia, Saunders, 1948.

⁶ Lionel Trilling, "The Kinsey Report," in The Liberal Imagination;
New York, Doubleday Anchor Books, 1953; p. 216.

⁷ This is not always true, since in some communities sex education in
schools has successfully weathered rather extreme conflicts. However, it
is the fear of this situation that keeps most adults silent.

⁸ Sigmund Freud, "Three Essays on Sexuality," Standard Edition of
the Complete Psychological Works 7:135–245; London, Hogarth, 1953.

⁹ It is clear that not all psychoanalysts hold these positions in whole
or in part. Unfortunately little effort has been devoted to redefinition.
A reconstruction of the Oedipus complex by Rado bears upon the first
point very directly. Sandor Rado, Psychoanalysis of Behavior: Collected
Papers; New York, Grune & Stratton, 1956; p. 197.

¹⁰ The functions of the sex hormones as an alternative energy source
in preparing the organism to receive sexual information is discussed
in the following work by John Money: "Components of Eroticism in
Man: I. The Hormones in Relation to Sexual Morphology and Sexual
Desire," J. Nervous and Mental Disease (1961) 132:239–248. "Sex
Hormones and Other Variables in Human Eroticism," in Sex and
Internal Secretions, edited by William C. Young; Baltimore, Williams
and Wilkins, 1961; pp. 1383–1400.

¹¹ René A. Spitz, with the collaboration of Katherine M. Wolf,
"Autoeroticism; Some Empirical Findings and Hypotheses on Three of
its Manifestations in the First Year of Life," in The Psychoanalytic Study
of the Child, 3/4:85–120; New York, Internat. Univ. Press, 1949.

¹² See the following works by Harry F. Harlow: "The Nature of
Love," Amer. Psychol. (1958) 13:673–685. "Love in Infant Monkeys,"

Scientific Amer. (1959) 200:68–74. "Sexual Behavior in the Rhesus Monkey," paper presented to the Conference on Sex and Behavior, Berkeley, Calif., 1961 (mimeographed). Harry F. Harlow and M. K. Harlow, "Social Deprivation in Monkeys," *Scientific Amer.* (1962) 207:137–146.

[13] This convergence has been noted by Spitz himself in René A. Spitz, "Autoeroticism Re-examined: The Role of Early Sexual Behavior Patterns in Personality Formation," in *The Psychoanalytic Study of the Child* 17:283–315; New York, Internat. Univ. Press, 1962.

[14] See footnote 12, Harlow and Harlow; p. 138.

[15] See footnote 14; p. 144.

[16] Bettye M. Caldwell, "The Usefulness of the Critical Period Hypothesis in the Study of Filiative Behavior," *Merrill Palmer Quart.* (1962) 8:229–242. It is implicit that prior to a certain point in time the organism may well be resistant to learning.

[17] An alternative formulation of the findings on infant behavior from a learning theory point of view may be found in Jacob L. Gewirtz, "A Learning Analysis of the Effects of Normal Stimulation, Privation and Deprivation in the Acquisition of Social Motivation and Attachment," in *Determinants of Infant Behavior,* edited by Brian M. Foss; New York, Wiley, 1961; pp. 213–290.

[18] The most thoroughgoing of the planners have been those who have used the Skinner Box with infants, but the outcomes of these experiments are still unclear.

[19] See the following papers by John Money, Joan G. Hampson, and John L. Hampson: "Hermaphroditism: Recommendations Concerning Assignment of Sex, Change of Sex, and Psychologic Management," *Bull. Johns Hopkins Hosp.* (1955) 97:284–300. "Sexual Incongruities and Psychopathology: The Evidence of Human Hermaphroditism," *Bull. Johns Hopkins Hosp.* (1956) 98:43–57. Joan G. Hampson, "Hermaphroditic Genital Appearance, Rearing and Eroticism in Hyperadrenocorticism," *Bull. Johns Hopkins Hosp.* (1955) 96:265–273.

[20] See footnote 19, 1955; p. 285.

[21] William C. Young, Robert W. Goy, and Charles H. Phoenix, "Hormones and Sexual Behavior," *Science* (1964) 143:212–218.

[22] Milton Diamond, "A Critical Evaluation on the Ontogeny of Human Sexual Behavior," *Quart. Review Biology* (in press).

[23] From studies cited in footnote 22.

[24] John L. Hampson and Joan G. Hampson, "The Ontogenesis of Sexual Behavior in Man," in *Sex and Internal Secretions,* edited by William C. Young; Baltimore, Williams and Wilkins, 1961; pp. 1401–1432.

[25] Robert R. Sears, Eleanor E. Maccoby, and Harry Levin, *Patterns of Child Rearing;* Evanston, Ill., Row, Peterson, 1957; pp. 176–217. See pp. 215–216 for the origin of the term *nonlabeling.*

[26] Sigmund Freud, "Transference," *Standard Edition of the Complete Psychological Works,* 16:431–447; London, Hogarth, 1963; p. 445.

[27] The chronic use of the term "motherfucker" by American Negro slum dwellers is a case in point. Rather than being directed toward anyone's "real" mother or calling to mind coitus with her, it has an extremely abstract referent. In its use in verbal games which function as outlets for aggression and therefore social ranking among males it

is clear that the reference is to womankind. See Roger D. Abrahams, *Deep Down in the Jungle;* Hatboro, Pa., Folklore Associates, 1964, for examples and discussion of urban Negro folklore, and especially pp. 259–262 for the meaning of this and other obscenities.

28 The work of Maslow supports this hypothesis. He shows that women who had higher dominance scores on a dominance-submission scale were more similar to men in other characteristics than similar to low-dominance women. It is quite likely that this shift in characteristics may have resulted from differences in the training for aggression rather than in training for sexuality. Abraham H. Maslow, "Dominance, Personality and Social Behavior in Women," *J. Social Psychology* (1939) 10:3–39; and "Self-Esteem (Dominance-Feeling) and Sexuality in Women," *J. Social Psychology* (1942) 16:259–294.

29 Bernard C. Glueck, Jr., "Early Sexual Experiences in Schizophrenia," in *Advances in Sex Research,* edited by Hugo G. Beigel; New York, Harper and Row, 1963; pp. 248–255. Karl Abraham, "The Experiencing of Sexual Traumas as a Form of Sexual Activity," *Selected Papers of Karl Abraham, M.D.;* London, Hogarth, 1927; pp. 47–63. Sandor Ferenczi, "Confusion of Tongues Between the Adult and the Child," *Internat. J. Psycho-Anal.* (1949) 30:225–230.

30 Adelaide M. Johnson and S. A. Szurek, "The Genesis of Antisocial Acting Out in Children and Adults," *Psychoanal. Quart.* (1952) 21:323–343. Edward M. Litin, Mary E. Griffin, and Adelaide M. Johnson, "Parental Influence in Unusual Sexual Behavior in Children," *Psychoanal. Quart.* (1956) 25:37–55.

31 See Johnson and Szurek, in footnote 30; p. 323.

32 See the case reports in Litin, Griffin, and Johnson, in footnote 30.

33 See Ferenczi, in footnote 29; p. 228.

34 Alfred C. Kinsey, Wardell B. Pomeroy, Clyde E. Martin, and Paul H. Gebhard, *Sexual Behavior in the Human Female;* Philadelphia, Saunders, 1953; p. 103.

35 See footnote 34; p. 717.

36 This has also been discussed by Albert Bandura and Richard H. Walters in *Adolescent Aggression: A Study of the Influence of Child-Training Practices and Family Interrelationships;* New York, Ronald, 1959; pp. 184–187.

37 I have already noted the lack of consensus about sexuality among adults who have at least had some sexual experience; how much more mysterious must sexual functions appear to the inexperienced child. The role of language as imposing order on the external world may be found explicitly in the works of Kenneth Burke and George Herbert Mead and implicitly in those of Erving Goffman.

38 See footnote 34; p. 107. Also see footnote 5; pp. 165–167.

39 See footnote 38; p. 167.

40 See footnote 38; p. 182.

41 There is a body of evidence that among young children there is a large amount of game and folklore material that is rapidly forgotten after puberty. A certain amount of this material is sexual; however, the folklorists who work with children usually fail to keep records of this, or if they do so, do not publish it. An interesting aspect of this material is its eternal character—that is, it is passed on from generation to generation; for example, children in England are currently singing a recog-

nizable variant of a song about Bonaparte popular in the early nine-teenth century. See Iona Opie and Peter Opie, *The Lore and Language of School Children;* London, Oxford, 1959; pp. 98–99. This evidence for the historical continuity of children's culture makes the contention in the earlier part of the paper concerning the change in the modern con-sciousness about children somewhat more complex; however, what seems to have happened is that the culture of children existed despite parental ignorance, and it had traditions of some viability independent of the adult community. It is unclear to what extent an adequate vocabu-lary for children would influence their overt behavior, but most likely it would not stimulate additional activity. This fear that is often expressed by parents is a function of their own anxiety and not necessarily related to the motives and drives of their children. Thus the parent placing himself in the role of the child presumes that exposure to certain types of stimulation or knowledge of certain types of behavior would cause the child to react in the same way as an adult would.

[42] A series of reports has appeared about a study of this sort con-ducted through the use of doll play and interviews with 200 children. The general good sense of these researchers is attested to in the follow-ing: " . . . no series of scientific terms can 'immunize' a child against the inevitable language of the street. The child may need both in order to become an effective member of his group." See the following papers by Jacob Conn: "Sexual Curiosity of Children," *Amer. J. Diseases Children* (1940) 60:1110–1119. "Children's Reactions to the Discovery of Genital Differences," *Amer. J. Orothopsychiatry* (1940) 10:747–754. "Children's Awareness of the Origins of Babies," *J. Child Psychiatry* (1948) 1:140–176. See also Jacob Conn and Leo Kanner, "Children's Awareness of Sex Differences," *J. Child Psychiatry* (1947) 1:3–57.

[43] Cited in Glenn Ramsey, "The Sex Information of Younger Boys," *Amer. J. Orthopsychiatry* (1943) 13:347–352.

[44] See footnote 43; p. 349.

[45] See footnote 43; pp. 349–350.

[46] Paul H. Gebhard, John H. Gagnon, Wardell B. Pomeroy, and Cornelia V. Christenson, *Sex Offenders: An Analysis of Types;* New York, Harper and Row, 1965.

[47] See footnote 43; pp. 350–351.

[48] See footnote 46. Also, the data for 5,000 college males is currently being analyzed at the Institute for Sex Research; this should provide some evidence about the experience of this social level.

[49] See footnote 36; pp. 150–154.

[50] All figures from Ramsey, footnote 43.

[51] See footnote 41; pp. 93–97.

[52] Richard Wright, *Black Boy;* New York, Signet, 1963; pp. 49–53.

[53] This also has been pointed out by Freud. "We are shown . . . above all, how the secret of sexual life begins to dawn on her indistinctly and then takes complete possession of the child's mind; how, in the con-sciousness of her secret knowledge, she at first suffers hurt, but little by little overcomes it." Sigmund Freud, *Standard Edition of the Com-plete Psychological Works* 14:341; London, Hogarth, 1963.

[54] Kurt H. Wolff, editor, *The Sociology of George Simmel;* Glencoe, Ill., Free Press, 1950; pp. 330–335.

[55] See footnote 5; pp. 394–417.

[56] See footnote 5. Ira Reiss, *Premarital Sexual Standards in America;* Glencoe, Ill., Free Press, 1960; pp. 126–145.

[57] See footnote 34; pp. 298–302. Winston Ehrmann, *Premarital Dating Behavior;* New York, Holt, 1959; pp. 32–36.

[58] Mervin B. Freedman, "The Sexual Behavior of American College Women: An Empirical Study and an Historical Survey," *Merrill Palmer Quart.* (1965) 11:33–48.

[59] See footnote 34; pp. 282–345.

[60] Robert R. Bell and Jack V. Buerkle, "Mother and Daughter Attitudes to Premarital Sexual Behavior," *Marriage and Family Living* (1961) 23:390–392.

[61] Erik H. Erikson, *Childhood and Society;* New York, Norton, 1950.

[62] The revision of Spock's classic in 1957 to include a greater concern with discipline is noted in Martha Weinman, "Now 'Dr. Spock' Goes to the White House," *The New York Times Magazine* (December 4, 1960) pp. 26, 120–121. The cause of the revision was "permissiveness running away with itself." The child-rearing column of the Magazine section of *The New York Times* is increasingly running to titles such as, "Relearning What Permissiveness Means," or "When Discipline is Called For." The column often translates psychiatric positions into layman's information.

[63] Many of these impressions come from personal interaction with psychiatrists, but the *J. Offender Therapy,* which is directed toward dealing with criminal populations explicitly, says what many therapists feel when confronted with these kinds of problems. See Ernst Schmidhofer, "Acting Up or Acting Out," *J. Offender Therapy* (1964) 8:1–4, or Mark D. Altschule, "The Alleged Value of Anti-Social Self Expression," *J. Offender Therapy* (1963) 7:73–74.

[64] Benjamin S. Spock, *The Pocket Book of Baby and Child Care;* New York, Pocket Books, 1946; p. 3.

[65] *Symposium on Sex Education,* edited by E. C. Cumings; New York, Amer. Social Hygiene Assn., November, 1957.

[66] Sigmund Freud, "Analysis Terminable and Interminable." *Standard Edition of the Complete Psychological Works* 23:216–253; London, Hogarth, 1964; pp. 233–234.

Sex Offenses: The Marginal Status of the Adolescent
ALBERT J. REISS, JR.

[1] Throughout this article, the sociological concept of adolescent is used interchangeably with the legal concept of juvenile. The context should make clear whether the concept is used primarily in the specialized sense of one discipline or the other.

[2] Appeals from the decisions rendered by a juvenile court are relatively rare, and particularly so for cases involving violations of sexual conduct norms. The relatively low rate of appeal from the decisions of a juvenile court itself reflects a social definition of the adolescent as a person whose best interest is protected by the court, so that the traditional safeguards for civil rights are unnecessary. This position needs careful examination, since many juveniles and their families are unaware of their legal rights in a juvenile hearing. The personnel in most juvenile jurisdictions make

no attempt to apprise juveniles of their rights and, in fact, often express obvious resentment when the juvenile is represented by counsel.

[3] ALFRED C. KINSEY, WARDELL B. POMEROY & CLYDE E. MARTIN, SEXUAL BEHAVIOR IN THE HUMAN MALE *passim* (1948) [hereinafter cited as KINSEY MALE REPORT]; ALFRED C. KINSEY, WARDELL B. POMEROY, CLYDE E. MARTIN & PAUL H. GEBHARD, SEXUAL BEHAVIOR IN THE HUMAN FEMALE *passim* (1953) [hereinafter cited as KINSEY FEMALE REPORT].

[4] KINSEY MALE REPORT 199.

[5] See, *e.g.,* Whyte, *A Slum Sex Code,* 49 AM. J. SOCIOLOGY 24 (1943). Investigation since Whyte's original statement of this sex code discloses that this might more appropriately be called the sex code of low-status persons in American society, whether or not they dwell in slums.

[6] See JAMES F. COLEMAN, SOCIAL STRUCTURES AND SOCIAL CLIMATES IN HIGH SCHOOLS chs. 3 and 4 (1959).

[7] Vincent, *Ego Involvement in Sexual Relations: Implications for Research on Illegitimacy,* 65 AM. J. SOCIOLOGY 287 (1959).

[8] See COLEMAN, *op. cit. supra* note 6, chs. 3 and 4.

[9] Most states specifically deny the juvenile court any power of conviction. See, *e.g.,* Mickens v. Commonwealth, 178 Va. 273, 278–79, 16 S.E.2d 641, 643 (1941), where the trial and punishment of juveniles for a specific offense is specifically prohibited.

[10] In the Matter of Arthur Lewis, 260 N.Y. 171, 183 N.E. 353 (1932).

[11] IND. ANN. STAT. § 10–4221 (1956); WYO. COMP. STAT. ANN. § 9–520 (1945).

[12] In order that the sexual act leading to pregnancy be socially visible, the boy and girl would have to be observed in intercourse. Only the girl's sexual deviation is socially visible, however, in the pregnancy that ensues from the act. There is a special problem here anyway, since the father's status can never be proved in any absolute sense, while that of the mother is determinable.

[13] For a detailed discussion of just how incest interferes with status and role expectations in family socialization processes, see TALCOTT PARSONS & ROBERT F. BALES, FAMILY SOCIALIZATION AND INTERACTION PROCESS 101–03, and 305–06 (1950).

[14] See Whyte, *supra* note 5, at 29.

[15] Mailer, *The White Negro,* 4 DISSENT 276 (1957).

[16] ALBERT J. REISS, JR., & A. LEWIS RHODES, A SOCIO-PSYCHOLOGICAL STUDY OF ADOLESCENT CONFORMITY AND DEVIATION ch. 9 (1959).

[17] See McKay, *The Neighborhood and Child Conduct,* 26 ANNALS 32 (1949).

[18] REISS & RHODES, *op. cit. supra* note 16, ch. 9.

[19] See CLARK E. VINCENT, UNWED MOTHERS (forthcoming).

[20] N. Y. PENAL LAW § 690.

[21] Investigation discloses that it is quite common among career-oriented delinquents in such large metropolitan areas as Chicago, Los Angeles, New York, and Washington, D.C., and smaller ones such as Nashville, Tenn. It is observed in smaller cities that attract large numbers of adult male homosexuals, such as the resort city of Hot Springs, Ark.

[22] See Ross, *The Hustler in Chicago,* I J. STUDENT RESEARCH 13 (1959).

[23] KINSEY MALE REPORT 224.

24 *Id.* at 166–74; KINSEY FEMALE REPORT 108–10.

25 KINSEY MALE REPORT 219–20; KINSEY FEMALE REPORT 518–29.

26 KINSEY FEMALE REPORT 326.

27 *Id.* at 325; PAUL W. TAPPAN, JUVENILE DELINQUENCY 264 (1949); Lane, *Illogical Variations in Sentences of Felons Committed to Massachusetts State Prison,* 32 J. CRIM. L. & CRIM. 171 (1941).

28 See BRUNO BETTELHEIM, TRUANTS FROM LIFE (1955); LOVE IS NOT ENOUGH (1950).

29 See FRITZ REDL & DAVID WINEMAN, CONTROLS FROM WITHIN (1952); CHILDREN WHO HATE (1951).

Sex Offenses: A Sociological Critique
STANTON WHEELER

1 Statutes defining sex offenses have been reviewed in a number of publications and will not be discussed in detail here. Major sources on which this discussion is based include ROBERT V. SHERWIN, SEX AND THE STATUTORY LAW (1949); MORRIS PLOSCOWE, SEX AND THE LAW (1951); Bensing, *A Comparative Study of American Sex Statutes,* 42 J. CRIM. L., & P.S. 57 (1951). See also Ploscowe, *Sex Offenses: The American Legal Context, supra* pp. 217–24.

2 MORRIS PLOSCOWE, SEX AND THE LAW 136–55 (1951).

3 EMILE DURKHEIM, ON THE DIVISION OF LABOR IN SOCIETY 73 (George Simpson transl. 1933).

4 *Ibid.*

5 Hart, *The Aims of the Criminal Law,* 23 LAW & CONTEMP. PROB. 401, 405 (1958). Hart also has emphasized the obligations imposed by community life, although these obligations are only indirectly caught up in his formal definition. See *id.* at 413, 426.

6 MORRIS PLOSCOWE, SEX AND THE LAW 197 (1951).

7 MODEL PENAL CODE art. 207 (Tent. Draft No. 4, 1955; Tent. Draft No. 9, 1959).

8 Committee on Homosexual Offenses and Prostitution, *Report,* CMND No. 247 (1957).

9 MODEL PENAL CODE § 207.1, comment at 207 (Tent. Draft No. 4, 1955).

10 EUSTACE CHESSER, LIVE AND LET LIVE 116 (1958).

11 From a 1949 Indiana statute, as described in CALIFORNIA DEP'T OF MENTAL HYGIENE, FINAL REPORT ON CALIFORNIA SEXUAL DEVIATION RESEARCH 45 (1954).

12 MODEL PENAL CODE 277–78 (Tent. Draft No. 4, 1955).

13 *Cf.* Fuller, *Morals and the Criminal Law,* 32 J. CRIM. L. & C. 624 (1942). Evidence on variation in sentences comes from a variety of sources and is summarized in Glueck, *Predictive Devices and the Individualization of Justice,* 23 LAW & CONTEMP. PROB. 463 (1958).

14 Murray, *Commons Debate on the Wolfenden Report,* 122 JUST. P. 816 (1958).

15 *Wolfenden Report in Parliament,* 1959 CRIM. L. REV. (Eng.) 38. The recommendations of the Wolfenden Committee are discussed in greater detail elsewhere in this symposium. Hall Williams, *Sex Offenses: The British Experience, infra* pp. 334–60.

16 All authorities are in agreement on the failures of legal controls, and the evidence is well known. Most states have almost no prosecutions under fornication, seduction, or adultery statutes. To quote Ploscowe, "Nowhere are the disparities between law in action and law on the books so great as in the control of sex crimes." MORRIS PLOSCOWE, SEX AND THE LAW 155 (1951). Nor is this a recent phenomenon. Geoffrey May cites data for the town of Groton, Mass., showing extremely high rates of fornication during the height of puritanism in the colonies. GEOFFREY MAY, SOCIAL CONTROL OF SEX EXPRESSION 254 (1930). When the Model Penal Code discussions review problems of enforceability, fairly good evidence for the claims is presented. When the discussions concern possible secular harms, claims are based largely on argument and opinion. See, *e.g.*, the discussion of adultery. MODEL PENAL CODE § 207.1, comment at 204–10 (Tent. Draft No. 4, 1955).

17 A similar problem is evident in discussions about the effectiveness of correctional techniques. It is fashionable to think of the "new penology" as based on rational, scientific investigation; yet, there is little evidence that current techniques are any more effective than those used in the past. Increasingly, evaluative research is carried out to test the effectiveness of various programs. Even the best of the studies are subject to methodological weaknesses that make for ambiguity in results, so that interpretations may be made consistent with the ideology of the interpreter. See Cressey, *The Nature and Effectiveness of Correctional Techniques,* 23 LAW & CONTEMP. PROB. 754 (1958).

18 ALFRED C. KINSEY, WARDELL B. POMEROY & CLYDE E. MARTIN, SEXUAL BEHAVIOR IN THE HUMAN MALE (1948) [hereinafter cited as KINSEY MALE REPORT]; ALFRED C. KINSEY, WARDELL B. POMEROY, CLYDE E. MARTIN & PAUL H. GEBHARD, SEXUAL BEHAVIOR IN THE HUMAN FEMALE (1953) [hereinafter cited as KINSEY FEMLE REPORT].

19 Kingsley Int'l Picture Corp. v. Regents, 360 U.S. 684 (1959).

20 PITIRIM A. SOROKIN, THE AMERICAN SEX REVOLUTION (1956).

21 A major review of changes in American values shows increasing discussion of sex and a rising interest in extramarital relationships revealed in content analyses of best sellers. See Kluckhohn, *Have There Been Discernible Shifts in American Values During the Past Generation?,* in ELTING E. MORRISON, THE AMERICAN STYLE 145 (1958). For changes of a similar sort during earlier decades, see Newcomb, *Recent Changes in Attitudes Toward Sex and Marriage,* 2 AM. SOC. REV. 659 (1937). For interesting essays on the subject, see ABRAM KARDINER, SEX AND MORALITY (1954).

22 KINSEY FEMALE REPORT 242–46.

23 KINSEY MALE REPORT 411–13.

24 *Id.* at 413–17.

25 An excellent review of the methodological problems in the Kinsey report on males is provided by WILLIAM G. COCHRAN, FREDERICK MOSTELLER & JOHN TUKEY, STATISTICAL PROBLEMS OF THE KINSEY REPORT (1954). These authors discuss the problem of establishing the stability of sexual patterns and caution against drawing more than tentative conclusions. *Id.* at 141.

26 The 1937 data are from *The Fortune Quarterly Survey: VIII,* Fortune, April 1937, pp. 111, 188–90. The 1959 results were supplied to the writer by Phillip K. Hastings, Director, The Roper Public Opinion

Research Center, Williams College, Williamstown, Mass. Results from these surveys demonstrate the dangers in inferring trends from comparison of older and younger generations at a single point in time. In both surveys, the older generation were somewhat less approving. The trend data suggest that this is largely a function of age, rather than a changing climate of opinion.

[27] Studies of moral values among samples of college students provide some evidence of change over recent decades. One study compared the responses of students in 1939 and in 1956 on an instrument designed to assess the perceived importance of certain characteristics in the ideal marriage mate. It found a decline in the importance attributed to chastity consistent with an assumed change from traditional to romantic and companionship factors as bases for mate selection. McGinnis, *Campus Values in Mate Selection: A Repeat Study*, 36 SOCIAL FORCES 368 (1958). A similar study, however, notes an increase in the severity of moral judgment regarding forms of promiscuity. See Rettig & Pasamanick, *Changes in Moral Values Among College Students: A Factorial Study*, 24 AM. SOC. REV. 856 (1959). While the increase in severity of judgment on three items dealing with sex was less than that for many other items, the values are still quite strong. For instance, "having illicit sex relations after marriage" was judged a more severe moral transgression than "nations at war using poison gas on the homes and cities of its enemy behind the lines"; or "a legislator, for a financial consideration, using his influence to secure the passage of a law known to be contrary to public interest."

[28] MODEL PENAL CODE § 207.1, comment at 206–07 (Tent. Draft No. 4, 1955).

[29] KINSEY MALE REPORT 347.

[30] *Id.* at 576–77.

[31] I wish to acknowledge the aid of the Roper Public Opinion Research Center in making the data available for analysis. Unfortunately, evidence on class distribution of responses for the 1959 item was not yet available for study.

[32] The socioeconomic labels are interpreted from an index used by the Roper agency and may not match the distinctions made in other studies. These distributions probably fail to catch the extreme top and bottom of the socioeconomic scale, where different patterns might emerge. Data are for white respondents only.

[33] Kinsey's own interpretations frequently were based on this assumption. Other examples are included in JEROME HIMELHOCH & SYLVIA FAVA, SEXUAL BEHAVIOR IN AMERICAN SOCIETY 175–205 (1955).

[34] SAMUEL A. STOUFFER, COMMUNISM, CONFORMITY, AND CIVIL LIBERTIES 89–108 (1955); Lipset, *Democracy and Working Class Authoritarianism*, 24 AM. SOC. REV. 482 (1959).

[35] See LISTON POPE, MILLHANDS AND PREACHERS (1942).

[36] ROBERT R. SEARS, ELEANOR E. MACCOBY & HARRY LEVIN, PATTERNS OF CHILD REARING 428 (1957).

[37] See Miller, *Implications of Urban Lower-Class Culture for Social Work*, 23 SOC. SERV. REV. 225 (1959); see also ALLISON DAVIS & JOHN DOLLARD, CHILDREN OF BONDAGE 272–90 (1940).

[38] See Kanin & Howard, *Postmarital Consequences of Premarital Sex Adjustment*, 23 AM. SOC. REV. 558 (1958); see also Ehrmann, *Influence*

of Comparative Social Class of Companion Upon Premarital Heterosexual Behavior, 17 MARRIAGE & FAMILY LIVING 48 (1955).

[39] A related point of misinterpretation hinges on Kinsey's use of an accumulative-incidence curve, which reflects single acts engaged in only during childhood, or perhaps on only one occasion as an adult. One can hardly assume that because an act has been committed at least once by the majority of the population, it is, therefore, regarded as culturally acceptable. Yet, this argument has apparently been used in court cases. See HIMELHOCH & FAVA, *op. cit. supra* note 33, at 244–50. On this basis, one would withdraw a large proportion of penal legislation, at least as it applies to males, including that governing tax evasion, malicious mischief, auto misdemeanors, disorderly conduct, and larceny. See Wallerstein & Wyle, *Our Law Abiding Law-Breakers,* 25 PROBATION 107 (1947).

[40] In response to the question reported in table II *supra.*

[41] Hohman & Schaffner, *The Sex Lives of Unmarried Men,* 52 AM. J. SOC. 501 (1947).

[42] KINSEY FEMALE REPORT 319.

[43] From the 1959 Roper survey reported in table I *supra.*

[44] See Palmore, *Published Reactions to the Kinsey Report,* 31 SOCIAL FORCES 165 (1952).

[45] Whyte, *A Slum Sex Code,* 49 AMER. J. SOC. 24 (1943).

[46] Ehrmann, *Premarital Sexual Behavior and Sex Codes of Conduct with Acquaintances, Friends and Lovers,* 38 SOCIAL FORCES 158 (1959).

[47] One of the major complaints in popular literature about the Kinsey research was the overly biological orientation and lack of attention to love and affection as basis for sex relationships. Some of Kinsey's results as well as those of other investigators suggest, however, that where the abstinence standard no longer exists, the emerging standard permits coitus when part of a stable, affectionate relationship. See Reiss, *The Treatment of Pre-Marital Coitus in "Marriage and the Family" Texts,* 4 SOCIAL PROBLEMS 334 (1957). An interesting recent study finds a high degree of ego involvement in premarital sexual relationships, particularly among middle-class women, and suggests some of the conditions that encourage intimacies for females in the middle and upper socioeconomic strata. See Vincent, *Ego-Involvement in Sexual Relations: Implications for Research on Illegitimacy,* 65 AM. J. SOC. 287 (1959).

[48] Contributing to and reflecting this trend is an increasing willingness on the part of some homosexuals to make their problems a matter for public concern. See, *e.g.,* PETER WILDEBLOOD, AGAINST THE LAW (1956). And note the signs of incipient pressure-group formation in the following quotation from the trade journal, One, published in Los Angeles: "No American Politician regards as humorous a millions votes.... Let's say the membership dues are ... fifty cents a month ... six dollars a year ... multiply that by a million and you have the gigantic fighting strength ... $6,000,000.... Nobody will care whose money it is ... that of screaming pansies, delicate decorators or professional wrestlers. Nobody will give a damn because this is the U.S.A. and money talks...." From the Sept. 1953 issue of One, as quoted in JAMES M. REINHARDT, SEX PERVERSIONS AND SEX CRIMES 32 (1957).

[49] See authorities cited, note 34 *supra.* These results refer largely to response to behavior clearly defined as deviant. Whether a given pattern

of behavior is recognized as deviant in the first place is a related, but separate, issue. At least in regard to mental illness, there is some evidence that lower-class persons with little education are less likely to recognize a particular behavior pattern as that of a mentally-ill person than are more educated, middle-class persons. See AUGUST B. HOLLINGSHEAD & F. C. REDLICH, SOCIAL CLASS AND MENTAL ILLNESS 171–93 (1958).

[50] STOUFFER, op. cit. supra note 34, at 26–57.

[51] Trends consistent with those noted above have been found for one item on sex criminals taken from a national survey. In response to the question: "What do you think is the best thing to do with sex criminals, send them to a hospital or a jail?," the younger and more educated were much more likely to choose the hospital. Significantly, a majority at all educational levels favored the hospital, as did a majority in all age groups up to age 45. See Woodward, Changing Ideas on Mental Illness and Its Treatment, 16 AM. SOC. REV. 443 (1951).

[52] See the discussion of proposed changes in legislation regarding deviate sexual intercourse. MODEL PENAL CODE § 207.5, comment at 276–81 (Tent. Draft No. 4, 1955).

[53] To be sure, there are weaknesses and pitfalls in the gathering and interpretation of opinions on controversial issues. But these problems are well known to experts in opinion-research and are subject to increasing control. One need not suggest that public opinion replace legislative and judicial opinion in order to see the value that can come from knowledge of public attitudes, especially in areas where presumed public response is explicitly considered in making important decisions. For a recent study and discussion of the use of opinion surveys and their application to one area of legal concern, see JULIUS COHEN, REGINALD A. H. ROBSON & ALAN BATES, PARENTAL AUTHORITY: THE COMMUNITY AND THE LAW (1958). This is not to suggest that public opinion studies are the only or necessarily the most appropriate means of establishing the relationship of public opinion to legal process. The University of Chicago Jury Project is one instance of a much different approach that promises to reveal some of the areas of agreement and disagreement between the response of judge and of jury to certain types of offenses. See Broeder, The University of Chicago Jury Project, 38 NEB. L. REV. 744 (1959).

[54] Sutherland, The Diffusion of Sexual Psychopath Laws, 56 AM. J. SOC. 142 (1950).

[55] Reports with detailed analyses of sex offender statutes and experience in their use include PAUL W. TAPPAN, THE HABITUAL SEX OFFENDER (1950) (prepared for the state of New Jersey); CALIFORNIA DEP'T OF MENTAL HYGIENE, FINAL REPORT ON CALIFORNIA SEXUAL DEVIATION RESEARCH (1954) [hereinafter cited as CALIFORNIA REPORT]; GOVERNOR'S STUDY COMM'N, REPORT ON THE DEVIATED CRIMINAL SEX OFFENDER (1951) (Michigan).

[56] TAPPAN, op. cit, supra note 55, at 36–42; CALIFORNIA REPORT 20–38.

[57] TAPPAN, op. cit. supra note 55, at 22–25. Tappan cites a New York study that found that only 7% of convicted sex offenders were re-arrested for sex offenses over a 12-year period. A recent California study also found 7% sex recidivism among sex offenders. See Frisbie, The Treated Sex Offender, FED. PROB., March 1958, p. 18.

[58] TAPPAN, *op. cit. supra* note 55, at 20–22. See also ALBERT ELLIS & RALPH BRANCALE, THE PSYCHOLOGY OF SEX OFFENDERS 32 (1956).

[59] For a beginning in this direction, see CALIFORNIA REPORT 142–47.

[60] TAPPAN, *op. cit. supra* note 55, at 15–16. Of course, a major problem has been that treatment has been almost totally lacking. Many states have passed laws requiring treatment without establishing treatment facilities. Beyond this, however, any treatment technique will have to be very effective if it is to reduce significantly the rate of recidivism, for the rate is already quite low.

[61] TAPPAN, *op. cit. supra* note 55, at 34.

[62] EDWIN POWERS, THE BASIC STRUCTURE OF THE ADMINISTRATION OF CRIMINAL JUSTICE IN MASSACHUSETTS 15–17 (United Prison Ass'n of Mass., Res. Div. Rep. No. 5, 1957).

[63] BENJAMIN KARPMAN, THE SEXUAL OFFENDER AND HIS OFFENSES (1954); JOSEPH PAUL DE RIVER, THE SEXUAL CRIMINAL (1950); REINHARDT, *op. cit. supra* note 48.

[64] For a clear, concise statement of the needs and uses of controls in psychiatric research. see COMM. ON RESEARCH, GROUP FOR THE ADVANCEMENT OF PSYCHIATRY, REP. No. 42, SOME OBSERVATIONS ON CONTROLS IN PSYCHIATRIC RESEARCH (1959). Neglect of the distinction between fact and hypothesis is illustrated in the following exchange in a discussion of a paper on sex psychopaths written by the psychiatrist Benjamin Karpman. One of the discussants, Albert Ellis, suggested that Karpman's propositions should be regarded as hypotheses rather than facts, and that evidence for some of them was lacking; to which Karpman replied: "I deny these allegations in toto. All of my statements are based on *actual clinical material;* I do not have one bit of theory." KARPMAN, *op. cit. supra* note 63, at 511–12, 525.

[65] ELLIS & BRANCALE, *op. cit. supra* note 58, at 94.

[66] See *id.* at 34, 38, 42, 46, 49, 56, 62. Two of the major categories excluded from the above review are statutory rape and incest. Ellis and Brancale provide convincing evidence of the essential normality of statutory rape offenders, and support the conclusions of Ploscowe and others that the age limit in such cases should be reduced. Evidence on incest cases suggests, as would be expected, that offenders are more like the aggressive than the passive offenders in terms of social and criminal background.

[67] The findings of the New Jersey study are, of course, subject to many weaknesses commonly found in sex offender research. As the authors of the study note, there is no way of knowing how their sample differs in background from sex offenders sentenced to state prisons or from those who are undetected. The number of cases is much too small, especially for the rapists, to place much confidence in the results. The characterizations of offenders, with the exception of prior arrest data, are undoubtedly colored by knowledge of which type of offense they committed.

[68] CALIFORNIA REPORT 132–35.

[69] *Id.* at 101–02.

[70] Ellis, Doorbar & Johnston, *Characteristics of Convicted Sex Offenders*, 40 J. SOC. PSYCH. 14 (1954).

[71] MARVIN E. WOLFGANG, PATTERNS IN CRIMINAL HOMICIDE 329 (1958).

[72] The psychiatrist Richard L. Jenkins has observed that "the differ-

ence between the law-abiding man and the rapist lies typically not in a difference of sex impulse, but in a difference of inhibition and consideration for the personality of others." Jenkins, *The Making of a Sex Offender,* in CLYDE B. VEDDER, SAMUEL KOENIG & ROBERT E. CLARK, CRIMINOLOGY 293, 295 (1953). The above observations seem consistent with this view, but are at variance with psychiatric analyses, which see even statutory rape as fundamentally tied up with the oedipus complex, representing an unconscious attack upon the parent. See, *e.g.,* DAVID ABRAHAMSEN, WHO ARE THE GUILTY? 184–85 (1952). Any theory that seeks to interpret sex aggression as a highly neurotic or psychopathic act must consider the prevalence of aggressive sexual acts among presumably normal populations of college students. See Kanin, *Male Aggression in Dating-Courtship Relations,* 63 AM. J. SOC. 197 (1957). The Kanin article points to some of the factors that may prevent these cases from becoming officially labeled as felonious aggressions.

[73] The culture of prison inmates provides insight into the differences between aggressive and passive sex offenders. No special status is conferred on aggressive offenders or those convicted of statutory rape. In fact, the latter are viewed as having "bum beefs" as a result of "pick on your own size" laws designed to allow promiscuous teen-agers to get off the hook when they become pregnant. Offenders who engage in nonviolent sex acts with children, on the other hand, are relegated to the bottom of the social structure and referred to in derogatory terms as "rapos"—so afraid of women they had to pick on children.

[74] See ROBERT K. MERTON, SOCIAL THEORY AND SOCIAL STRUCTURE 131–94 (rev. ed. 1957).

[75] JOHN LEWIS GILLEN, THE WISCONSIN PRISONER 107–16 (1946); Reimer, *The Background of Incestuous Relationship,* in VEDDER, KOENIG & CLARK, *op. cit. supra* note 72, at 301.

[76] WOLFGANG, *op. cit. supra* note 71, at 245.

[77] The Model Penal Code expresses recognition of these elements in suggesting that where a woman loses capacity to control her own conduct by voluntary use of intoxicants or drugs, any resulting intercourse cannot be charged as rape, although it can be under most existing statutes. MODEL PENAL CODE § 207.4, comment at 248–49 (Tent. Draft No. 4, 1955).

[78] ELLIS & BRANCALE, *op. cit. supra* note 58 at 78.

Prostitution
WAYLAND YOUNG

[1] Oxford University Press, 1947.

[2] *The Commentaries of Pius II,* "Memoirs of a Renaissance Pope," London, 1960 (New York, 1961), p. 35.

[3] *La Retorica delle Puttane,* Cambrai, 1642, pp. 115–116.

[4] London, 1955.

[5] See note 6 below.

[6] In England a distinction is made between the *ponce* who runs the girl's life in general, and the much rarer *pimp* who actively solicits men to go to her. In America the word *pimp* covers both classes. Perhaps

the American *sweet daddy* is the closest to British ponce, but it is more colloquial.

The Self-Image of the Prostitute
NORMAN R. JACKMAN, RICHARD O'TOOLE, AND GILBERT GEIS

¹ W. A. Bonger, *Criminality and Economic Conditions* (Boston: Little, Brown, 1916), pp. 321–56.

² Robert E. Park and Ernest W. Burgess, *Introduction to the Science of Sociology* (Chicago: Univ. of Chicago Press, 1921); Park, Burgess, and Roderick D. McKenzie, *The City* (Chicago: Univ. of Chicago Press, 1925); Nels Anderson, *The Hobo: The Sociology of the Homeless Man* (Chicago: Univ. of Chicago Press, 1923); Walter C. Reckless, *Vice in Chicago* (Chicago: Univ. of Chicago Press, 1933).

³ Kingsley Davis, "The Sociology of Prostitution," *American Sociological Review*, 2:744–55 (Oct., 1937).

⁴ Edwin H. Lemert, *Social Pathology* (New York: McGraw-Hill, 1951), p. 233.

⁵ W. I. Thomas, *The Unadjusted Girl* (Boston: Little, Brown, 1924).

⁶ Karl Abraham, *Selected Papers on Psycho-Analysis* (London: Hogarth Press, 1927), p. 361.

⁷ Edward Glover, "The Abnormality of Prostitution," in A. M. Krich, ed., *Women* (New York: Dell, 1953), pp. 247–73; and Glover, *The Psychopathology of Prostitution* (London: Institute for the Study and Treatment of Delinquency, 1957).

⁸ Harold Greenwald, *The Call Girl* (New York: Ballantine Books, 1958), p. 94.

⁹ Frank S. Caprio, *Female Homosexuality* (New York: Citadel, 1954).

¹⁰ T. Agoston, "Some Psychological Aspects of Prostitution; The Pseudo-Personality," *International Journal of Psycho-Analysis*, 26:62–67 (1945).

¹¹ Helen Deutsch, *The Psychology of Women* (New York: Grune and Stratton, 1944), vol. 1.

¹² Cf. David W. Maurer, "Prostitutes and Criminal Argots," *American Journal of Sociology*, 44:546–50 (Jan., 1939). On rationalization by juvenile delinquents, see Gresham M. Sykes and David Matza, "Techniques of Neutralization: A Theory of Delinquency," *American Sociological Review*, 22:664–70 (Dec., 1957).

¹³ During the jail interviews only the investigating team was present. In two night club interviews patrol car officers were also present but not in a position to hear the conversation.

¹⁴ We were not concerned with the literal "truth" of respondents' statements. We accepted the statements at their face value since we were concerned with the prostitutes' self-image, however fantastic. Where pertinent, however, we have employed police records for validation or further information.

¹⁵ Gresham M. Sykes and David Matza, *loc. cit.*

¹⁶ J. Walton Yinger, "Contraculture and Subculture," *American Sociological Review*, 25:625–35 (Oct., 1960).

¹⁷ Muzafer Sherif and Hadley Cantril, *The Psychology of Ego-Involvements* (New York: Wiley, 1947), p. 387.

Apprenticeships in Prostitution
JAMES H. BRYAN

[1] H. Benjamin, "Prostitution Reassessed," *International Journal of Sexology*, 26 (1951), pp. 154–160; H. Benjamin & A. Ellis, "An Objective Examination of Prostitution," *International Journal of Sexology*, 29 (1955), pp. 100–105; E. Glover, "The Abnormality of Prostitution," In A. M. Krich, editor, *Women*, New York: Dell Publishing Company, Inc., 1953; M. H. Hollander, "Prostitution, The Body, and Human Relatedness." *International Journal of Psychoanalysis*, XLII (1961), pp. 404–413; M. Karpf, "Effects of Prostitution on Marital Sex Adjustment," *International Journal of Sexology*, 29 (1953), pp. 149–154; J. F. Oliven, *Sexual Hygiene and Pathology*, Philadelphia: J. B. Lippincott Co., 1955; W. J. Robinson, *The Oldest Profession in The World*, New York: Eugenics Publishing Co., 1929.

[2] H. Greenwald, *The Call Girl*, New York: Ballantine Books, 1960.

[3] H. S. Becker, *Outsiders: Studies in the Sociology of Deviance*, New York: Free Press of Glencoe, 1963. Also see *The Other Side*, H. S. Becker, editor, New York: Free Press of Glencoe, 1964. P. London, *The Modes and Morals of Psychotherapy*, New York: Holt, Rinehart and Winston, Inc. 1964. For recent trends in personality theory, see N. Sanford, "Personality: Its Place in Psychology" and D. R. Miller, "The Study of Social Relationships: Situation, Identify, and Social Interaction." Both papers are presented in S. Koch, editor, *Psychology: A Study of a Science*, Vol. 5, New York: McGraw-Hill Book Co., Inc. 1963.

[4] Evelyn Hooker, "The Homosexual Community." *Proceedings of the XIV International Congress of Applied Psychology*, 1961, pp. 40–59. See also 'A. Reiss, "The Social Integration of Queers and Peers," *Social Problems*, 9 (1961), pp. 102–120.

[5] D. W. Maurer, *The Big Con*, New York: Signet Books, 1940. H. S. Becker, *Outsiders, op. cit.* E. H. Sutherland, *The Professional Thief*, Chicago: University of Chicago Press, 1937. A. R. Lindesmith, *Opiate Addiction*, Evanston: Principia Press, 1955.

[6] This definition departs somewhat from that offered by Clinard. He defines the call girl as one dependent upon an organization for recruiting patrons and one who typically works in lower-class hotels. The present sample is best described by Clinard's category high-class independent professional prostitute. M. D. Clinard, *Sociology of Deviant Behavior*, New York: Rinehart & Co., Inc., 1957.

[7] E. Reid, and O. Demaris, *The Green Felt Jungle*, New York: Pocket Books, Inc., 1963.

[8] H. Greenwald, *op. cit.* W. Pomeroy, *Some Aspects of Prostitution*, unpublished paper.

[9] A point also made in the autobiographical account of a retired call girl. Virginia McManus, *Not For Love*, New York: Dell Publishing Co., Inc., 1960, p. 160.

[10] Two of the pimps denied that this was very often so and maintained that the girls will solicit them. The degree to which they are solicited seems to depend upon the nature and extent of their reputations. It is difficult to judge the accuracy of these reports as there appears to be a strong taboo against admitting to such solicitation.

[11] C. Winick, "Prostitutes' Clients' Perception of the Prostitute and Themselves," *International Journal of Social Psychiatry*, 8 (1961–62), pp. 289–297.

[12] H. S. Becker, Blanche Geer, and E. C. Hughes, A. L. Strauss, *Boys In White*, Chicago: University of Chicago Press, 1961.

[13] The statements made by prostitutes to previous investigators and mental helpers may have been parroting this particular value structure and perhaps have misled previous investigators into making the assumption that "all whores hate men." While space prohibits a complete presentation of the data, neither our questionnaire nor interview data suggest that this is a predominant attitude among call girls.

[14] There is, from the present study, little support for the hypothesis of Reckless concerning the association of experience trauma and guilt with abruptness of entry into the occupation. W. C. Reckless, *The Crime Problem*, New York: Appleton-Century-Crofts, Inc., 1950.

[15] The topic of solicitation will be dealt with in a forthcoming paper.

[16] In the unpublished paper referred to above, Pomeroy has indicated that, of 31 call girls interviewed, only 23% reported never experiencing orgasms with customers.

[17] The fee-splitting arrangement is quite common at all levels of career activity. For example, cooperative activity between two girls is often required for a particular type of sexual contract. In these cases, the girl who has contracted with the customer will contact a colleague, usually a friend, and will obtain 40%-50% of the latter's earnings. There is suggestive evidence that fee-splitting activities vary according to geographical areas and that Los Angeles is unique for both its fee-splitting patterns and the rigidity of its fee-splitting structure.

[18] Needless to say, however, all of the sample of call girls who were asked for status hierarchies of prostitution felt that the street-walker had both less status and a less complex job. It *may* well be that the verbal exchange required of the call girl requires greater knowledge than that required of a street-walker, but the nonverbal skills required of the street-walker may be considerably greater than those of the call girl.

The Homosexual Community
EVELYN HOOKER

[1] The brevity of this paper on a problem of such broad dimensions is due to the fact that it was written for oral presentation (1961) within specified time limits. It is highly over-simplified and fragmentary, especially in the description of complex social phenomena and the development of a theoretical framework to account for them. A radical and complete revision in greatly expanded form would be required to fully correct these and other inadequacies and to bring it up to date.

[2] This statement refers to studies at the human level and is a rough generalization about the relative proportion of publications in which the content focuses on etiology, personality patterns and psychodynamics, or treatment of homosexuality in individuals (or aggregates of individuals), as contrasted with those in which the focus is on social patterns in groups, societies, or collectivities.

[3] A study of the total homosexual community would, of course, in-

clude homosexual women. The relations between homosexual men and women in private social gatherings, in bars, and in homosexual organizations are not discussed in this brief paper, but are, of course, important features of the total project—although the focus is on the collective aspects of male homosexuality.

[4] For the concept of the 'community' as outlined in this sentence, I am indebted to Johnson (1955).

[5] For this concept, I am indebted to Harold Garfinkel. My very large indebtedness to Dr. Garfinkel in the development of the concepts used in this paper cannot be explicitly and adequately documented.

[6] Suggested by Erving Goffman in a personal communication.

[7] For the term 'common understandings,' I am indebted to Harold Garfinkel. The meanings of the term as he uses it are to be found in his 1964 paper.

References
1. Garfinkel, H. The routine grounds of everyday activities. *Soc. Prob.*, 1964, *11*, 225–250.
2. Hooker, E. A preliminary analysis of group behavior of homosexuals. *J. Psychol.*, 1956, *42*, 217–225.
3. Hooker, E. The adjustment of the male overt homosexual. *J. proj. Tech.*, 1957, *21*, 18–31.
4. Hooker, E. Male homosexuality in the Rorschach. *J. proj. Tech.*, 1958, *22*, 33–54.
5. Hooker, E. What is a criterion? *J. proj. Tech.*, 1959, *23*, 278–281.
6. Johnson, R. The nature of the minority community: internal structure, reactions, leadership, and action. Unpublished doctoral dissertation (Cornell University), 1955.
7. Leznoff, M., and Westley, W. A. The homosexual community. *Soc. Prob.*, 1956, *3*, 257–263.
8. Riesman, D. *Individualism Reconsidered*. Glencoe, Ill.: The Free Press, 1954, p. 529.

The Homosexual Community

MAURICE LEZNOFF AND WILLIAM A. WESTLEY

[1] Kinsey reports that 37 per cent of the total male population have at least some overt homosexual experience to the point of orgasm between adolescence and old age; 30 per cent of all males have at least incidental homosexual experience or reactions over at least a three year period between the ages of 16 and 55; 25 per cent of the male population have more than incidental homosexual experience or reactions for at least three years between the ages of 16 and 55; 18 per cent of the males have at least as much of the homosexual as the hetereosexual in their histories for at least three years between the ages of 16 and 55; 4 per cent of the white males are exclusively homosexual throughout their lives, after the onset of adolescence. Homosexual practices are reported among all occupational groups with the percentage for professionals approximately 50 per cent lower than those of other groups. Further confirmation of the distribution of homosexuals among all social strata was obtained from police files and the testimony of homosexuals.

[2] Access to this homosexual community was obtained through a client at a social welfare agency.

[3] A stable social and sexual relationship between two homosexuals is frequently referred to as "marriage."

[4] The substitution of the female for the male pronoun is a common practice within homosexual groups.

[5] William A. Westley, "Violence and the Police," *American Journal of Sociology*, 59 (July, 1953).

[6] National Opinion Research Center, *Opinion News*, 9 (September, 1947), 3–13.

[7] The Burning Flame refers to a bar which tended to draw its clientele from secret homosexuals; the Red Room was the acknowledged gathering place of overt homosexuals.

[8] Robert is the leader of an overt group of which the respondent was a member at the time he was contacted.

[9] Our data with respect to the prevalence of this role are incomplete. However, homosexuals regularly refer to the queens of other cities, suggesting that the practice is widespread.

[10] The adoption of feminine names is a widespread practice among all homosexuals interviewed.

[11] The queen of the overt group studied maintained an address book containing the names of approximately 3,000 homosexuals scattered across North America.

The Social Integration of Queers and Peers
ALBERT J. REISS, JR.

[1] Arthur V. Huffman, "Sex Deviation in a Prison Community," *The Journal of Social Therapy*, 6 (Third Quarter, 1960), pp. 170–181; Joseph E. Fishman, *Sex in Prison*, New York: The Commonwealth Fund, 1930; Donald Clemmer, *The Prison Community*, Boston: The Christopher Publishing House, 1940, pp. 260–273.

[2] William Marlin Butts, "Boy Prostitutes of the Metropolis," *Journal of Clinical Psychopathology*, 8 (1946–1947), pp. 673–681; H. Laurence Ross, "The 'Hustler' in Chicago," *The Journal of Student Research*, 1 (September, 1959), pp. 13–19; Jens Jersild, *Boy Prostitution*, Copenhagen: C. E. Gad, 1956 (Translation of *Den Mandlige Prostitution* by Oscar Bojesen).

[3] H. Laurence Ross, *op. cit.*, p. 15.

[4] The distinction made here is not intended to suggest that other types of hustlers do not also define themselves in other deviant roles. Hustlers may occupy a variety of deviant roles which are classified as delinquent or criminal; they may be "hooked," blackmailers, thieves, etc.

[5] I am indebted to Ned Polsky for bringing Rechy's stories to my attention.

[6] John Rechy, "The Fabulous Wedding of Miss Destiny," *Big Table*, I, Number 3 (1959), p. 15.

[7] John Rechy, "A Quarter Ahead," *Evergreen Review*, Vol. 5, No. 19 (July-August, 1961), p. 18.

[8] For a definition of the types of conformers and deviators see Albert J. Reiss, Jr., "Conforming and Deviating Behavior and the Problem of

Guilt," *Psychiatric Research Reports,* 13 (December, 1960), pp. 209–
210, and Albert J. Reiss, Jr. and Albert Lewis Rhodes, "The Distribution
of Juvenile Delinquency in the Social Class Structure," *American Sociological Review,* Vol. 26, No. 5 (October, 1961), pp. 720–732.

9 See, for example, Maurice Leznoff and William A. Westley, "The
Homosexual Community," *Social Problems,* 3 (April, 1956), pp. 257–
263.

10 *Ibid.,* p. 258.

11 H. Laurence Ross, *op. cit.,* p. 15.

12 The cues which lead to the queer-peer transaction can be subtle
ones. The literature on adult male homosexuality makes it clear that
adult males who participate in homosexual behavior are not generally
socially visible to the public by manner and dress. Cf., Jess Stearn,
op. cit., Chapters 1 and 3.

13 *Op. cit.,* pp. 260–261.

14 Ross notes that, failing in the con-man role, some hustlers resort to
extortion and blackmail since they provide higher income. See Ross, *op.
cit.,* p. 16. Sutherland discusses extortion and blackmail of homosexuals
as part of the practice of professional thieves. The "muzzle" or "mouse"
is part of the role of the professional thief. See Edwin Sutherland, *The
Professional Thief,* Chicago: University of Chicago Press, 1937, pp. 78–
81. See also the chapter on "Blackmail" in Jess Stearn, *op.'cit.,* Chapter
16.

15 Jess Stearn, *op. cit.,* p. 47.

16 Albert J. Reiss, Jr., "Sex Offenses: The Marginal Status of the
Adolescent," *Law and Contemporary Problems* 25 (Spring, 1960), pp.
322–324 and 326–327.

17 Albert Cohen, Alfred Lindesmith and Karl Schuessler (editors),
The Sutherland Papers, Bloomington, Indiana: Indiana University Press,
1956, p. 31.

18 It is not altogether clear why mouth-genital fellation is the only
sexual act which is tolerated in the peer-queer transaction. The act
seems to conform to the more "masculine" aspects of the role than do
most, but not all possible alternatives. Ross has suggested to me that it
also involves less bodily contact and therefore may be less threatening
to the peers' self-definitions. One possible explanation therefore for the
exclusiveness of the relationship to this act is that it is the most masculine
alternative involving the least threat to peers' self-definition as non-
hustler and nonhomosexual.

19 Talcott Parsons in *The Social System* (Glencoe: The Free Press,
1951, Chapter III) dicusses this kind of role as " . . . the segregation
of specific instrumental performances, both from expressive orientations
other than the specifically appropriate rewards and from other components of the instrumental complex" (p. 87).

20 Walter Miller, "Lower-Class Culture as a Generating Milieu of
Gang Delinquency," *The Journal of Social Issues,* 14 (1958), No. 3, p. 9.

The Development of the Homosexual Bar as an Institution
NANCY ACHILLES

1 Albert Cohen, "The Study of Social Disorganization and Deviant

Behavior," *Sociology Today*, ed. Robert Merton, Leonard Broom and Leonard Cottrell (New York: Basic Books, 1959), p. 471.

² Donald W. Cory, *The Homosexual in America* (New York: Castle Books, 1951), p. 120.

³ 86'd means to be evicted from some public place, usually a bar.

⁴ *San Francisco Chronicle*, November 1, 1963, p. 4.

⁵ *San Francisco Chronicle*, October 25, 1963, p. 2.

⁶ *LCE News*, April 3, 1963, p. 3.

⁷ A leather bar is one where the patrons wear motorcycle clothes, often made of leather. This type of bar is sometimes associated with sado-masochism.

⁸ Faggot is a derogatory term for an extremely effeminate male homosexual, who flagrantly displays his effeminacy.

⁹ Butch means having a masculine appearance or character or the playing of a masculine role. When applied to the male, it is a complimentary term indicating a lack of effeminacy. Applied to the female, it connotes a masculine appearance, demeanor, and the playing of the masculine role.

¹⁰ Hell's Angels is a group of motorcyclists and their girl friends who often invade the less genteel gay bars. Their habitual attire is leather jackets, ragged pants, gold hoop earrings, and bandanas wrapped about the head, pirate fashion. Members of the Community firmly maintain that the Hell's Angels are not gay, but hang around the bars as perennial troublemakers.

¹¹ A male homosexual's "sisters" are his good friends, with whom he has an asexual relationship. The term is used infrequently and always jokingly.

¹² Mary is an affectionate, but slightly deprecating, nickname which male homosexuals use in addressing one another.

The Lesbians: A Preliminary Overview
WILLIAM SIMON AND JOHN H. GAGNON

¹ P. H. Gebhard, J. H. Gagnon, W. B. Pomeroy, and C. V. Christenson, *Sex Offenders: An Analysis of Types*, New York, Harper & Row, 1965, pp. 155–205.

² It should be kept in mind that the production of a public sexual language and a public sexual imagery remains largely a male activity. As a consequence, pornography is made by males for other males.

³ A. C. Kinsey, *et al., Sexual Behavior in the Human Female*, Philadelphia, Saunders, 1953, pp. 642–689.

⁴ Irving Bieber, *et al., Homosexuality, a Psychoanalytic Study*, New York, Basic Books, 1962, 358 pp.; Cornelia B. Wilbur, "Clinical Aspects of Female Homosexuality" in Judd Marmor, ed., *Sexual Inversion*, New York, Basic Books, 1965, pp. 268–281.

⁵ A. C. Kinsey, *et al., op. cit.*, pp. 446–452.

⁶ *Ibid.*, pp. 669–670.

⁷ Simone de Beauvoir, *The Second Sex*, trans. and ed. by H. M. Parshley, New York, Knopf, 1953, pp. 421–422.

⁸ See J. H. Gagnon, "Sexuality and Sexual Learning in the Child," reprinted in this volume, pp. 15–42.

Index

LIBRARY
OF
MOUNT ST. MARY'S
COLLEGE
EMMITSBURG, MARYLAND

72-73   12 11 10 9 8 7 6 5

111757

JUL 8 - 1974